JUST GIVING

Just Giving

Why Philanthropy
Is Failing
Democracy
and How It Can
Do Better

Rob Reich

PRINCETON UNIVERSITY PRESS

PRINCETON AND OXFORD

Copyright © 2018 by Princeton University Press

Published by Princeton University Press
41 William Street, Princeton, New Jersey 08540
6 Oxford Street, Woodstock, Oxfordshire OX20 1TR

press.princeton.edu

All Rights Reserved

Library of Congress Control Number: 2018954909
ISBN 978-0-691-18349-7

British Library Cataloging-in-Publication Data is available

Editorial: Rob Tempio and Matt Rohal
Production Editorial: Jenny Wolkowicki
Jacket Design: Amanda Weiss
Production: Jacqueline Poirier
Publicity: Tayler Lord
Copyeditor: Joseph Dahm

This book has been composed in Adobe Text Pro

Printed on acid-free paper. ∞

Printed in the United States of America

10 9 8 7 6 5 4 3 2 1

For Marie Olszewski

CONTENTS

Acknowledgments   xi

Introduction   1
Philanthropy Today   7
Philosophers on Philanthropy   11
On the Terms "Philanthropy" and "Charity"   19
Plan of the Book   20

1   Philanthropy as an Artifact of the State:
    Institutional Forms of Philanthropy   24

   *The Liturgical System and the Amazing Antidosis
   Procedure in Democratic Athens*   29

   *The Islamic Waqf: Precursor to the Contemporary
   Philanthropic Foundation*   35

   *Eighteenth- and Nineteenth-Century Resistance
   to Foundations*   45

      Anne-Robert Turgot   46

      John Stuart Mill   54

   Conclusion   62

2 Philanthropy and Its Uneasy Relation to Equality   65

Philanthropy and Equality   67

An Overview of Giving in the United States   72

Philanthropy and Tax Policy   74

   Equality and the Treatment of Donors   78

   Equality and the Distribution of
   Charitable Giving   82

Private Foundations   90

*When Philanthropy Generates Greater Inequality:
The Plutocracy of the PTA*   94

Conclusion   103

3 A Political Theory of Philanthropy   106

A Simple Framework   110

Justifications for Tax Incentives   114

   Tax Base Rationale   115

   Efficiency Rationale   119

   Pluralism Rationale   128

Conclusion   133

4 Repugnant to the Whole Idea of a Democratic Society?:
On the Role of Foundations   135

*The Birth of the Private Foundation in the
United States*   137

What Is a Foundation For?   140

Foundations as Institutional Oddities   144

   Foundations Lack Accountability   144

   Foundations Lack Transparency   147

Donor-Directed Purpose in Perpetuity   147

Foundations Are Generously Tax-Subsidized   148

The Case for Foundations   152

Pluralism   153

Discovery   159

Conclusion   167

5   Philanthropy in Time: Future Generations
and Intergenerational Justice   169

Just Savings and Intergenerational Assistance   175

The Reproduction of Social Capital Argument   178

The Precaution against Remote Risks Argument   184

The Discovery Argument   190

Conclusion   193

Conclusion   195

Notes   201

Bibliography   223

Index   233

ACKNOWLEDGMENTS

Writing is a solitary endeavor. Philosophy is conducted best through dialogue. Writing something philosophical therefore produces an interesting tension: the need to be alone alongside the need for intellectual company. I want to record my thanks to the many people who talked with me about the ideas in this book.

I have had the good fortune to work with some exceptional undergraduate and graduate students on various aspects of this project. I thank Emma Leeds Armstrong, Jess Asperger, Aysha Bagchi, Alyssa Battistoni, Nita Bhat, Marilee Coetsee, Hilary Cohen, Lacey Dorn, Jamie Doucette, Meredith Ely, Josh Freedman, Emily Gerth, Alec Hogan, Wouzbena Jifar, Katie Keller, Yoon Jee Kim, David Louk, Jenna Nicholas, Ramya Parthasarathy, Solveij Praxis, Ranjana Reddy, Priti Sanghani, Jessica Sequiera, Matt Smith, Julia Spiegel, Stefanie Sutton, and Tony Wang.

I am deeply grateful to the many friends and colleagues who discussed this project with me, who entertained and frequently criticized and improved my tentative ideas. The book could not have been written without Danielle Allen, Joanne Barkan, Eric Beerbohm, Alexander Berger, Lila Corwin Berman, Corey Brettschneider, Mark Brilliant, Phil Buchanan, David Callahan, Josh Cohen, Chiara Cordelli, Checker Finn, Archon Fung, Julia Galef, Kristin Goss, David Grusky, William Howell, Stanley Katz, Larry Kramer, David Laitin, Gara LaMarche,

Ted Lechterman, Jacob Levy, Steve Macedo, Ray Madoff, Johanna Mair, Alison McQueen, Maribel Morey, Josh Ober, Kieran Oberman, Timothy Ogden, Tomer Perry, Miranda Perry Fleischer, Jeff Raikes, Julie Rose, Jennifer Rubinstein, Debra Satz, Emma Saunders-Hastings, William Schambra, Melissa Schwartzberg, Gary Segura, Seana Shiffrin, Ben Soskis, Robert Taylor, Megan Tompkins-Stange, Susan Verducci, Jeremy Weinstein, and Leif Wenar. Special thanks to John Tomasi, who suggested the title.

Josh Cohen and Deb Chasman at *Boston Review* provided a venue for my early ideas about the role that private foundations play in a democratic society. Their editorial guidance was invaluable, and their assembly of respondents in the magazine's forum discussion stimulated a healthy debate that continues to shape my thinking.

I want particularly to thank my extraordinary colleagues at the Stanford Center on Philanthropy and Civil Society (PACS), where many portions of this book were presented in draft form, including Woody Powell, Paul Brest, Lucy Bernholz, and Bruce Sievers. Special gratitude to Kim Meredith and Annie Rohan Wickert, whose tireless efforts to support the work of PACS made all of these conversations possible.

I shared an early version of the entire manuscript with Elizabeth Branch Dyson, whose astute comments vastly improved it. Two anonymous reviewers commissioned by Princeton University Press offered excellent suggestions as well.

Larissa MacFarquhar encouraged me to write in a way that would bring the ideas to an audience beyond other scholars and helped me see how I might do that. Henry Timms provided guidance about how to present these ideas to philanthropists and nonprofit leaders. Both read portions of the manuscript in its final stages, giving last-minute advice when I was so buried

in the details that I could no longer see what if anything was interesting about what I'd written.

This is a book that contains no shortage of criticism about philanthropy and the policies that shape it. It may seem surprising, then, for me to express thanks for the various forms of philanthropic support I received while writing this book. First and foremost, I am grateful to Stanford University, whose resources are provided in no small measure through generations of philanthropic gifts, for the intellectual setting in which all of the ideas expressed here were first born and sent out on toddler legs. Second, I am grateful for the support of various foundations and individuals whose gifts to the Center on Philanthropy and Civil Society offered me a no-strings-attached opportunity to write about philanthropy, to present these ideas before audiences of nonprofit and philanthropic leaders, and funded our vibrant interdisciplinary community.

Rob Tempio at Princeton University Press was a model editor, and Joseph Dahm was an excellent copy editor.

My family has lived with this project for nearly a decade and heard me discuss the ideas more times than they care to admit. They have been my deepest source of support and confidence that I had something worth saying.

My grandmother, Marie Olszewski, was born in Germany in 1917, arrived in the United States in 1938 without the ability to speak a word of English. Her fierce and critical mind—as lively today as it ever has been—is the wellspring of my own questioning spirit. I dedicate this book to her with gratitude, admiration, and boundless love.

Portions of this book have appeared elsewhere, though I have significantly revised much of the older material. Thanks to the following for permissions. "A Failure of Philanthropy: American Charity Shortchanges the Poor, and Public Policy

Is Partly to Blame," *Stanford Social Innovation Review*, Winter 2005, 24–33; "Philanthropy and Its Uneasy Relation to Equality," in *Taking Philanthropy Seriously: Beyond Noble Intentions to Responsible Giving*, ed. William Damon and Susan Verducci (Bloomington: Indiana University Press, 2006), 27–49; "Toward a Political Theory of Philanthropy," in *Giving Well: The Ethics of Philanthropy*, ed. Patricia Illingworth, Thomas Pogge, and Leif Wenar (Oxford: Oxford University Press, 2011), 177–195; "Philanthropy and Caring for the Needs of Strangers," *Social Research* 80 (2013): 517–538; "Repugnant to the Whole Idea of Democracy: On the Role of Foundations in Democratic Societies," *PS: Political Science and Politics* 49 (2016): 466–471; "On the Role of Foundations in Democracies," in *Philanthropy in Democratic Societies: History, Institutions, Values*, ed. Rob Reich, Chiara Cordelli, and Lucy Bernholz (Chicago: University of Chicago Press, 2016), 64–81; "Philanthropy and Intergenerational Justice," with Chiara Cordelli, in *Institutions for Future Generations*, ed. Iñigo González-Ricoy and Axel Gosseries (Oxford: Oxford University Press, 2016), 228–244.

JUST GIVING

Introduction

"Your fortune is rolling up, rolling up like an avalanche! You must keep up with it! You must distribute it faster than it grows! If you do not, it will crush you, and your children, and your children's children!"[1] So wrote Frederick Gates to sixty-seven-year-old John D. Rockefeller in 1906. Rockefeller was the founder of Standard Oil, a corporation that had generated a colossal fortune and made him the richest man in the world. For some years already, Rockefeller had relinquished the day-to-day operations of the company and was dedicating an increasing amount of his time to charitable giving. Gates was Rockefeller's main and trusted advisor on business and philanthropic matters.

In the 1880s, as Rockefeller's wealth accumulated, he was trailed constantly and contacted daily by ordinary people seeking charitable favors. "Neither in the privacy of his home nor at his table, nor in the aisles of his church, nor during his business hours, nor anywhere else," wrote Gates, "was Mr. Rockefeller secure from insistent appeal."[2] His lawyer once told Congress that

Rockefeller received four to five hundred letters per day, most asking for a donation. One steamliner from Europe delivered five thousand letters soliciting funds, and after one especially large Rockefeller gift was announced, the following month the oil magnate received more than sixty thousand letters asking for charity. Rockefeller, a devout Christian, prided himself on dispensing gifts to the genuinely needy, but the volume of requests made impossible any cursory examination much less serious review of each appeal. Shortly after making the founding grant to establish the University of Chicago in 1890, Rockefeller decided he needed full-time philanthropic guidance. He sought the assistance of Gates, a former Baptist minister who had been involved in the creation of the University of Chicago, and Gates became Rockefeller's chief advisor in 1891.

By the early 1900s, Rockefeller's ever-growing fortune had attained Everest-like proportions, peaking in 1916 at more than $1 billion.[3] Gates knew that Rockefeller wished to give away most of his wealth. And Gates realized that at such a mountainous scale, responding to individual appeals for donations was impracticable. Gates was further concerned that unless Rockefeller devised some grand plan, his heirs would be left to disburse the money without his guidance and, therefore, with uncertain results. To match the size of his wealth, it was necessary to do more than accelerate the pace of giving. He would have to shift from retail charity to wholesale philanthropy, he would have to seek to address root causes of social ills rather than provide direct relief through alms, and he would have to pursue a broad mission with a global vision.

Working together, Rockefeller and Gates soon devised a plan for something novel: to create a general-purpose philanthropic foundation whose mission would be nothing less, and nothing more specific, than to benefit humankind. The proposed mis-

sion was "to promote the well-being and advance the civilization of the people of the United States and its territories and possession and of foreign lands in the acquisition and dissemination of knowledge; in the prevention and relief of suffering and in the promotion of any and all of the elements of human progress."[4] Such a mission would permit Rockefeller and his handpicked trustees to undertake virtually any project they deemed worthy.

Rockefeller, like any other person, was free to make donations to other people or to existing organizations. But Gates imagined creating an entity more enduring, living beyond Rockefeller's lifetime, that would be administered by a small body of experts. It would be a variation on the idea of an existing legal form, the perpetual charitable trust. Gates was well aware of the significance of the proposed trust for democratic life. The foundation would be so large that its "administration would be a matter of public concern, public inquiry, and public criticism."[5]

As with the creation of any charitable trust, to establish this new foundation would require a charter, or formal permission to incorporate, from a public body. Although it likely would have been easy to obtain a charter from the New York state legislature, Rockefeller and his advisors were concerned that a state charter would impose limits on their foundation's size and purpose. State legislatures frequently capped philanthropic endowments at $3 million and insisted upon narrowly defined purposes. In light of their national and global aspirations, Gates recommended that Rockefeller look beyond New York and seek the imprimatur of the U.S. Congress.

In 1909 Rockefeller took the first concrete steps toward the establishment of his general-purpose foundation by conferring more than seventy thousand shares of his company, worth more than $50 million (roughly $1.3 billion in 2018 inflation-adjusted dollars), to a new entity, the Rockefeller Foundation.

He appointed three trustees: his son, his son-in-law, and Frederick Gates. A further $50 million transfer was planned to bring the total endowment to $100 million.

Rockefeller and his advisors then sought congressional approval of a bill to incorporate the foundation and sanction its size, open-ended purpose, and local, national, and international scope of activity.

The philanthropist immediately encountered fierce criticism in Washington. Some stemmed from resistance to Rockefeller's extraordinary wealth, obtained from the monopolistic business practices of Standard Oil and its stubborn resistance to labor unions, and from animus against the man himself. "No amount of charities in spending such fortunes," observed former U.S. president Theodore Roosevelt, "can compensate in any way for the misconduct in acquiring them." The sitting U.S. president, William Taft, called on Congress to oppose the creation of the foundation, describing the effort as "a bill to incorporate Mr. Rockefeller." American Federation of Labor president Samuel Gompers carped, "The one thing that the world would gratefully accept from Mr. Rockefeller now would be the establishment of a great endowment of research and education to help other people see in time how they can keep from being like him."[6]

Other critics focused not on Rockefeller the man or his business practices but on the very idea of a seemingly limitless foundation. Testifying before the Commission on Industrial Relations in 1912, Reverend John Haynes Holmes, a well-known Unitarian minister who served for many years as the board chair of the American Civil Liberties Union, said,

I take it for granted that the men who are now directing these foundations—for example, the men who are representing the Rockefeller foundation—are men of wisdom, men

of insight, of vision, and are also animated by the very best motives. . . . [M]y standpoint is the whole thought of democracy. . . . From this standpoint it seems to me that this foundation, the very character, must be repugnant to the whole idea of a democratic society.[7]

A U.S. senator went still further. The chairman of the Industrial Relations Commission, Frank Walsh from Missouri, opposed not merely Rockefeller's foundation, but all large foundations. Writing in 1915, Walsh challenged "the wisdom of giving public sanction and approval to the spending of a huge fortune thru such philanthropies as that of the Rockefeller Foundation. My object here is to state, as clearly and briefly as possible, why the huge philanthropic trusts, known as foundations, appear to be a menace to the welfare of society."[8]

The concerns expressed by Holmes and Walsh were hardly eccentric. For many Americans, foundations were troubling not because they represented the wealth, possibly ill-gotten, of Gilded Age robber barons. They were troubling because they were considered a deeply and fundamentally *antidemocratic* institution, an entity that would undermine political equality, convert private wealth into the donor's preferred public policies, could exist in perpetuity, and be unaccountable except to a handpicked assemblage of trustees.

Over the course of several years, Rockefeller and his advisors lobbied friends and allies in Congress to support the chartering of his proposed foundation. Political opposition was stiffer than they had anticipated and arrived from some whom they had expected to be supporters rather than critics, such as Harvard president emeritus Charles Eliot, who publicly spoke out against the federal charter. Rockefeller's family attorney, Starr Murphy, who had drafted the initial federal charter bill,

met with critics and, working closely with several senators and with Rockefeller's full endorsement, eventually redrafted the bill to incorporate a host of provisions that would allow for significant public oversight of the proposed foundation and limit its size.

A cap of $100 million would be placed on the assets of the Rockefeller Foundation. In order to prevent the endowment from growing over time and to ensure that the foundation would distribute some of its assets, all income earned from the endowment would be required to be spent annually. The duration of the foundation's activities would be limited; it would be required to spend down its entire principal after fifty years (with permission to extend to one hundred years if both two-thirds of the trustees and the U.S. Congress so approved). And governance of the foundation would be subject to partial public oversight. Members of the board of trustees would be subject to a veto by a majority of a congressionally appointed board consisting, in the initial proposal, of the president of the United States, the president of the Senate, Speaker of the House, chief justice of the U.S. Supreme Court, and the presidents of Harvard, Yale, Columbia, Johns Hopkins, and the University of Chicago.[9] Anxiety about the democracy-corrupting influence of a large and unaccountable private foundation was to be allayed by creating a legal template that limited the size and life span of the foundation and imposed a form of public governance on its operation.

Rockefeller scheduled a clandestine meeting with President Taft to ask for his support, and Rockefeller's advisors redoubled their efforts to win allies in Congress. In 1913, the House of Representatives passed the redrafted bill to charter the Rockefeller Foundation, yet opposition in the Senate remained firm. Despite efforts lasting several years and the offer of significant

further concessions to concerned lawmakers, the federal charter failed.

In short order, Rockefeller turned to the New York state legislature, removing each of the amendments offered in the U.S. Congress. The bill was approved and signed into law in May 1913, and the Rockefeller Foundation was officially chartered and open for philanthropic business.

Philanthropy Today

Contrast Rockefeller's reception in Congress and the court of public opinion with the ceaseless praise given to the philanthropists of our age. Rather than asking about the purposes of charity and power of philanthropists, we tend instead to celebrate donors, large and small, for their generosity. We ought however to be asking, what is the role of philanthropy in a liberal democratic society, and what role *should* philanthropy play?

These are questions worth asking no matter the circumstances. Under present circumstances—astonishing growth of philanthropy in the past century, especially the rise of large private fortunes sometimes converted into large philanthropic foundations—they are questions we should pose with greater interest and urgency.

One reason is that philanthropy is a form or exercise of power. In the case of wealthy donors or private foundations especially, it can be a plutocratic exercise of power, the deployment of vast private assets toward a public purpose, frequently with the goal of changing public policy. In the United States and elsewhere, big philanthropy is often an unaccountable, nontransparent, donor-directed, and perpetual exercise of power. This is something that fits uneasily, at best, in democratic

societies that enshrine the value of political equality. No wonder that Reverend Holmes described the idea of the Rockefeller Foundation as "repugnant to the whole idea of a democratic society."

But there is a second reason to focus attention on philanthropy. Giving money away does not happen in a vacuum. Contemporary philanthropy in democratic societies is embedded within a set of legal rules that structure and encourage it. Whether, when, to whom, and how much people give is partly a product of laws that govern the creation of nonprofit organizations, charitable trusts, private and community foundations, and so on, and spell out the rules under which these may operate; that set up special tax exemptions for philanthropic and nonprofit organizations, and that frequently permit tax exemptions for individual and corporate donations of money and property; that enforce donor intent, often beyond the grave, creating philanthropic projects and entities that can exist, in principle, in perpetuity. What, if anything, might justify such policies?

And consider one aspect of these policies. It may seem that philanthropy is just voluntary activity, a result of the exercise of individual liberty. A moment's reflection suggests otherwise. It is indeed voluntary, but in many countries philanthropy is a tax-subsidized activity, partly paid for by all taxpayers. Strictly speaking, then, donors are not exercising a liberty to give their money away; they are subsidized to exercise a liberty they already possess. Unlike the Rockefeller and Carnegie era when enormous philanthropic entities were created without any tax concessions for doing so (because the personal income taxation had yet to be adopted; it would arrive only in 1917), today philanthropy is partially underwritten by the state through a complex web of advantageous tax laws that apply to donors as

well as to nonprofit organizations and private foundations. In the United States, for example, subsidies for charitable contributions cost citizens at least $50 billion in forgone federal tax revenue in 2016.

Examining philanthropy and the array of policies that shape it is even more important in light of current economic conditions. We live now in a second gilded age, with income and wealth inequality approaching levels from the early twentieth century. Growing inequality might be a foe to civic comity, but it is a friend to private philanthropy. In 1930 in the United States approximately two hundred private foundations possessed aggregate assets of less than $1 billion. In 1959 there were more than two thousand, in 1985 just over thirty thousand private foundations. As of 2014 the number was nearly one hundred thousand, with total capitalization of more than $800 billion.[10]

What Carnegie and Rockefeller were to the early twentieth century, Gates and Buffett and their fellow Giving Pledge signatories are to the twenty-first century. The last decade of the twentieth century witnessed the creation of unprecedentedly large foundations like the Gates Foundation. The combined assets of the Gates Foundation and a separate Gates Trust, which holds donations from Bill and Melinda Gates and contributions from Warren Buffett, totaled more than $80 billion in 2016, placing the foundation at roughly sixty-fifth in the world on a list of total GDP, ahead of most countries in Africa. It's not just a U.S. phenomenon. Large philanthropic entities dot the globe: the Wellcome Trust in the United Kingdom, the Li Ka Shing Foundation in Hong Kong, the Azim Premji Foundation in India, the Carlos Slim Foundation in Mexico, the Robert Bosch Foundation in Germany. And it's not just billionaires and their mega-foundations that command attention. The last three decades witnessed a boom in millionaires that fueled

unprecedented growth in small foundations, both in number and in assets. Foundations are no longer controversial but mundane and commonplace.

The scope of philanthropy goes far beyond the grant making of foundations. Despite the eye-popping size of large foundations and the growth in the total number of foundations, the overwhelming majority of total giving, at least in the United States, comes from living donors making charitable contributions. Americans donated more than $390 billion to eligible nonprofit organizations in 2016. Of that total, giving by living individuals accounted for $281 billion, or 72 percent. Estimates suggest that nearly all Americans donate some amount of money every year. A small donor does not wield the same kind of power as does a big philanthropist. Yet the distribution of small giving in the aggregate matters a great deal, fueling the operation of a significant slice of nonprofit organizations, and small donors enjoy the same discretion as a big philanthropist and also benefit from tax incentives for their giving. Any consideration of philanthropy must go beyond the Rockefellers and Gateses of the world and attend to the amount and significance in a democratic society of ordinary charitable giving.

Finally, we should ask what all this philanthropic activity is funding. Philanthropic resources sometimes complement and sometimes counteract public choices about the allocation of public or taxpayer funds. Individuals direct their private resources to support social benefits of myriad kinds, including poverty relief, education, animal welfare, health care, cultural and artistic expression, religion, international aid, scientific research, think tanks, and associational organizations of a thousand different stripes. In the United States, a kaleidoscopic nonprofit sector of more than one million organizations, accounting for roughly 10 percent of the labor force, absorbed

more than $390 billion in 2016, a sum larger than the gross domestic product of many small countries.

Philosophers on Philanthropy

A small scholarly literature attempts to document the historical evolution, scope, and breadth of philanthropy both domestically and globally. A more popular literature aims at criticism of the practice of philanthropy or, in a friendlier manner, at suggestions to philanthropists about how to do more and do better with philanthropic donations. Advice abounds to donors about how to give strategically or more smartly, and so too does advice to leaders about how to improve the effectiveness of charitable organizations.

In order to be in a position, however, to criticize existing modes of philanthropy, or to offer advice about how to improve it, we must have some background standard on which to base our criticism or suggested improvement. We must shift from thinking about what the role of philanthropy *is* in a liberal democratic society to what the role of philanthropy *should be*. And on this topic there is almost no systematic thinking, scholarly or otherwise. It may go too far to say that we first need a *theory of philanthropy* in order to comment intelligently on the topic. Yet that is the subject and aspiration of this book.

In many respects, asking how best to give is an ancient question, one that arises in all societies, not just in liberal democracies. It was Aristotle, after all, who wrote, "To give away money is an easy matter and in any man's power. But to decide to whom to give it, and how large, and when, and for what purpose and how, is neither in every man's power nor an easy matter."[11]

Aristotle notwithstanding, philanthropy has rarely been a topic of serious inquiry, especially in contemporary philosophy.

To the extent that philanthropy has been a subject of serious research in philosophy, it has been the province of moral philosophers and moral psychologists. Their approach provides one answer to Aristotle's question. In seeking to explore the morality of giving, they tend to focus on the perspective of individual donors. This frame gives rise to questions such as: When is giving obligatory? To whom and how much should one give? Is anonymous giving more praiseworthy than its alternative? Does individual motive matter in evaluating giving? What role, if any, does philanthropy play in an account of personal virtue? Peter Singer's argument that individuals in developed countries have especially demanding obligations to assist those in desperate poverty is but one well-known example of such an approach.[12]

These are natural and important questions, and since large majorities of people make philanthropic donations and volunteer time every year, they are asked as often, I would think, by ordinary people as by moral philosophers. Taking this approach is to ask questions about *private, individual morality*. It is to ask about how you or I should practice philanthropy.

This book takes a different approach. I make questions about philanthropy a compelling topic of inquiry for *public morality*, or for *political* in addition to *moral* philosophy. The practice of philanthropy raises distinctive questions of political philosophy that have not often been asked, much less well answered.

To be sure, political philosophers, and especially political scientists, have in the past generation addressed questions concerning associational life and civil society, offering evidence about changes in associational patterns and civic engagement and arguments about their importance to the flourishing of democratic societies.[13] Philanthropy, in the form of donations and volunteer time, constitutes an especially important input—

the essential fuel—of associational life. Moreover, the general phenomenon of giving away money and volunteering is both ubiquitous and universal. Yet political philosophers have neglected the topic of philanthropy.

From the perspective of political rather than moral philosophy, different and important questions arise: What attitude should a state have toward the preference of individuals to give away money for a public purpose? What role, if any, should philanthropy have in the funding or distribution of essential goods and services? When is philanthropy an exercise of power deserving of democratic scrutiny? Is philanthropy always remedial or second best to justice? How, when, and should the state frame, shape, subsidize, limit, or block individual preferences to give money away? Under what circumstances and for what purposes, if any, should associations be granted a corporate form with special tax treatment, as a nonprofit organization, for example?

Cast in this manner, the phenomenon of philanthropy presents unavoidable and fundamental questions of political philosophy. I therefore develop a *political theory* of philanthropy. In so doing, I provide a framework through which we can evaluate what the role of philanthropy in a liberal democratic society should be. More precisely, by the end of the book we will be in a better position to assess the array of actual and possible institutional arrangements that structure, encourage, and give shape to the philanthropic activity of individuals and nonprofit organizations and that, in turn, play a large role in associational life and indeed in democratic life more generally. Is philanthropy in its different forms compatible with liberal democratic ideas? Can philanthropy, in current or alternative forms, support a flourishing democratic society? The arguments provided here will set the foundation on the basis of which criticisms,

sometimes very sharp ones, will be made of contemporary philanthropy. It should not be obvious, after all, that philanthropy is always and everywhere a good thing.

Many people today, especially donors, think that skepticism or criticism of philanthropy is wrongheaded or impertinent. The explanation offered is that when we think about philanthropy, we frequently assume it to be a form, even a paradigmatic form, of virtuous behavior. We might think this for many reasons: because certain kinds of philanthropic activity are commanded or commended by religion; because philanthropy reflects prosocial or altruistic motives, and such motives are socially desirable or praiseworthy; because philanthropy can have good effects, or be a vehicle for producing unambiguously good things in the world, such as reducing poverty or assisting the disadvantaged. These reasons all have some merit.

Another explanation is also at work to account for the high esteem in which philanthropy is usually held. That explanation is to view philanthropy always in comparison to other things that individuals might do with their resources. Supporters of philanthropy stress that rather than giving money away, individuals simply could have saved their wealth or consumed newer and flashier goods. Relative to consumption—going shopping and buying things—and relative to investment—seeking financial returns on one's assets—philanthropy will always come out looking good. Here's the thought: rather than buying a third car, a second home, a first jet, the wealthy person opted to give her money away, and that choice deserves only praise. The same could be said of ordinary donors, those who make small gifts in lieu of, say, purchasing fancy coffee every day. Surely the decision to give money away—even if the motive is not pure, even if the result is ineffective—deserves praise when compared to the identically wealthy person who opts not to engage in philanthropy.

In developing a political theory of philanthropy, it is precisely this view I want to dislodge. I don't wish to deny that relative to consumption or investment, giving money away to others might be a more praiseworthy act. I want to suggest that the comparison to other things that we could do with our money is not the only way to evaluate philanthropy. We need to think, for example, about philanthropy as part of a larger political economy of marketplace and corporate activity, of government spending and public agencies; as a potential exercise of power that warrants democratic scrutiny; as having the potential to help the poor while also entrenching a wealthy elite. And we need to consider whether the legal rules that structure philanthropy—also a form of power, in this case the state's—are justifiable. Finally, I want to suggest, as we will see later, that philanthropy can also be a form of ordinary and self-interested consumption.

What do I mean, then, by a political theory of philanthropy? From my earlier discussion, I hope it is clear that I mean to shift attention away from private morality, away from straightforward ethical assessments of the decisions that individuals make about whether to give away money or property, and to whom, and how much. I mean instead to explore the *public morality of giving.*

A political theory of philanthropy views philanthropic activity as sitting in a variety of relationships to the state. First, it considers the effect of philanthropic activity on the state and on other citizens. For example, philanthropy is sometimes described as private action in the public interest, the direction of private assets to produce public benefits. In this respect, philanthropy has unavoidable political dimensions. What effect does this private action have on the body politic? How does it change, if at all, the relationship among citizens, especially

between donor and recipient? Further, can philanthropy undermine or crowd out legitimate state interests? Might philanthropy be an exercise of private power with objectionable public consequences? Are the strings that donors sometimes attach to gifts objectionably paternalistic? Does donor direction beyond the grave throttle the agency of future generations to channel philanthropic assets? Is perpetuity a defensible time horizon for philanthropy? Does big philanthropy undermine political equality?

Second, a political theory of philanthropy will focus our attention not on individual philanthropic activity and its political dimensions but on the institutional arrangements or regulatory structure of philanthropy, such as the legal rules concerning the creation of nonprofit entities, such as public charities and philanthropic foundations, and the tax treatment of philanthropic gifts. It will provide a framework for assessing the design and performance of the legal rules that shape philanthropy. Under what circumstances would these rules be justifiable? What alternative rules might be compatible with, or required by, the ideals of liberal democratic justice?

This latter set of questions is of particular importance. The basic institutional structure of any society—its legal and political and economic arrangements—has a profound effect on the lives of citizens who are subject to them. They help to establish the basis on which people relate to one another, facilitate their cooperation for mutual benefit, assign to them a variety of rights and liberties, and set the terms for the distribution of various benefits and burdens. But these arrangements are not handed down from the heavens or derived from natural law. They are the products of political decision making, matters of convention, and could be otherwise. One of the primary aims of a political theory, it is often said, is to establish the grounds

on which to favor one set of legal, political, and economic rules over another. This is frequently assumed to be the task of a general theory of justice, and of course different theories of justice offer different arguments about how to choose among rival social schemes and rules.

A political theory of philanthropy focuses our attention on the variety of legal rules that structure and encourage philanthropic activity and prompts us to question whether they are compatible with justice and supportive of democracy. To illustrate further, here are three separate domains that will be discussed at different places in this book.

- *Tax treatment of donations*: Should charitable donations be subject to any favorable tax treatment? If yes, should the tax ramifications be what they are today? Is the charitable contributions deduction defensible?
- *Defining the nonprofit sector*: How should a democratic society define what counts as a nonprofit or nongovernmental organization? Relative to the status quo, should there be stricter or looser criteria for what organizations qualify for status as a public charity or private foundation, perhaps to better reflect redistributive or other aims?
- *Limiting philanthropy*: Are there some kinds of private donations that should be constrained or disallowed, independent of whether they are favored by a tax concession? What time horizons, if any, should orient or limit philanthropy?

This book is called *Just Giving* and I mean, of course, to pick up on a double entendre.

When is giving *just*? Under what conditions, if any, does giving promote, or at least stand compatible with, liberal

democratic justice? How should we understand the relationship between philanthropy and justice? For some philosophers, the relationship is problematic. Will Kymlicka argues, for instance, that justice supersedes charity in importance and that our obligations as citizens to fulfill and realize justice through political institutions effectively subsume any reasons we might have to perform acts of charity. The demands of justice are obligatory and crowd out the space for charity, which is praiseworthy but voluntary. At best, says Kymlicka, charity is a second-best response to unjust inequalities.[14] In chapters 3 and 4, I develop an account that makes space—and not just on a second-best basis—for philanthropy and charity in liberal democratic societies. Philanthropy, under certain circumstances and structured by certain policies, I will argue, has an important, first-best role to play.

And are individuals really just *giving*? I have already described several ways in which philanthropy is not just *giving*. Philanthropy can be the pursuit of self-interest (seeking social status or civic honor, for instance), consumption, or an exercise of power, sometimes an objectionable exercise of power; when undertaken by the wealthy, it can be the expression of plutocratic voice in a democratic society. In many respects, this latter idea is an old and familiar line of criticism. Left-wing critics, especially those of a Gramscian bent, have long attacked philanthropy as but another self-interested means of the powerful to continue their domination over the poor and to entrench the ideological interests of the wealthy in all of society.[15] To the extent that the state is involved in supporting philanthropy, it would merely be abetting the philanthropic actions of the powerful and reinforcing their already dominant position.

I take up questions in all of these areas. I offer a short description of the chapters below, but here's a preview of the main

argument. Many of the legal rules that structure philanthropy in the United States and in many other countries, such as the tax deduction for charitable contributions, are difficult or impossible to justify. In this respect, the book is often critical of contemporary philanthropy. In order to identify what kinds of legal rules would be better, the political theory of philanthropy I develop offers separate treatments of individual philanthropy and the role of private philanthropic foundations, arguing that the institutional arrangements that shape each should emphasize different goals. In the case of individual philanthropy— ordinary giving by individuals, something that virtually all people do every year—I argue that these goals are pluralism and the decentralization of power in the definition and production of public goods. In the case of foundations, I argue that the goal is what I call "discovery," an experimentalist approach to funding and assessing long-time-horizon policy innovations that, if successful, can be presented to a democratic public for approval and incorporation into state policy or, alternatively, adopted into a market economy by corporate actors. The upshot is that philanthropy should not be considered a remedial activity, a second-best approach to the aims of justice in a liberal democracy. It can promote, in a first-best sense, the aims of liberal democracy, and when it does, it is compatible with and plays an essential role in a flourishing liberal democratic state.

On the Terms "Philanthropy" and "Charity"

One terminological note merits a comment. Though some seek to distinguish philanthropy from charity, usually on the ground that philanthropy seeks to attack the root causes of social problems whereas charity aims to provide direct assistance, or on the ground that philanthropy refers to private foundation

activity whereas charity refers to individual donations, I use the two here interchangeably. The reason for doing so is not because I think the putative distinctions between the two are necessarily spurious. The reason is that, however disambiguated, both philanthropy and charity refer to a common activity, namely giving away money or property for some other-regarding purpose. Moreover, whatever one understands by philanthropy and charity, both are regulated and governed by a common institutional framework of laws and public policies. The law currently makes no, or very little, distinction between philanthropy and charity, and since questions about the justification of the relevant institutional arrangements that structure philanthropy form my quarry, in general I make no distinction either. When distinctions between philanthropy and charity are necessary to make in order to account for differences in institutional treatment, I indicate so.

Plan of the Book

Philanthropy is as old as humanity, but it has long been intertwined with social norms and the legal rules of states. In this respect, philanthropy is not an invention of the state but can be viewed as an artifact of the state. In chapter 1, "Philanthropy as an Artifact of the State," I examine a variety of ways that different states have organized, and taken different attitudes toward, philanthropic activity. I bring three historical episodes to the fore, examples rarely included in conventional histories of philanthropy: the liturgical system and *antidosis* procedure in classical democratic Athens; the creation in Islamic societies of the *waqf*, a precursor to the modern foundation; and stark criticisms of foundations made in the eighteenth and nineteenth centuries by French Enlightenment thinker Anne-Robert Tur-

got and Britain's John Stuart Mill. These brief accounts reveal how, in other historical eras, philanthropy has been understood to have political implications and how state policies have been designed to structure, both promoting and containing, philanthropic activity.

In chapter 2, I turn from historical episodes of the interaction between philanthropy and the state to the contemporary institutional arrangements that shape philanthropy. I do so with an eye toward assessing these arrangements in relation to the value of equality, and my conclusion is that, contrary perhaps to expectation, philanthropy sits uneasily with equality. Both the policy instruments and the distribution of giving reflect little if any concern with egalitarian distribution. Philanthropy, we will learn, is directed with surprising *infrequency* to the relief of poverty and assistance for the disadvantaged. My main focus is on the United States, but many of the general U.S. policies—such as tax benefits for philanthropy—exist in other liberal democratic societies.

Chapter 3, "A Political Theory of Philanthropy," presents a general framework for assessing what I take to be a universal and ubiquitous phenomenon in need of analysis: how ought a liberal democratic state consider the preference of individuals to give their money or property away for a philanthropic purpose? In light of the fact that nearly all liberal democracies provide advantageous tax treatment for philanthropic donations and organizations, I explore what might justify such policies. They amount, I claim, to subsidizing the exercise of liberty to give money away. A respect for the liberty of individuals to give away money or property that is legitimately theirs is one thing, subsidizing its exercise is another. Three potential justifications for a subsidy are presented—a tax base rationale, an efficiency rationale, and a pluralism rationale—and I spell out the normative

implications of each. I conclude that the efficiency and pluralism rationales both have some merit, but that they lead to different implications for what kinds of nonprofit organizations should be eligible for tax-incentivized donations. In this respect, I provide a positive case for an important role that philanthropy can and should play in liberal democratic societies. The arguments offered also suggest that none of the rationales supply a justification for many of the policies, described in chapter 2, that structure philanthropy in the United States today.

In the fourth chapter, "Repugnant to the Whole Idea of a Democratic Society? On the Role of Foundations," I consider a particular form of philanthropy that is relatively recent in origin, small in size relative to total giving overall, but large and growing in power and influence: the general-purpose grant-making private foundation. I draw upon the largely forgotten story of John D. Rockefeller's contentious effort in the early twentieth century to win approval from the U.S. Congress for a federal charter to establish the Rockefeller Foundation. That foundations in the early twentieth century needed to be authorized by a democratic body in order to be incorporated reflects the tension that was seen between the plutocratic voice of a private foundation and a democratic society that prizes the political equality of citizens. Extending the framework in the preceding chapter, I examine the role and legitimacy of private foundations in liberal democratic societies. Many of the legal permissions currently enjoyed by foundations, such as low accountability and transparency, generous tax treatment, and protection of donor intent in perpetuity, warrant exacting normative scrutiny. Yet foundations can survive such scrutiny, I argue, provided they operate in a particular role, namely as "discovery" mechanisms for innovations in social policy that the state and market are unlikely to undertake.

The final chapter, "Philanthropy in Time: Future Generations and Intergenerational Justice" (written with Chiara Cordelli), considers philanthropy, both individual giving and the
activity of private foundations, as a vehicle for intergenerational
justice. Liberal democratic justice offers powerful reasons to
treat intergenerational *philanthropic* transfers of wealth differently from intergenerational *family* transfers of wealth. Setting
up a foundation that lives beyond one's death is different from
transmitting wealth, in the form of an inheritance, to one's
heirs. Whereas the latter should be limited or forbidden in the
interest of intergenerational equality, the former should, under
certain circumstances, be permitted or encouraged in the interest of intergenerational justice. Philanthropy, unlike the family,
can play three important roles in promoting justice for future
generations. It can, first, complement political institutions that
aim to secure the reproduction of social capital over time. Second, it can supplement political institutions in fulfilling what
John Rawls called the "just savings principle," especially as a
hedge against remote, low-probability but highly consequential
risks (such as potentially cataclysmic natural disasters). Third,
as developed in the previous chapter, the intergenerational
existence and potential long-time-horizon outlook of private
philanthropic foundations can counteract built-in features of
short-termism and presentism in the democratic process.

1

Philanthropy as an Artifact of the State

INSTITUTIONAL FORMS
OF PHILANTHROPY

The practice of philanthropy is as old as humanity. People have been giving away their money, property, and time to others for millennia.

The classic work of French sociologist Marcel Mauss illuminated the ubiquity of gift giving in archaic or primitive societies. Mauss identified what he called the gift exchange, a form of exchange contrasted with market exchange. Gift exchange was not merely ubiquitous; Mauss argued that gift giving revealed the deeper structure of social relations and that gifts were embedded within a morality of obligation and reciprocity. Moral norms about giving, receiving, and reciprocating informed gift economies, which in turn helped to establish social order and hierarchy. Gift giving was frequently, perhaps always, competitive and strategic. Gift exchange in this sense does not directly

map onto the idea of charity or philanthropy, though of course philanthropy can also be understood as competitive and strategic and also as an exercise of power that reveals underlying social structures and hierarchies.[1]

In a brief and tantalizing passage, Mauss suggested that during times of surplus, expectations about generosity shift and the wealthy come to be seen as obligated to the poor. Here begins, he says, a theory of alms, in which the "ancient morality of the gift" is changed into a "principle of justice."[2] We shall pursue this idea—the distinction between charity and justice—in the next chapter.

In this chapter, our aim is to examine how social norms are always at work in the activity of philanthropy. Philanthropy has an ineliminable moral and political undercurrent. And there is a rich tradition of scholarship, partly stimulated by Mauss, on the gift and its relationship to charity and justice. As I mentioned at the outset, however, my aim in this book is not an exploration of the morality of giving as such—whether, when, where, and to whom individuals should give, and how gifts should be received and reciprocated, if at all. My aim is to develop a political theory of philanthropy, to explore what kind of institutional arrangements should define and structure philanthropy. My particular interest is the fit between philanthropy and contemporary theories of justice that involve commitments to liberal democracy, which is to say commitments to the values of liberty and equality. One might say that I aim to examine the norms, drawn from the independent standing of liberal democratic justice, that ought to inform the institutional setting in which philanthropy takes place.

Seen this way, philanthropy is more than the sum total of individual philanthropic acts. It is also an institutionalized practice of privately funding the production of goods that have prosocial or

public benefits. In this respect, philanthropy is not an invention of the state but ought to be viewed as an artifact of the state. We can be certain that philanthropy would not have the form it takes in the absence of the various norms, laws, and policies that help to define and structure it. In the modern-day United States and most other developed countries, this much should seem obvious. The contemporary practice of philanthropy involves tax incentives to give money away. More generally, laws govern the creation of nonprofit organizations and foundations, and they spell out the rules under which these organizations may operate. The legal codification, for example, of the nonprofit corporation, as distinct from the for-profit corporation, is a relatively recent phenomenon. In the United States, laws for incorporation as a not-for-profit corporate entity began in the late nineteenth century.[3]

Tax incentives for making philanthropic gifts are also relatively new—dating back in the United States to 1917 and the institution of a federal income tax. Yet states of all different kinds have long done more than simply respect the liberty of individuals to make philanthropic donations. Philanthropy should not be understood in the simplistic manner of an array of activities that take place within a framework of nonintervention by the state: philanthropy as nothing more than the aggregation of private individual decisions to give money away. Instead, philanthropic behavior, both individually and collectively, must be understood as embedded in political institutions, laws, and public policies, the sum total of which help to give shape, structure, and social meaning to philanthropy.

That this is so should seem obvious. Philanthropy is hard to imagine, for instance, without political arrangements concerning property and lawful transfer of property. Such arrangements are necessary, after all, to understand when something can be donated, treated as one person's legitimate possession

in order to give to another person or entity. Even if the political attitude toward the philanthropic inclinations of individuals is simple governmental forbearance, such an attitude depends on a background legal infrastructure about property and, quite frequently, much more, such as taxation, a legal codification of recognized charitable purposes, and institutional arrangements concerning bequests, trusts, and endowments and their permissible size and duration.

Typical histories of philanthropy often begin by making reference to the Greek origin of the word "philanthropy" (love for humanity) and the religious, specifically Judeo-Christian, roots of charity, referring to a spiritual calling to assist the poor and sick. Think here of the biblical commitment to tithing or of the passage "it is more blessed to give than to receive" (Acts 20:35). And standard histories virtually always make mention of the passage in medieval England of the Elizabethan Statute of Charitable Uses in 1601. This law was among the first to define what would be recognized as official, that is, politically sanctioned and supported, charitable purposes, with the aim of assigning the state some authority over the creation and expenditure of the many private charitable trusts that had been created, lodged most frequently within a church, and directed at many different purposes. Here we see quite plainly the interaction between the state and the practice of philanthropy.

In this chapter, I provide a short tour of different political arrangements that have organized the phenomenon of philanthropy. Philanthropy may be a universal and time-immemorial activity, but because its practice is embedded within different social norms and structured by different institutional arrangements, it takes on different forms in different places at different times. This is what I mean by the idea that philanthropy is not an invention but an artifact of the state.

My purpose is threefold. First, I demonstrate the deep and underappreciated history of the different attitudes or approaches, as encapsulated in laws and social norms, toward philanthropy. Philanthropy has long been embedded within political systems, and so its practice must be understood in relation to the state. I give examples of how states have organized and codified philanthropy through law, calling attention to a variety of institutional design mechanisms for its practice. Second, I refute an idea that is too frequently assumed today, namely that philanthropy is just the expression of the liberty of individuals, a freely and voluntarily undertaken activity in which the state plays no role at all. This is false; philanthropy depends on laws about, among other things, property, transfer, trusts, donor intent, and taxation and, quite frequently, on codifications of state-sanctioned charitable purposes. Third, I use these historical episodes as a springboard for what follows in the next chapter: an examination of the laws and policies that structure giving in the contemporary era, focusing primarily on the United States. This will provide the backdrop for my development, in chapter 3, of a political theory of philanthropy for modern liberal democratic states.

What follows therefore is not a concise history of philanthropy. It is a selective tour of three different episodes in the history of philanthropy that illustrate the relationship between philanthropy and the state or the public rather than private morality of philanthropy. These are the liturgical system and *antidosis* procedure in ancient democratic Athens, the creation of the *waqf*, a forerunner to the private foundation, in Islamic societies, and the surprising attitudes of a French enlightenment thinker, Anne-Robert Turgot, and of British philosopher John Stuart Mill, about laws concerning foundations. I have chosen examples that I find interesting rather than merely

familiar—there are ample accounts of the religious roots of charity and the etymological roots of philanthropy. And I have chosen examples that demonstrate both institutional support for as well as resistance to philanthropy.

The Liturgical System and the Amazing Antidosis Procedure in Democratic Athens

One of the most remarkable episodes in the history of the relationship between philanthropy and democracy dates back to ancient democratic Athens. Ancient Greek city-states, as in any society, contained different economic classes or social strata. Athens developed a system whereby wealthy citizens were expected to make voluntary contributions to various state projects that were of benefit to the entire citizenry, or *demos*. It developed a system, in other words, in which private donations for the production of public benefits were routine.[4]

This is known as the liturgical system. A liturgy is the private funding by wealthy citizens of state services and activities, and it was one of the principal mechanisms through which the state funded itself and the public services it provided. According to some estimates, the sum total of liturgies accounted for more than half of all state revenue in fourth-century Athens.[5] The central role of liturgies demonstrates how the wealthy were expected to return part of their wealth in service to the community.

The Greek liturgy was, as one scholar describes it, "compulsory philanthropy."[6] It generally fell into one of two categories: festival liturgies, the underwriting of civic plays or choral dramas, known as *choregia*, or athletic competitions, known as *gymnasiarchia*; and military liturgies, the funding of defense and war needs. Military liturgies primarily involved

the funding of naval warships, called *triremes*, and the donor who outfitted and maintained the ship and its crew usually became its captain, or *trierarch*. This latter arrangement was known as the *trierarchy*.

The liturgical system in Athens cannot be understood apart from deeply seated social norms in ancient Greece that prized competition, honor, and virtue. Wealthy citizens sometimes competed for the privilege of liturgical service, expecting in return for their donations both honor and gratitude for their status as a civic benefactor. Motive in providing the liturgy was important; to receive honor and gratitude, gifts had to be provided in the spirit of benefitting the body politic, or demos, rather than for personal gain or status maintenance. In the absence of the appropriate civic spirit, benefactors could fail to receive favor from their fellow citizens and, more threateningly, by jurors in any court appearances. They could even be punished by courts. In this respect, liturgies can be seen as an instance of what Mauss observed about gift giving: the gift represents and reflects norms of obligation and reciprocity. Ober comments, for instance, "Gifts to the state in the form of liturgies and the sense of gratitude jurors would feel for the good done the state can therefore be seen as an elaboration at a national level of a giver/recipient relationship between individuals, a relationship that continued to function alongside the system of state liturgies."[7]

Yet, as Ober's final clause suggests, the liturgical system was also given particular expression by democratic Athens in its laws and institutions. The liturgy took on special form and meaning within the democratic *polis*. Gabrielsen observes in his masterly *Financing the Athenian Fleet*, for instance, that "the Athenian liturgical system in the classical period was firmly attached to democracy."[8] Significant democratic reforms came

to Athens around 480 BC—the creation of election to public offices by lottery, for example. During this period, what was once the voluntary prerogative of the wealthy under oligarchy to undertake liturgies became regulated by law. "In addition to its principal intention, which was to reduce (but not completely eliminate) aristocratic influence, the democratic constitution embodied the requirement that affluent households expend part of their wealth on the city through the fiscal conduits of the liturgy system."[9]

New democratic laws provided that liturgical service for the funding of festivals could be assigned to wealthy citizens rather than performed voluntarily. Reliance on civic norms that wealthy individuals would make donations, in the proper spirit, in return for honor and gratitude was eclipsed, and liturgies more frequently were allocated to particular citizens by democratic rulers. Honor and gratitude would still attach to liturgical service, but the element of voluntary provision receded, even if never eliminated completely. Liturgies in democratic Athens became a system of public finance via private contribution, something akin to a system of taxation. According to Ober, by the fourth century voluntary liturgical service continued for some civic benefactions but the state also began to assign liturgical service to wealthy individuals on some kind of rotating schedule.[10]

Nowhere was this more visible than in the funding mechanism for military liturgies, in particular the construction and outfitting of Athenian warships, known as the *trierarchy*, and in the *antidosis* procedure, the latter of which comes as an astonishment to any contemporary observer of philanthropy.

Festival liturgies happened on a regular schedule; athletic competitions and dramatic performances were held during different seasons and at predetermined intervals. But the

financial demands of military liturgies such as the trierarchy were less predictable because the need for certain numbers of warships was not constant, growing or diminishing depending on whether Athens found itself at war. With limited alternative mechanisms for taxation and public finance, democratic Athens developed a complicated system of philanthropic funding for military needs, involving elements of voluntarism and compulsion.

Funding a warship (*trireme*) and becoming its captain (*trierarch*) could occur in a number of different ways. First, a wealthy citizen could volunteer for the public service, privately funding the warship itself and volunteering as the captain of the ship. Undertaking this burden was a source of honor and civic status. But wealthy individuals could also be appointed to the trierarchy. The Athenian state kept registers of wealthy people, and if one had not performed a liturgy recently, which typically qualified a person for temporary exemption, the state could select that person to donate for the provision of a warship and perform the needed service. If appointed, the wealthy individual could accept and would then donate for the liturgy and serve as captain. However, the appointed wealthy person was not obligated to accept by law. He had other options and could not immediately be coerced by the state to serve.

Instead of accepting the appointment, one option was the antidosis, in which the appointed person could attempt to resist liturgical service by pointing out the fact that other citizens with even greater resources were not volunteering and had not performed any significant liturgy recently. One could seek, in other words, to transfer responsibility for the liturgy to a fellow citizen of greater means. But simply pointing out that other citizens were wealthier and therefore presumably more able to afford the donation was not enough. The appointed person

had to name a particular individual as a potential replacement. At this point in the process, the wealthier person so named could accept the liturgy, gaining public recognition both for his superior wealth and as a civic benefactor, and then the initial person would be exempt and the liturgical service would proceed with the newly named person as the funder. Or the wealthier person could refuse.

And here is where things become especially interesting. If the challenger refused, the initially appointed person could offer to exchange estates with the wealthier person and, with that person's estate now in his possession, carry out the liturgy. If the challenger refused to swap estates, the matter would then be referred to a court hearing with peers serving as jurors. The court would then decide which of the two disputants would carry forth the liturgy.

Of course, for the person challenged, resorting to a court resolution risked three things: first, the refusal to perform the liturgy despite possessing superior resources could bring shame and dishonor; second, the court could order an exchange of estates, depriving the wealthier man of his superior resources in addition to the sting of civic dishonor; and third, the court could punish the person who refused to perform the liturgy.[11] Thus, the disputants had powerful reasons not to involve the court and to work out the performance of the liturgy privately. Refusing a challenge, according to Gabrielsen, meant "automatically agreeing to exchange properties with the challenger."[12]

The design of the liturgical appointment system and antidosis procedure counts as an ingenious institutional design mechanism for philanthropy.[13] It amounted to the private provision of a quintessentially public good, military defense, in this case the Athenian navy. And it was tied distinctively to democracy and the limitation of aristocratic influence. Ober

describes the imposition of forced liturgies upon the rich "as a democratization of the donation system. As long as liturgies were voluntary, the state had little effective control over the donors, since all voluntary donors would expect *charis* [gratitude] from the demos when they gave money to the state. When liturgies were made regular and were legally required, however, the demos obtained effective control over at least every very rich man's property. The individual who gave only what was demanded by the state, and then grudgingly, was not deserving of the demos' *charis*. By making *charis* more difficult to obtain, forced liturgies shifted the balance of wealth-power in the favor of the masses."[14]

Overall, the mechanism of the liturgical appointment system and antidosis procedure had three important effects within democratic Athens. It served, first, to help prevent wealth concealment and avoidance of taxation, for if challenged to perform a liturgy and one professed to be resource-constrained, the appointed person, who was likely to have better knowledge than public officials of a neighbor's true wealth, could exchange estates with the neighbor and then perform the liturgy. The system gave officials visibility into the comparative wealth of the Athenian elite. Second, it furnished Athens with the funds it needed for essential public services while in effect delegating to the wealthy the decision about who would provide the funds. No wealthy citizen could claim, therefore, that he bore an unfair philanthropic burden for civic finance since he could always challenge a wealthier citizen to perform the liturgy. Third, and therefore, it created some democratic control over wealth while still preserving certain privileges for the wealthy, such as honor, gratitude, and status as a civic benefactor. Gabrielsen's conclusion is apt: the process can be understood as "the domestication, under Athenian democracy, of the aristocratic warrior."[15]

Obviously, there is no modern analogue of the liturgical system and certainly not of the antidosis procedure.[16] Even so, contemporary echoes of these distant Athenian norms are not impossible to find. I have in mind what is sometimes called patriotic philanthropy, in which wealthy citizens make donations not to private nonprofit organizations but to the state itself in a spirit of civic benefaction.[17] Whatever the case, the century-long existence of the liturgical system and antidosis procedure in democratic Athens attests to a distinctively democratic institutional design for the organization and regulation of private funding of public benefits. The episode reveals an interesting and deep relationship between philanthropy and a democratic state.

The Islamic Waqf: Precursor to the Contemporary Philanthropic Foundation

The main contemporary English-language reference guide for scholars of philanthropy, *The Nonprofit Sector: A Research Handbook*, contains a lengthy historical overview of philanthropy and nonprofits called "The Nonprofit Sector in Historical Perspective: Traditions of Philanthropy in the West." There is but one recent philosophical treatment of philanthropy, edited by the distinguished philosopher J. B. Schneewind, *Giving: Western Ideas of Philanthropy*.[18] Both texts announce a focus on the West, aspire to a comprehensive treatment, and discuss Jewish, Christian, and ancient Greek and Roman roots of philanthropy. Neither contains any discussion at all about Islamic practices of philanthropy.

This is peculiar in light of the fact that Islam was born in seventh-century Arabia, which was at that time under Byzantine influence and had resident Christians and Jews. Byzantine religion and culture were also infused with the legacy of

Greece, which connects the origins of Islam with the ancient Greek world. As a result, the Holy Book of Islam, the Qur'an, whose text was fixed when the prophet Muhammad died, reveals deep influence from Judeo-Christian traditions. If by "Western traditions" one means to pick out a shared cultural genealogy, rather than simple geographical location, Islamic philanthropic traditions should be counted as part of, or at least deeply connected to, the West.

My point here is that the absence of Islam from standard scholarly explorations of the history of philanthropy is a lamentable mistake. Its etymological roots notwithstanding, philanthropy is exclusively rooted neither in the ancient Greek world nor in the Judeo-Christian past. Examples of private giving for prosocial or public purposes can be found everywhere. And examples of such giving that involve well-developed institutional arrangements to define and support philanthropy also exist outside of the geographically defined West.

One significant but underappreciated historical tradition is the early development in Islam of the *waqf*, a legal and institutionally defined charitable endowment that was a central component of Islamic civilization for centuries. The waqf is especially interesting because its institutional arrangement makes it a kind of precursor to the modern philanthropic foundation.[19] The waqf represents an institutional design for channeling private resources for the production of public benefits.

My focus here is on the waqf, but it is not the only relevant example to illustrate distinctively Islamic traditions of philanthropy. For example, as commanded in the Qur'an, one of the five main pillars of Islam is *zakat*, or mandatory almsgiving. Little historical evidence remains to document how zakat worked in practice, but the intent of the practice is clear: zakat is obligatory, analogous to the practice of tithing, and was intended to

be collected by a central Muslim authority that would distribute the funds to benefit eight separate classes of recipients, including the poor. In addition to zakat, the Qur'an also commends the performance of voluntary giving, called *sadaqa*.[20] Zakat was basically a religious tax payment whereas sadaqa was more varied in quantity and purpose; it could be given anywhere and at any time, though it was frequently tied to a calendar of occasions for voluntary giving. Both zakat and sadaqa were understood to be a demonstration of one's piety, and their practice continues today.

In contrast to zakat and sadaqa, which were present at the birth of Islam and discussed in the Qur'an, the waqf developed in the ninth or tenth century, is unknown in the Qur'an, and was designed to provide enduring public benefits for society during the life and *beyond the death* of the donor. The mechanism of the waqf was simple. A living man or woman could create a waqf by relinquishing ownership of private property, usually real estate but sometimes just cash, for the support of a designated social service or other beneficiary. Waqfs were permanent, meant to provide revenue in perpetuity, and once established were irrevocable. Creating a waqf out of private property funded public benefits, but also conferred some private advantage: the establishment of a property as a waqf usually shielded it from taxation; and waqfs were often publicly associated with their donors so that, like the Greek liturgy, benefactors gained social recognition and status in addition to demonstrating their piety.

Waqfs could be established for a great variety of purposes, including nonreligious purposes, though the social service or beneficiary had to be sanctioned by Islamic law. Many had the spirit of almsgiving. Typical waqfs were founded to support specific buildings, such as mosques or schools, or to provide funds for soup kitchens, hospitals, orphanages, tombs, and

shelters for travelers. Because the waqf was intended to exist in perpetuity, the initial donor also appointed a manager of the waqf and defined a process for managerial succession. Local judges could intervene in cases where the manager deviated from the donor's intent or mismanaged the assets placed under his trust. The endowment deed of each waqf—sometimes an ornamental certificate listing the intended beneficiary of the donor and the appointed manager—would be registered with local judges or authorities. Scholars have mined the many thousands of these waqf deeds to create a detailed picture of the institutional design and operation of the waqf over many centuries. Whereas sadaqa and, to a lesser extent, zakat were informal acts of charity, infrequently leaving behind a paper trail of documentation and frequently prizing anonymity, the creation of a waqf was more formal, more transparent, and more public insofar as waqf deeds were recorded by local authorities and insofar as the frequent purpose of a waqf was to endow and sustain a well-known building, such as a mosque.

The number of waqfs accumulated over time, and they quickly became integral to Islam. Scholars describe the waqf as "a defining feature of Islamic civilization" that would become a source of "cross-civilizational emulation." By the end of the tenth century, observes the historian Marshall Hodgson, the waqf replaced zakat as nothing less than "the vehicle for financing Islam as a society." Most of the major Middle Eastern mosques constructed in the Middle Ages were funded and sustained by the waqf system. Virtually every soup kitchen in the Ottoman Empire was provisioned by a waqf. Istanbul, the largest city in Europe in the late seventeenth century, had a waqf-financed entity that served food to an estimated thirty thousand people per day. Waqfs also supported smaller beneficiaries, including hostels for religious pilgrims, public bazaars,

water wells, bakeries, and a neighbor who owed taxes, and id-iosyncratic beneficiaries such as the support of donkeys, stray cats, and dowries for poor girls.[21]

By the 1800s, records document the existence of twenty thousand waqfs in the Ottoman Empire generating annual revenue equivalent to one-third of annual state revenue. Beyond their provision of particular social services and public benefits, one indicator of the significance of waqfs is the percentage of total real estate property designated as a waqf. According to some scholars, an examination of detailed land records and waqf deeds reveals that when the Republic of Turkey was founded in 1923, upward of 75 percent of all arable land had been set aside in waqfs. Smaller but nevertheless still significant percentages—on the order of one-third of all land—could be found in nineteenth-century Tunisia, Algeria, and Egypt.[22] The waqf system was not a marginal institutional arrangement for the private provision of social benefits sanctioned by Islam; it was a central and enduring feature of Islamic society.

Like the liturgical system in classical Athens, waqfs were a mechanism for the private provision of public goods. Emblematic of this fact is the existence of a waqf dedicated to the establishment and operation of a lighthouse, the paradigmatic example of the modern economic definition of a public good as nonrivalrous (consumption by one person does not diminish supply for another) and nonexcludable (no one can be excluded from use of the good). Citizens of all kinds, poor and wealthy, relied upon waqfs for the construction and maintenance of mosques and schools and for basic social services.

The waqf was in the first instance not a political creation but a religious one. A waqf was an independent entity defined, recognized, and regulated by religious custom and law, a private and pious individual creation with a public-facing purpose.

But of course this took place within Muslim political systems in which politics and religion were tightly coupled: Islamic law was the basis of political law, the latter could not contradict the former, and political elites and religious elites were interconnected. Moreover, the religious origin of the waqf served two important political functions. First, the institutional design of the waqf created a legally sanctioned and supported flow of private funds for social services of many different kinds, and did so in a way that facilitated their intergenerational provision, extending often across many centuries. Second, the public benefits provided by waqfs persisted not only across generations but also often through shifts in political arrangements. Individual waqfs could survive political upheaval in large part due to their design and purpose: the religious and legal obligation of the waqf manager was to honor the founder's intentions in perpetuity, and the establishment of a waqf was understood socially to be a pious act. After establishing a waqf, the endowed property was considered to belong not to the donor but to God. Rulers or state officials could threaten to confiscate waqf assets or redirect their intended purpose, but not without appearing impious.[23] If the assets of a waqf belonged to God and were intended to provide important social services in perpetuity, interfering with a waqf was politically risky for any ruler; such interference had to be justified in terms of legal Islamic principles, and these systematically favored the waqf rather than the opportunistic ruler. Embedded in this way within Islam, the waqf was insulated from shifting political winds and even from dramatic changes in political regimes. For these reasons, waqfs were among the most enduring of *all* Islamic institutional arrangements.

Over the course of centuries, there evolved three basic kinds of waqfs: imperial, charitable, and family. The labels are

somewhat misleading, for all three kinds shared the same legal form and were all charitable, in that their purpose was to provide enduring benefits for others. The labels are meant to capture something about differences in the kind of donor and the kind of recipient. So-called imperial waqfs were created by members of the ruling Muslim class, a sultan and his relatives, for example, or by other high state officials. Imperial waqfs had a wide class of beneficiaries. Some of the largest waqfs were imperial, consisting of waqf complexes, typically a large parcel of land with a mosque and associated charities such as a madrasa and soup kitchen. Charitable waqfs could be created by any man or woman, including Jews and Christians living in Muslim territories, ranged considerably in size, had a great diversity of purposes, all of which had to be sanctioned by Islamic law, and funded social benefits for a broad population. Material benefits from charitable waqfs almost never flowed to their founders. Family waqfs could also be created by any man or woman, but directed the benefits of the property for the intergenerational support of family members and were a mechanism for the preservation of family wealth. All three kinds of waqfs required the donor to appoint a manager, and for family waqfs the manager would often be a salaried family member who would receive a percentage of the waqf's annual income.[24]

Today, waqfs continue to exist in many Islamic societies, though their prevalence and legal status have changed dramatically, primarily because of the effects of nationalization, modernization, and rationalization of the state in the nineteenth and twentieth centuries and, not least, of the effects of British colonialism in India and French colonialism in Algeria. Modern states began to assume greater responsibility for the provision of social services, diminishing the need for waqfs while simultaneously driving up demand for generating tax revenue, and

partly because large percentages of land had been assigned to waqfs, colonialists sought to free up property for their own purposes and settlement, altering the legal status of the waqf. In the nineteenth century, the Ottoman Empire centralized the administration of waqf assets, and in the twentieth century, the modern waqf emerged via legal reforms in Turkey, Egypt, and other predominantly Muslim states, which permit a waqf to be founded by a group, to undertake fund-raising, and to invest assets in the commercial marketplace. In this form, the waqf is a more conventional nongovernmental organization.

The modern evolution of the waqf is, however, not my concern here. For my purposes, what makes discussion of the waqf important is the similarity between the waqf and the contemporary private foundation in the United States and many other countries. Charitable waqfs and, to a lesser extent, family waqfs anticipate many of the institutional features and social functions of a philanthropic foundation, and waqfs therefore deserve recognition as one of the most important institutional precursors to the contemporary foundation.[25] Like a waqf, the private foundation consists in the legally sanctioned establishment of an endowment whose assets and income-generating revenues are directed to fund a wide variety of public benefits. Like a waqf, the assets of a private foundation are generally exempt from taxation, and therefore the decision to establish a foundation can be understood as a mechanism for sheltering wealth from taxation. Like a waqf, the private foundation enshrines fidelity to donor intent and does so beyond the death of the donor. Neither the managers of a foundation nor state officials can abrogate donor intent by redirecting the assets of a foundation to purposes not designated by the donor. Like a waqf, both the donor's directives and the assets of a foundation are legally designed to last *in perpetuity*. Like the waqf system,

the provision of public benefits through private foundations constitutes a form of limiting the authority of the state by decentralizing the production and distribution of public goods. Limiting the power of the state as the main or sole determinant and provider of public goods might itself be construed as a benefit, but decentralization provides additional benefits: donors differ in their preferences about what charitable purposes to pursue, and this permits funding public benefits that might be politically risky or impossible for the state to pursue.

And finally, like a waqf, including a family waqf, the private foundation, especially in the form of the family foundation (one of the most common kinds of foundations), can be used to produce a variety of benefits for one's own family. These include not just the ability to shelter wealth from taxation or confiscation, but also the permission to employ family members in the management of the endowment and distribution of funds. This is a routine practice among small family foundations in the United States. Beyond these material benefits, the creation of a private foundation, like that of a charitable or family waqf, is a mechanism for generating social status and recognition. Foundations are frequently named after their donors, as is true with waqfs, and this confers status as a civic benefactor. Donors can moreover seek a certain form of immortality by insisting upon naming rights in return for donations. Founders of waqfs often did the same, naming structures endowed by their gifts after themselves and even insisting, as a condition of a gift to establish and support a mosque, that ritual prayers conclude with a commemoration of the donor's benevolence.[26]

In summary, the institutional form of the waqf anticipates by many centuries, in a non-Judeo-Christian context, a number of core features of the contemporary private philanthropic foundation: a permanent endowment whose revenues are designed

to provide public benefits, tax protections for the endowment, legal protections for adhering to donor intent, permission to exist in perpetuity, conferral of both material and status advantages to the donor and the donor's family, with the aggregate result that the supply of public benefits is partly decentralized. The waqf system stands, as does the private foundation, as a widely used mechanism for the private provision of public goods through a permanent endowment.

One obvious difference between the waqf system and both the liturgical system of classical Athens and the private foundation of the contemporary United States is that the waqf was not embedded within democratic political arrangements. The waqf system was not entirely divorced from questions about democracy, however. There is significant scholarly controversy about whether the widespread creation of waqfs, the considerable amount of untaxed land that accumulated in waqfs over time, and their institutional features that inscribed donor intent and perpetual existence help to explain why democracy did not take root earlier in Islam. Timur Kuran has argued, for example, that the waqf system bears chief responsibility for sustaining autocracy and retarding democracy in the Middle East. Kuran's explanation is complex and controversial, but among the reasons he emphasizes is the rigidity and inflexibility of the waqf system, where each waqf was harnessed in perpetuity to purposes assigned by an initial donor and legally blocked from alteration or adaptation to evolving social needs.[27] Kuran views the institutional legacy of the waqf as a hindrance to democracy. That waqfs bear more than a passing resemblance to contemporary philanthropic foundations—something he fails to register—raises, at least to my mind, interesting questions about the compatibility of foundations with democratic societies.

The suitability of foundations for democratic societies was a concern, it turns out, for two prominent eighteenth- and nineteenth-century intellectuals interested in democracy and representative government, French Enlightenment intellectual and royal official Anne-Robert Turgot and British philosopher, parliamentarian, and civil servant John Stuart Mill. To their efforts in resisting the influence, and sometimes very existence, of foundations I now turn.

Eighteenth- and Nineteenth-Century Resistance to Foundations

If the waqf was an institutional precursor to the contemporary private philanthropic foundation, it is not the only such historical antecedent. The idea of a foundation as the legally recognized dedication of private assets to the provision of some civic benefit dates to antiquity. Most such foundations, as in the case of waqfs, were perpetual endowments or, in modern parlance, operating foundations, philanthropic bodies that did not themselves make grants to other entities but instead directly provided and sustained a particular benefit for the community, such as a hospital, soup kitchen, school, orphanage, church, and so on.

The widespread adoption of such perpetual endowments, coupled with their accumulation over centuries, eventually gave rise in the eighteenth and nineteenth centuries to resistance and criticism. The background context, of course, is the Enlightenment, with its characteristic suspicion of religious authority and ambition to deploy reason on behalf of social progress. Across Europe in the early 1700s grew unease with *mortmain* (literally "dead hand"), perpetual and inalienable corporate ownership of real estate, most frequently that of the

church. Such unease was partly motivated by rising skepticism of the church and resistance to its power. It was also motivated by concern that the rights of donors, even after their death, were unduly elevated over the rights of heirs; the establishment of a perpetual foundation by a wealthy family was thought to cheat descendants of inheritances that were properly theirs. This mattered not merely because the alleged rights of heirs were being neglected, but also because philanthropic activity by the wealthy threatened national security.

To the contemporary ear, this comes across as bizarre. How could philanthropy threaten national security? The answer is that only private property owners, rather than stewards of a philanthropic endowment, would be likely to defend their property from foreign invasion. The intergenerational transfer or inheritance of land and wealth, not the establishment of philanthropic endowments, was thought essential to creating the appropriate incentive structure for citizens who would be called upon to uphold national defense.[28]

ANNE-ROBERT TURGOT

> I do not fear to say that were we to weigh the advantages and disadvantages of all the foundations in Europe, perhaps there would not be found one which would stand the test of an enlightened scrutiny.

An entirely different attack on foundations was launched in the mid-eighteenth century by Anne-Robert Turgot.[29] Turgot was a contemporary of Voltaire and Rousseau, a mentor to Condorcet, a hero to the French *philosophes*, and royal minister of the navy and controller-general to King Louis XVI from 1774 to 1776. Condorcet wrote an admiring biography shortly after

Turgot's death. Alongside Adam Smith, whose *Wealth of Nations* appeared in 1776, Turgot is considered one of the founding fathers of economics as an independent social science.[30] Today he is perhaps best remembered for his ideas about human and social perfectibility. Turgot was the founder of the ideology of progress, the idea that basing political authority, social organization, and public policy on reason would bring about constant improvement, that humans and civilization were capable of steady betterment. He represents the philosophical taproot of rational meliorism.

Here our concern is with his 1756 contribution, "Fondation," to the famous *Encyclopaedie* of Diderot.[31] Turgot viewed foundations not as injurious to the rights of heirs or as impediments to national security. He saw them as massively inefficient and, over time, grossly ineffective and vainglorious vehicles for social improvement. Foundations fail to promote social progress, he thought. Instead, they actually retard progress and should therefore be swept away.

Turgot's article is most frequently invoked as an early example of the argument that certain forms of charity can actually perpetuate the existence of the poor. Less appreciated is that Turgot's skepticism about alms for the poor is but one portion of a frontal attack on the very existence of private foundations. Turgot attacked not just the particular philanthropic projects of wealthy donors but the very idea that foundations could be useful. His intention, he announced at the start of his short entry, was to examine "the utility of foundations in general, in respect to the public good, and chiefly to demonstrating their impropriety." He enumerated several reasons, drawn out of the "philosophic spirit of the age," that delivered nothing less than a thunderous denunciation of foundations old and new: "I do not fear to say that were we to weigh the advantages and

disadvantages of all the foundations in Europe, perhaps there would not be found one which would stand the test of an enlightened scrutiny."[32]

Turgot offered four separate arguments against foundations. First, he claimed that though the intentions of philanthropic founders might be admirable, the effect of foundations was often negative. Charitable provision for the needy was not to be celebrated if it failed to address the source of the need. Worse, foundation support is often given "to a few individuals against an evil the cause of which is general, and sometimes the very remedy opposed to the effect increases the influence of the cause." Here Turgot laid out the case that charity can set in a dynamic that subsidizes idleness, neglects the underlying cause of a problem, and provides reason to beneficiaries to remain objects of charitable need. Thus, says Turgot, where philanthropic resources are most abundant "misery is more common and more widely spread than elsewhere."[33] Turgot's sentiments here echo across time, finding similar expression in Tocqueville's *Memoir on Pauperism*, in which he claimed that "any measure which establishes legal charity on a permanent basis and gives it an administrative form thereby creates an idle and lazy class." We can also find threads of Turgot in Henry David Thoreau's memorable passage, "There are a thousand hacking at the branches of evil to one who is striking at the root, and it may be that he who bestows the largest amount of time and money on the needy is doing the most by his mode of life to produce that misery which he strives in vain to relieve."[34]

Second, Turgot criticized foundations as frequently nothing but projects for the self-aggrandizement of donors. To establish a foundation, he writes in the opening lines of his article, "is to assign a fund or sum of money in order to its being employed in perpetuity for fulfilling the purpose the founder had in view,

whether that purpose regards divine worship, or public utility, or the vanity of the founder—often the only real one, even while the two others serve to veil it." Foundations, in short, are vehicles to promote the honor and reputation of the donor, not disinterestedly motivated projects for the private provision of public goods. Philanthropists cloak in virtue what is actually vanity, even as their foundations fail to address the root of social ills. In a sarcastic aside that might well apply still today, Turgot observes the "splendor of the buildings" and the "pomp connected with some of the grand foundations" and says their social utility might favorably be valued at "one hundredth part of the whole cost."[35]

Third, Turgot voiced strong objection to the legal arrangement that permitted foundations to exist in perpetuity and for the intent of the initial founder to determine the purpose of the philanthropic fund across generations. This is his most fundamental criticism. He suspends the first two objections and supposes that the social effects of the foundation at inception are positive and supposes that motives of the founder are praiseworthy. Even in such circumstances Turgot rejects the idea that permanently dedicated endowments will retain their utility. He offers two distinct reasons for this. One is that the management of a foundation tends toward degeneration as it is handed down from the donor to a series of trustees, whether those trustees be family members or professional stewards. "Founders deceive themselves," says Turgot, "if they imagine that their zeal can be communicated from age to age to persons employed to perpetuate its effects." It is but wishful thinking for the initial creator of a philanthropic endowment to believe that his successors will maintain the vision and effectiveness of the foundation. Turgot's criticism is a familiar one today; we often hear in contemporary debates about private foundations that

the founder would be appalled to discover what his grandchildren or professional managers have done. Echoing Turgot, for example, economist Gary Becker complains that U.S. foundations have a lamentable tendency to become politically liberal over time and that professionally trained managers and trustees wander from the founder's initial political convictions.[36]

The second reason Turgot offers against perpetual endowments eschews reliance on predictions of mission drift—an argument contingent on claims about probable empirical outcomes—and rejects perpetuity on principle. Assume, writes Turgot, that a foundation at its origin has "incontestable utility" and that fail-safe precautions have been taken against its degeneration. Even in such cases foundations are objectionable because perpetual existence is objectionable. No person is so wise as to be able to anticipate the needs of future generations; no foundation's purpose, endowed in perpetuity, could guarantee its social utility. And yet the law demands fidelity to donor intent and protection of assets across generations. Thus, for Turgot, "the very immutability which the founders have succeeded in giving it is still a great public impropriety, because time brings about new revolutions which will sweep away the utility the foundation once fulfilled and will render its continued operation even injurious."[37] Turgot's background views about social perfectibility and constant progress are clear here. Even if well managed, a foundation is shackled by law to the donor's initial intent. The philanthropy of even enlightened founders, driven by the purest of motives, eventually becomes dead weight over the course of time as conditions change, social problems evolve, and new needs arise. Foundations conceivably can be valuable entities in the short run, but the logic of *perpetual* foundations requires that they be abolished and swept aside. His tone becomes sharper as Turgot concludes his essay,

No work of man is made for immortality; and since foundations, always multiplied by vanity, would in the long run, if
uninterfered with, absorb all funds and all private properties, it would be absolutely necessary at last to destroy them.
If all the men who have lived had had a tombstone erected
for them, it would have been necessary, in order to find
ground to cultivate, to overthrow the sterile monuments
and to stir up the ashes of the dead to nourish the living.[38]

What lesson, then, did Turgot draw from his broadside attack
on permanent philanthropic endowments? It was a simple lesson, actually. He recommended that political authorities assume the right to ban the creation of new foundations and to
modify and, if necessary, to annul the terms by which existing
foundations operate. The political institutions that gave definition to and recognition of permanent endowments should be
altered. He offered strong endorsement for a 1749 edict of the
French king that blocked the formation of new foundations except those that were approved by the Crown (an edict quickly
undone by legal loopholes and exceptions).[39] More dramatically, because "public utility is the supreme law," Turgot argued
that no social convention or superstition about the intention of
the donor should temper the right of the state to interfere with
philanthropic corporate bodies. He went still further. Private
entities—and here Turgot meant of any kind, philanthropic or
otherwise—were not products of nature or protected by natural law. "They have been formed by society, and they ought
not to exist a moment after they have ceased to be useful."[40]
Corporations are not independent of the state but are conven-
tions of the state, and for any entity to warrant a corporate
charter, it must serve a clear public interest.[41] Philanthropy in
the form of the establishment of an endowment to provide

some kind of public benefit might meet the test of social utility, but the end could be pursued and accomplished by simply letting individuals give their money away. There was no need for the incorporation and legal recognition of a foundation. The institutional form that had persisted for centuries and had permitted permanent endowments with the dead hand of the donor defining the purpose of the endowment in perpetuity had to be swept aside.

By the end of the eighteenth century, criticism of perpetual foundations was commonplace. Enlightenment thinker par excellence Immanuel Kant echoed Turgot's conclusions in 1797: "Even perpetual foundations for the poor, and educational institutions, cannot be founded in perpetuity and be a perpetual encumbrance upon the land because they have a certain character specified by the founder in accordance with his ideas; instead the state must be free to adapt them to the needs of the time."[42] No foundation, even those dedicated to admirable ends and constituted by well-intentioned donors, should live forever. Perpetuity unduly binds future generations and undermines the ultimate political authority of the state.

The views expressed by Turgot (and Kant) strike a contemporary sensibility as politically radical. Current laws in the United States and in many other countries do not merely permit the establishment of permanent endowments with a mission defined in perpetuity but favor or stimulate the creation of such endowments with tax benefits.[43] Turgot's views were also radical at the time, and for a reason it is harder from our current vantage point to appreciate. Turgot aimed not merely to visit "destruction" upon foundations, to undermine the legal status of permanent endowments, and to assert the right of the state to modify or abolish corporate entities, but also to attack the Catholic Church in France, which was the wealthiest and most

powerful corporate body in the French kingdom and was the source, and frequent beneficiary, of a vast number of endowments. To the Enlightenment rationalists, the corrosive legacy of the Church was not simply the promulgation of religious superstition among gullible believers but, more practically, the generations-long accumulation of capital and land that was locked up in perpetual endowments. Virtually every small town in France, no matter how rich or poor, had a parish with a foundation whose assets supported church activities, such as masses for the dead, facility maintenance, housing for priests, and so on.[44] Montesquieu had proposed in his 1748 *Spirit of the Laws* to leave existing religious endowments and real estate intact but to prevent the Church from acquiring new lands, even if they were to be set aside as philanthropic endowments. Voltaire was bolder, claiming that Church property actually belonged to the nation and proposed that any Church property be nationalized if doing so was determined to be in the public interest.[45] Turgot's essay, the fifth and final contribution he would make to the *Encyclopaedie*, followed shortly thereafter. His ideas represented those of the *philosophes* more generally and were widely disseminated. They had a potent effect. It was only a few decades later, in October 1789, on the eve of the French Revolution, that Talleyrand proposed nationalizing all ecclesiastical property, for which the pope promptly excommunicated him. And in December 1789 the Assembly passed legislation that put all Church estates at the nation's disposal and followed this with the sale to the public of the Church's corporate lands.

For my purposes here, the broader context of French society and the actual consequences of his ideas are certainly relevant but not of chief interest. What Turgot provides us is an early and important set of objections to permanent philanthropic

endowments. These objections arose out of Enlightenment thought and were directed, in the main, at diminishing the power of the Catholic Church and establishing a new political and social order in France based on reason and the idea of progress. These were ideas that in a different country and in different circumstances and with a democratic setting in mind John Stuart Mill, the great champion of individual liberty, would pick up and modify in the next century.

JOHN STUART MILL

> There is no fact in history which posterity will find it more difficult to understand, than that the idea of perpetuity, and that of any of the contrivances of man, should have been coupled together in any sane mind.

Mill wrote three essays about foundations over the course of thirty years. His most significant statement on the subject, "Corporation and Church Property," was published in 1833 in a periodical called the *Jurist*.[46] It was also issued as an anonymous pamphlet in the same year under the more telling title "Corporation and Church Property Resumable by the State." Mill's general argument was that endowments should be permitted, in some cases even celebrated, but that they should never be perpetual and that the state must always retain the right to intervene in a philanthropic endowment. He rejected Turgot's deprecation of the very existence of foundations and developed instead a framework for understanding how a democratic government could, and should, make endowments socially useful. The baseline principle is summarized best in a passage in his 1873 *Autobiography* reflecting on his early views about foundations: "The paper in the Jurist, which I still think

a very complete discussion of the rights of the State over Foundations," asserts the doctrine, wrote Mill, "that all endowments are national property, which the government may and ought to control."[47] Mill's allegiance to utilitarianism leads him to a view deeply critical of the actual operation of foundations at that time yet leaves room for a principled defense of their existence.

In the 1833 essay Mill responds directly to Turgot, whom he holds in such high regard—expressing "deep reverence for this illustrious man" and describing him as "the great and good Turgot"—that he seems almost embarrassed to be in modest disagreement. "That eminently wise man," wrote Mill, "thought so unfavourably of the purposes for which endowments are usually made, and of the average intelligence of the founders, that he was an enemy of foundations altogether."[48] Mill excuses Turgot's mistake as an understandable reaction to the great number of ineffectual or harmful foundations in France and the lamentable power of the Catholic Church, which was "irreconcilably hostile to the progress of the human mind." He is in full agreement with Turgot that foundations count among the "grossest and most conspicuous abuses of the time" and yet concludes that the great evils of foundations exist not because there are foundations "but because those foundations were perpetuities."[49] It was this point Mill wished to dispute, and in his characteristic mode and Victorian prose, Mill provides a classic philosophical exposition of the case against perpetual endowments and the case in favor of time-delimited endowments. Mill's essays amount to a framework for understanding how a liberal democratic state should treat the historical practice of the establishment by wealthy persons or corporate entities, especially the church, of philanthropic endowments.

It is worth examining Mill's arguments in some detail, not merely for the clarity with which he sets out his case but for the

refreshing lack of reverence or sentiment he has for philanthropy. Mill sings no hymns of praise to the wisdom of wealthy
men or to the public spirit of philanthropic entities. Mill identifies his question with precision—what are the rights and duties
of a legislature with respect to endowments and foundations?
And his answer is unambiguous; there is "no moral hindrance"
to a legislature in interfering with endowments, even if such
interference amounts to "a total change in their purposes."[50]
His exposition is philosophical, by which I mean he is chiefly
concerned with the moral principles at stake that make the
inquiry general. But he admits to a practical motivation too: a
"most pressing" need for the public and the British Parliament
to decide what may and should be done with the property of
the church and of other public corporations. There is therefore
a question of political ethics—would state control over foundations amount to a violation of liberty, property, and first principles of justice? There is also a practical question—because permanent endowments already exist, under what circumstances,
and to what end, may a government assert control over a foundation? The practical question is worth addressing only if the
answer to the philosophical question is to defend state control
over foundations. So Mill focuses the lion's share of his attention on the general and philosophical question.

In so doing, Mill sets aside consideration of the projects and
motives of individual philanthropists. If foundations as a class
are to be found objectionable, it should not be on grounds that
one dislikes or disapproves of the particular interests of a donor.
Let any person have an opinion on any foundation, and yet
separate from the mind, says Mill, all impression or evaluation
of the character of the donor or the purposes of the endowment. "We have our opinion, like other people, on the merits

or demerits of the clergy, and other holders of endowments. We shall endeavor to forget that we have any."[51]

Having thus cleared the terrain of the brush of mere opinion and personal prejudice and established the clear ground of principle on which to proceed, Mill begins his inquiry by taking note of the "exceedingly multifarious" purposes for which foundations have in many different countries been created. Schools, hospitals, orphanages, and almshouses, monasteries and universities, corporations local and national in scope, funded by money or real estate—all have been part of the tradition of foundations that direct what had once been the private assets of an individual to a public purpose in perpetuity. Should it ever be permitted, Mill asks, for the government to interfere with this purpose or to appropriate the foundation's assets?

His answer is immediate and blunt. Finding it "so obvious" that he can scarcely conceive how any "earnest inquirer" could think otherwise,[52] Mill asserts that the founder's intentions in establishing an endowment should be legally protected only for his lifetime and perhaps a very short duration thereafter. No foundation should have its purpose fixed forever.

In light of Mill's direct references to Turgot, we can surmise that Mill drew directly in his reasoning from Turgot. The two shared a principle of social utility and a rationalist's desire to establish political institutions on the basis of reason. Thus, like Turgot, Mill argues that circumstances change, societies evolve, old needs dissipate, and new needs arise, and no founder could ever be so wise as to infallibly predict the future. To permit foundations to exist in perpetuity amounts to making "the dead, judges of the exigencies of the living" and that "under the guise of fulfilling a bequest" a foundation transforms a "dead man's intentions for a single day" into a "rule for subsequent centuries."[53]

Summoning all his rhetorical powers to signal the strength of his conviction, Mill concludes,

> There is no fact in history which posterity will find it more difficult to understand, than that the idea of perpetuity, and that of any of the contrivances of man, should have been coupled together in any sane mind: that it has been believed, nay, clung to as sacred truth, and has formed part of the creed of whole nations, that a signification of the will of a man, ages ago, could impose upon all mankind now and for ever an obligation of obeying him—that, in the beginning of the nineteenth century, it was not permitted to question this doctrine without opprobrium.[54]

Mill rejects eternal rights of founders and funders, and sweeps aside any claim that in interfering with a foundation the state is engaging in a violation of property rights. The dead have no property rights, Mill claims. Neither do the trustees of a foundation, who serve as successors to the initial founder and are obliged to carry out the founder's purposes. To the extent there is any property interest, Mill says the property belongs to the intended beneficiaries of the endowment, the people for whom the foundation had been created. It is therefore "no crime to disobey a man's injunctions who has been dead five hundred years."[55] To the objection that Mill's argument amounts to a defense of robbing the church or expropriation of someone else's property, he replies that it is not the clergy but the congregants who own the church's endowments and that it is permissible for the state to act on behalf of these congregants to redirect the purposes of the endowment, if need be, to their own benefit. Mill is scoring some easy points here, and only later does he confront the real legal obstacle and objection to his position. That objection is that the church is a corporation,

and foundations of many kinds have been incorporated by the state. Corporations are legal personifications and can possess property, and therefore it is the church as a corporate body that would be robbed were the state to expropriate any church endowment and redirect it to some ostensibly more socially useful purpose. This line of reasoning would apply as much today as it did in Mill's time. Mill concedes the point, namely that the church is a corporate body with legal claims of personhood and ownership. His reply is straightforward, a paradigmatic expression of Mill's Socratic impulse: "Because the law is so, does it follow that it ought to be? Or that it must remain protected against amendment?" Mill's response, in effect: the law is morally bad and should be changed. Neither dead persons nor corporate entities should be entitled to any rights, or at least rights of the same kind of significance that attach to living persons. Mill announces here a striking claim: "The only moral duties which we are conscious of, are toward living beings, either present or to come; who can be in some way better for what we do or forbear." Should a government push aside the alleged rights of founders, of trustees, or of corporate bodies themselves, would trouble Mill not at all. To the contrary, he would "sleep with an untroubled conscience the sleep of the just; a sleep which the groans of no plundered abstractions are loud enough to disturb."[56]

Mill concludes by explaining under what circumstances and for what purposes the government ought to intervene in a perpetual endowment. He gives two criteria to guide intervention: first, that intervention is warranted only for purposes of social utility and, second, that when a government intervenes, it should do so by hewing as closely as possible to the intentions of the founder. Mill is concerned not to authorize state action that would permit confiscation of endowments for

any purpose at all, especially for purposes that might tempt legislators looking for means to pay off state debts or diminish burdens of taxation more generally. These criteria, and Mill's discussion of them, are less significant for my purposes than his reasoning against perpetual foundations and his endorsement of time-limited foundations that serve to support and enhance democratic government. This latter aspect of Mill's argument is especially important, for it provides an example, like that of the liturgical system in classical Athens, of how the rules and norms that structure philanthropy can render its activities supportive of democratic ideals.

Foundations need not merely be scrutinized by the state to ensure their social usefulness; a society that fosters philanthropic endowments in a particular manner can improve upon democratic governance. Mill offers three distinct reasons why foundations, especially educational and cultural endowments, directed solely by the preferred projects of donors so long as their preferences are not guaranteed in perpetuity, can play a salutary social role.

First, governments are fallible, and though it is important for the state to undertake its own projects and to express its preferences about the provision of various goods, it should not block or deter others from attempting to provide the same goods in different ways or different goods altogether. "A government," Mill says, "when properly constituted should be allowed the greatest possible facilities for what itself deems good; but the smallest for preventing the good which may come from elsewhere."[57]

Second, Mill points out that under democratic government, where, unlike the cases of monarchies or aristocracies, citizens have a formal political voice in what the government does, and, through elections, authorize its activities and hold public offi-

cials accountable, it is "the opinion of the majority that gives the law." Therefore, permitting the creation of time-limited foundations affords minority opinions a voice and a public hearing. It permits minorities a mechanism to produce the kinds of public goods that they cannot manage to convince a majority to authorize through elected representatives. In so doing, minorities can attempt to persuade the majority and shift provision of their preferred goods to the public purse. Even if they fail in persuading others, Mill says they are still a "convenient mode of providing for the support of establishments which are interesting only to a peculiar class, and for which, therefore, it might be improper to tax the whole community."[58]

Third, democratic states that permit the creation of foundations undertake what we could call Millian "experiments in living." It might be the case that particular foundations are genuinely eccentric and contribute little, if anything, to the greater part of the public. It is the activities of foundations in the aggregate, however, that command democratic attention. When private individuals have permission to make public expression of their individual, and even idiosyncratic, views about the public interest not only through their voices but through their wallets, it not merely gives place to minorities but is an important mechanism of social progress. Private foundations in the aggregate can supply variety, diversity, and experimentation in a never-ending conversation and contestation about what counts as a public good or a worthy social project. In an 1869 essay on endowments that revisits Mill's 1833 remarks on church property, Mill issues a ringing defense of such endowments: "What is called tampering by private persons with great public interests . . . means trying to do with money of their own something that shall promote the same objects better. . . . It is healthy rivalry."[59] I shall return to, and develop in greater

detail, Mill's reasoning in my later discussion of foundations in chapters 4 and 5.

Conclusion

Upon reading Turgot and Mill on the subject of foundations, it is impossible not to have the impression that the authors are scathing in their assessment of the actual operation of many endowments, especially those that are old and belong to and benefit the church (often one and the same). The tone of Turgot's and Mill's essays is caustic and denunciatory. Both agree that the long-standing practice of legal sanction of permanent endowments and respect for the intent of founders in perpetuity has deleterious social consequences. They reason not merely from the evidence presented to them by the actual practices of endowments in France and England and elsewhere. They also state their case as a matter of principled argument: societies evolve, needs change, and for there to be the prospect of social progress, the present should never be tethered to the design and purpose of founders long dead. Dead men should wield no power over the living or the unborn, and it does no damage to them to modify or annul their philanthropic projects in favor of the interests of the present day. Perpetual private philanthropic foundations, no matter how enlightened the founder, are scandalous.

In the end, however, Mill, but not Turgot, offers redemption of the foundation, so long as it is appropriately governed and constrained by law. Foundation assets are never to be considered the property of the donor or the trustees; founders ought to have no rights to block state scrutiny of and intervention in foundation assets and activities. And no government should permit foundations to exist in perpetuity. Yet when individuals

can create foundations that exist for their lifetimes, or perhaps for a limited duration thereafter, foundations can contribute to healthy democratic societies. Permitting private funding of what individuals believe to be in the public interest is legitimate because government is not infallible. Foundations can also lift up minority interests and permit public expression of idiosyncratic preferences without any burden on the public purse. And finally, foundation activity in the whole can amount to fulsome experimentation and innovation. Democracies would be wise, Mill thinks, to create public policies that structure and regulate philanthropic endowments along these lines.

Private giving for the provision of public goods has a long history. I have here avoided retelling a history of philanthropy that roots its practice in Judeo-Christian ideas of charity, makes dutiful reference to one of the early legal codifications of official charitable purposes—the 1601 Elizabethan Statute of Charitable Uses—and goes on to mention Tocqueville's famous description of the United States as a nation of joiners, and ends, usually, with the creation of the American general-purpose, grant-making, private foundation in the early twentieth century by Andrew Carnegie, Russell Sage, and John D. Rockefeller. I have instead emphasized that although philanthropy is a ubiquitous and universal phenomenon, it is shaped and structured by social norms and public policy. The design of institutions, formal and informal, matters a great deal for what counts as philanthropy, how philanthropy is practiced, who its beneficiaries are, and how it relates to the state. Philanthropy is not an invention of the state but an artifact of it.

The overview here of three episodes in different parts of the world in very different eras—of the liturgical system in classical Athens, of the development and significance of the waqf in Islamic civilization, and of the eighteenth- and nineteenth-century

debates about perpetual endowments by Turgot and Mill—provides an antidote to any historical amnesia that might suggest philanthropy, as it is practiced today, is a novel phenomenon. It also suggests that when we think about philanthropy, we ought not consider and evaluate it only, or even primarily, as the decision of an individual to give money away for a public purpose. We must also consider philanthropy as an act with political dimensions, in the sense that philanthropy can be an expression of political power, as in the case of Athenian liturgists who garnered civic honor through their private giving, and in the sense that philanthropy is shaped by political arrangements, as in the case of the legal recognition of the waqf. Put differently, wealthy elites can pose problems for democratic politics, even—and perhaps especially—when elites direct their wealth toward the public sphere. Wise democratic governance seeks, when possible, to redirect elite influence, as with classical Athens, so that it might act on behalf of the demos or to contain it, as with Turgot's and Mill's arguments against perpetual foundations.

The norms and policies that give definition to philanthropy are contingent, not inevitable, and the short history here reveals different attitudes and institutional designs, drawn from political rather than private morality, to support, permit, or limit philanthropy of different kinds. In a liberal democratic state, public policies require public justification. In the next chapter, we turn toward an examination of the array of contemporary policies that regulate philanthropy and explore its connection to justice and, in particular, to the ideal of equality.

Philanthropy and Its Uneasy Relation to Equality

One could begin an inquiry into what might count as just institutional arrangements for philanthropic giving by starting with matters of abstract principle.[1] What are the demands of liberal democratic justice, and what do they imply, if anything, for the practice of giving money away? How should philanthropy be understood with respect, for example, to especially important liberal democratic ideals such as liberty and equality? And then, without ever making reference to existing institutional practices or actual patterns of philanthropic giving we see before us, one might craft a blueprint of institutional arrangements for philanthropy that are derived from considerations of justice. One could proceed, to use a phrase invoked with some frequency in contemporary political philosophy, at the level of so-called ideal theory.[2] This would be to ask the question, what role, if any, should philanthropy play in a perfectly just society?

My approach will be somewhat different. I do not in any way eschew analysis of abstract principle, but neither do I wish

to ignore the diversity of institutional arrangements one can find in actual liberal democratic societies and that play a highly consequential role in giving shape to the direction of private resources for public benefits. It is useful, I find, to have reference points to real-world institutional design and performance both in order to make evaluations about whether institutions live up to the demands of justice *and* in order to explore and assess matters of justice themselves.

A growing debate has emerged among political philosophers about reasoning in ideal versus nonideal modes and whether there are important methodological differences between the two. Some philosophers criticize the method of working only at the level of ideal theory. In Amartya Sen's description, political philosophy is better conducted in a "comparative" rather than "transcendental" mode; his aspiration is to focus attention on comparisons of real or possible institutional arrangements, within or across societies, in order to effectuate improvements, to make the world a little more just. Other philosophers argue that the very idea of ideal theory is bankrupt.[3]

I see no good reason to take sides here, and I do not attempt to referee this debate.[4] It is perhaps more my intellectual predisposition, not a principled conviction that ideal theorizing should be resisted, that I prefer to begin, at least in part, from real-world settings and the importance of identifying and attempting to diminish or eliminate actual injustice.

In the previous chapter, I considered three historical episodes that illuminate different institutional designs intended to structure philanthropic activity. In this chapter, we turn our attention to present-day institutional arrangements. Many of these arrangements are obscure, buried and expressed in the arcane jargon of the tax code. They are no less powerful a shaper

of philanthropic behavior, however, for their obscurity. In this chapter I take stock of the array of philanthropic policies, especially within tax law, and assess them in relation to one of the core ideals of liberal democratic societies, equality. The decision to focus attention on equality is nonaccidental: for many people and in many historical traditions, philanthropy has something to do with providing for the poor and disadvantaged. This is especially so, of course, if the term one is analyzing is "charity," which denotes voluntary assistance for those in need. For the average person, charity is synonymous with almsgiving. Moreover, independent of history and etymology, if we ask ourselves what kind of philanthropy a liberal democratic society might wish to produce, a focus on equality could lead us to believe that public policies should structure philanthropy so that it assists the poor and disadvantaged.

The setting I inhabit is the United States, and although I avail myself on occasion of comparisons to philanthropic policy arrangements in other countries, and to earlier eras in the United States, my chief reference point will be contemporary U.S. policies. This should not count as a significant liability for non-American readers, I hope, partly because other countries frequently seek to emulate American philanthropy, and therefore it should be of interest whether it would be desirable to do so, and because many (though certainly not all) of the policy arrangements I describe in this chapter are identical or similar to those in other liberal democratic societies.

Philanthropy and Equality

There's a conventional story to tell about philanthropy and its relation to liberty and equality. The story is this. Philanthropy

is thought to be tightly connected to liberty. This is so for two reasons. First, philanthropy is voluntary. Whereas the state can mandate and coerce behavior, activity within the philanthropic sector is not compelled. Indeed, charitable actions that are coerced are thought not to be instances of charity at all. It is no coincidence that philanthropic organizations are part of what is typically called the voluntary sector or the independent sector. Second, the exercise of liberty includes freedom to associate, which, famously in the American context, has resulted in the inclination for people to join together to address and solve social problems. Philanthropy is not only an activity of free persons, but when the state protects the freedoms of individuals, it sometimes becomes a group activity. To illustrate this latter point, commentators tend to produce any number of Tocqueville citations, especially the familiar line about Americans being a nation of joiners.[5]

Philanthropy is also thought to be tightly connected to equality. This is so because the quintessentially philanthropic act—and the virtue in the philanthropic act—is often said to consist in providing for the poor or disadvantaged or in attacking the root causes of poverty or disadvantage. Certainly this is historically true of various traditions of charity—think of the imperative to assist the poor in various religious traditions, the practice of almsgiving, and the famous 1601 Elizabethan Charity Law that codified official charitable purposes, most of which involved directing charitable resources to those considered the deserving poor. And many believe it is true today: that the philanthropic sector in modern society is justified at least in part because of its redistributive or, to invoke an archaic but wonderful term, "eleemosynary" aims.[6] Philanthropy results in the lessening of inequality between rich and poor, either

through direct transfers from the rich to the poor or through efforts to improve structural conditions so that the poor will no longer need to rely on charity for basic sustenance.

This story, linking philanthropy to both liberty and equality, is an attractive one. And it contains some truth. My aim in this chapter, however, is to complicate this rosy story. I show how the rosy story holds far less frequently than we ordinarily think it does and that philanthropy has an especially rocky relationship with equality. I argue that philanthropy is not often a friend of equality, can be indifferent to equality, and can even be a cause of *in*equality.

More specifically, I argue that philanthropy sits uneasily with an egalitarian norm in two different respects. Equality is wanting, first, on the input or supply side of philanthropy. The public policies that regulate philanthropic giving treat donors in deeply unequal ways. The policy instruments in the United States designed to structure giving are, as we will see, powerfully inegalitarian, amplifying the voice and preferences of the wealthy over and above their already louder voice in virtue of the size of their fortunes. And equality is wanting, second, on the output or demand side of philanthropy. Contrary to popular impression, the distribution of charitable giving *does not* predominantly benefit the poor. And in some cases philanthropy actually produces or exacerbates inequality. When we consider philanthropy and its relationship to liberty and equality in the U.S. context, therefore, it is far easier to discern the story that connects philanthropy to liberty than to equality. Indeed, American policy not merely respects the liberty of individuals to make philanthropic gifts but subsidizes the exercise of that liberty.

These observations constitute, I hasten to add, no decisive objection to the practice of philanthropy in general or to the

policies that structure it, for there are a variety of justifications for philanthropic endeavors, some of which depend not at all on philanthropy being redistributive or eleemosynary. I explore these other justifications in later chapters.

In some sense, I hope to make a familiar point about liberty and equality and apply it to philanthropy. The familiar understanding about liberty and equality sets these two ideals in tension with one another. On the one hand, protecting the liberty of individuals inevitably brings about distributive inequality. Some people are savers, others spenders. When people are free to lead their lives as they please, the cumulative impact of the choices they make will leave them in unequal positions, be it with respect to income, wealth, education, opportunity, and so on. On the other hand, promoting equality seems to require significant interference with the liberty of individuals. To make people equal with respect to some opportunity or material outcome, the state needs either to redistribute goods from some people to others (e.g., through tax and transfer policies) or to curtail the liberty of some for the benefit of others. Some believe that the former is tantamount to the latter; Robert Nozick infamously described taxation as "on a par with forced labor."[7]

The liberal democratic state, on this interpretation, cannot maximally realize both liberty and equality, for the promotion of one sometimes comes at the expense of the other. In Isaiah Berlin's clever phrase, "Total liberty for the wolves is death to the lambs."[8] If the tension between liberty and equality is unavoidable, then philanthropy cannot unproblematically embrace both liberty and equality. The familiar story about philanthropy with which I began must be more complicated.

As described earlier, my focus here is not on the motives or actions of individual donors but on the political institutions in

and through which philanthropy takes place. An underlying theme of this book is that we can assess not only the actions and motives of individuals as donors—an evaluation of private morality—but also the institutions that structure philanthropy—an evaluation of public morality. One might go further: a complete assessment of the private morality of giving depends on clarity about the public morality of giving. Can the motive of a donor be understood apart from tax incentives that are in the self-interest of the donor and that reward philanthropic behavior?

But such a claim is not necessary for my argument here. I simply recognize that, though philanthropy may be as old as humanity itself, its setting in modern societies—as well as in ancient social orders such as classical Athens or premodern Islam—embeds it firmly within the political institutions of the state. Public policies of many different kinds shape and structure philanthropy. The most obvious examples in the United States are the charitable contributions deduction and the legal definition of different kinds of nonprofit organizations. In the language of an economist, these produce "distortions" in individual behavior and in the philanthropic sector.[9] Philanthropy would not have the form it currently does in the absence of the various laws that structure it and tax incentives that encourage it.

The chapter proceeds as follows. The first section offers a short descriptive overview of philanthropy in the United States. I turn then to the complex interplay between philanthropy and the tax code. I examine the variety of institutional arrangements that shape philanthropy with an eye to their implications for the two dimensions of equality mentioned earlier: the egalitarian norm on the input or donor side and the egalitarian norm on the output or distributive and beneficiary side. In each case, I focus attention on the ways in which the public policies

governing philanthropy are at best indifferent to equality and at worst deeply inegalitarian. In the final section, I provide an illustration of how philanthropy can be causally implicated in the worsening of inequality: the case of private donations to public schools.

An Overview of Giving in the United States

It is often said that Americans are the world's most generous citizens. The claim is based upon the large amount of money given away every year by Americans, approximately $390 billion in 2016, a figure that has risen more or less constantly for the past forty years.[10] See Figure 2.1.

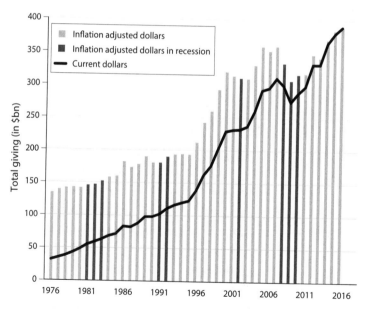

FIGURE 2.1. Total Giving: 1976–2016. *Source*: Giving USA Foundation, "Giving USA 2017."

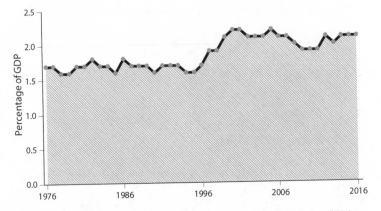

FIGURE 2.2. Giving as Percentage of GDP. *Source*: Giving USA Foundation, "Giving USA 2017."

The United States has many more citizens than other highly industrialized countries, so the absolute amount given ought not be an especially significant metric. A better metric to substantiate the claim that Americans are especially generous is the total amount donated as a percentage of gross domestic product (GDP), about 2 percent, a figure that has remained more or less constant over forty years, even during recessions, and that compares favorably to statistics from other countries. (See Figure 2.2). Perhaps more telling, donations for several decades have hovered at roughly 2 percent of disposable net income.[11]

As shown in Figure 2.3, four primary sources account for the roughly $390 billion donated in 2016: living individuals, bequests by individuals at their death, corporate foundations, and philanthropic foundations. Gifts by living individuals account for the vast majority of donations at 72 percent, reflecting the fact that the incidence of charitable giving in the United States is indeed widespread. According to recent studies, nearly 90 percent of American households make charitable donations.[12]

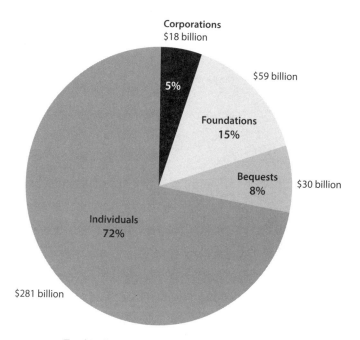

Total Dollars Contributed = $390 billion

FIGURE 2.3. 2016 Charitable Contributions by Source (in Billions of Dollars). *Source*: Giving USA Foundation, "Giving USA 2017."

Philanthropy and Tax Policy

Americans might in some respect be a most generous people. But the intertwining of charitable giving with the tax code— the tax concessions available for charitable giving—also makes the United States the most generous country in terms of subsidizing charitable activity.

What are the institutional arrangements in the tax code that give shape to philanthropy in the United States and that provide such generous subsidies? Here we necessarily confront some

arcane and technical information. I keep the discussion brief and jargonless to the extent possible.

Nonprofit organizations and philanthropic foundations enjoy an array of substantial tax benefits at the federal level. The details and levels of these benefits have changed from time to time, either when Congress passed legislation directly affecting nonprofits and foundations or when Congress passed legislation making changes in the rates of taxation for individuals, estates, and corporations. The rules are often very complicated, but the underlying mechanisms that supply the tax advantage are simple and have been the same for decades.[13] First, nonprofit organizations, including private foundations, which are a specific kind of nonprofit organization, are tax-exempt entities. They are not generally subject to tax on income or revenue (e.g., donations or grants made to the organization or fees collected in the performance of their function, such as tuition payments to universities). There are more than twenty-five different categories of nonprofit, tax-exempt organizations in U.S. law, including social welfare organizations, fraternal societies, employee benefit associations, business leagues, chambers of commerce, veterans organizations, cemetery companies, black lung benefit trusts, and teacher retirement fund associations. The list reads, perhaps unsurprisingly, not as the product of a rationalized system or coherent theory of nonprofit organizations but as a sedimentary history of the slow accumulation over many years of incremental changes and additions to the law.

Second, for a specific and large class of nonprofit organizations, those called 501(c)(3)s after the section of the tax code that defines them, contributions of cash or property to the nonprofit organization are *tax-deductible* for the individual or corporation making the contribution. There are two kinds of 501(c)(3)

organizations: "public charities" that receive a substantial portion of their income from the general public or from government, and "private foundations" that receive most or all of their income from a small number of donors and use payouts from an endowment to fund their grant-making activity. The vast majority of nonprofit organizations in the United States are 501(c)(3) public charities, and they are the public face of the charitable or nonprofit sector. More importantly, the provision of tax-deductible donations to public charities and private foundations is perhaps the most well-known institutional incentive for charitable activity, and some version or another of this incentive has existed since the creation of a federal income tax by the U.S. Congress in 1917. In addition to these two basic mechanisms (i.e., tax exemption for nonprofit organizations and tax deductibility for donations to public charities and private foundations), nonprofit organizations are also exempt from tax on investment income; private foundations pay a small 2 percent excise tax on net investment income, generally coming from endowments. Finally, and nontrivially, nonprofit organizations of all kinds are generally exempt from property taxation at the state and local levels.

Expressed in the abstract language of the tax code, it is hard to appreciate just how significant an intervention into charitable and philanthropic behavior these tax laws are. To get a better picture, consider what the tax laws mean in concrete terms for a would-be donor. The mechanism of a tax deduction for a donation creates a subsidy by the government at the rate at which the donor is taxed. So a person who occupies the top tax bracket—39 percent in 2017—would find that a $1,000 donation actually costs her only $610. The government effectively pays $390 of her donation, subtracting this amount from her tax burden. Similar incentives exist for the creation of donor-advised funds and private and family foundations, and for contributions

to community foundations, where donations and bequests to a foundation are deducted from estate and gift taxation.

In extending these tax incentives, federal and state treasuries forgo tax revenue. Had there been no tax deduction on the $1,000 contribution, the state would have collected an additional $390 in tax revenue. Or to put it differently, tax incentives for philanthropy constitute a kind of spending program or "tax expenditure."[14] Just as a direct spending program has an effect on the annual budget of the United States—Congress allocating funds for defense spending, for example—so too does a tax deduction affect the national budget. In fact, the fiscal effects of a direct spending program and a tax expenditure are exactly the same. In Suzanne Mettler's apt phrase, federal policy driven by tax expenditures rather than direct spending constitutes the "submerged state," obscured from public view and accountability but with powerful distributional consequences.[15]

Tax incentives for philanthropy are one of the largest tax expenditures for individuals in the U.S. tax code, and they amount to massive federal and state subsidies for the operation of philanthropic and charitable organizations and to the individuals and corporations that make donations of money and property to them. These tax policies have been described as "the world's most generous tax concessions" for charity. One economist observes that "no other nation grants subsidies at such a high level or across so many types of activities."[16]

With this description of the tax policies that structure philanthropy in place, let us now consider whether the ideal of equality is playing any role in the institutional design of the policies. I examine the question in two respects: from the supply side or donor's perspective, or how the policies treat donors; and from the demand or beneficiary side, or how the policies shape the distribution of charitable giving.

EQUALITY AND THE TREATMENT OF DONORS

Two inequalities inhere in the current structure of the preferential tax treatment of nonprofits and philanthropies. First, the charitable contributions deduction is available only to those individuals who itemize their deductions, people who opt not to take the so-called standard deduction on their income tax. This effectively penalizes, or fails to reward and provide an incentive for, all people who do not itemize their deductions, a group that constitutes roughly 70 percent of all taxpayers.[17] Thus the low-income renter who does not itemize her deductions but makes a $500 donation to a public charity receives no tax concession, while the high-income house owner who makes the same $500 donation to the same public charity can claim a deduction. One might think that it is predominantly high-income earners, and therefore itemizers, who make charitable contributions, but this is false. Nearly all American households—a remarkable 90 percent—make charitable contributions every year. And low-income individuals give away more money as a percentage of their income than does everyone else except the very wealthiest.[18] The consequence is that a great many people are capriciously excluded from the tax deduction simply because they do not itemize deductions on their return. If the incentive is meant to recognize or stimulate charitable giving and the production of public benefits, what reason is there to limit the incentive to itemizers? Why should your $100 donation to a charitable organization be deductible, and therefore subsidized, while my $100 donation to the same charitable organization goes unsubsidized simply because I cannot avail myself of itemized deductions? They may be identical donations to the identical organization producing the identical social benefit, yet the two donations are treated differently under the law because of itemization status.

Taxable income	Itemization status	Tax bracket	Net cost of a dollar donation
$0–$18,650	✗	10%	$1.00
$18,650–$75,900	✗	15%	$1.00
$75,900–$153,100	✗	25%	$1.00
$153,100–$233,350	✓	28%	$0.72
$233,350–$416,700	✓	33%	$0.67
$416,700–$470,700	✓	35%	$0.65
$470,700+	✓	39.60%	$0.60

FIGURE 2.4. Cost per Dollar of a Charitable Contribution for Married Taxpayers Filing Jointly, 2017. *Source*: Adapted and updated from Clotfelter, "Tax-Induced Distortions."

I can discern no reason the benefit of the charitable contributions deduction should turn on this contingency.

Second, the tax subsidy given to those who do receive the deduction possesses what is known as an "upside-down effect." The deduction functions as an increasingly greater subsidy with every higher step in the income tax bracket. Those at the highest tax bracket (39.6 percent in 2017) receive the largest deduction, those in the lowest tax bracket (10 percent in 2017) the lowest. As two scholars wryly noted, in such a system "the opportunity cost of virtue falls as one moves up the income scale."[19] Figure 2.4 illustrates how the progressivity of the tax code translates, perversely but as a matter of mathematical logic, into a regressive system of tax deductions: the wealthiest garner the largest tax advantages.[20] Compounding this oddity is a variant of the objection offered above. Identical donations to identical recipients are treated differently by the state depending on the donor's income; a $500 donation by the person in

the 39 percent bracket costs the individual less than the same donation by a person in the 10 percent bracket. Since the same social good is ostensibly produced in both cases, the differential treatment appears totally arbitrary. If anything, lower income earners might seem to warrant the larger subsidy and incentive in order to lower the cost of their charitable giving; in light of the declining marginal utility of additional dollars for people at the top of the income scale, they can afford a "higher price" for charitable donations than can poor people. The upside-down phenomenon is not specific to the tax deduction for charitable donations, of course. Deductions in general massively favor the wealthy. In 2013, over two-thirds of all tax deductions were claimed by the wealthiest decile of earners.[21]

Both of these features of the tax code are arbitrary and unfairly benefit the well-off. The structure of the tax code vis-à-vis charitable donors treats individuals unequally, differentially rewarding people at various income levels for identical donations to identical nonprofit organizations. Low-income individuals either are excluded from the benefit of a deduction (because they do not itemize) or receive a smaller subsidy for the same charitable contribution (because of the upside-down effect). This is so because the tax code, as applied to donors, arbitrarily discriminates between individuals on the basis of a characteristic—status as itemizers or tax bracket position—that is unrelated to the purpose of the preferential tax treatment in the first place.

The upshot is that the donor-facing charitable giving policies in the tax code are deeply *inegalitarian*: they systematically favor the rich in providing them larger benefits. The choice of the charitable contributions deduction as the preferred tax policy for philanthropy introduces a potent plutocratic bias. It's of course true that wealthy people give away more money in absolute terms than do poor people. But why should public policy

differentially reward the rich over the poor? Why should more than two-thirds of the tax expenditures for charitable giving be attached to the giving preferences of the wealthiest 10 percent of Americans? The relevant issue here, therefore, is not just that the incentive applies unequally to donors of different tax-filing statuses and income levels; it's that the public funds forgone in the tax deduction are flowing disproportionately to the favored charitable organizations of the rich. Tax policy in the realm of charity favors the wealthy and, by extension, weights the preferences of the wealthy over those of the poor in the nonprofit organizations they fund. The 1 percent receive a tax policy megaphone and the poor no or little policy amplification.

In theory, it would be quite simple to remedy this unfairness. Policies could allow non-itemizers to deduct their charitable contributions from their income. Better, since this solution would still leave the upside-down effect in place, policies could allow all donors an identical nonrefundable and capped tax credit, rather than a tax deduction, for donations. This fix would be of the greatest marginal value to lower income individuals but would still be an equivalent subsidy for all persons. The U.S. Congress has at times debated versions of both remedies, but neither has ever become law. I return to these proposals in the next chapter.[22]

Even if we eliminated these inegalitarian aspects of the tax code, however, important questions about the structure of charitable tax policy would remain. The focus would turn from evaluating whether tax laws treat the supply side of philanthropy in a justifiable way—the donors—to whether the institutional design of the incentive works in a way to encourage the social benefits that democratic societies wish to provide and to deter any particular ills they wish to avoid. This is important for more than the obvious reason that we wish for public policies of any sort to bring about good rather than bad. It is also important because

in providing tax concessions to philanthropy, the state is not merely permitting and setting guidelines within which philanthropy takes place—offering the state's imprimatur to every charitable nonprofit and philanthropic foundation and charitable donation and bequest—but is in a fiscally meaningful way actively participating in what nonprofits and foundations and donors do. If the state is actually funding, through a tax expenditure, some philanthropic bad, it makes the state partially complicit in the bad action and outcome of the philanthropist. It is no exaggeration to say that as philanthropy is currently structured, when philanthropists do harm, so too does the state.

For the same reasons, when charitable giving is wasted, producing no social benefit at all, it is false to say of such a situation that a donor or foundation simply squanders its own assets and to remark, "Too bad for the donor or the foundation but no loss to the rest of us." Instead, we should recognize that the individual or foundation squandered assets that, had there not been tax concessions, would have been the public's in the form of tax revenue. The wasting of philanthropic assets is the wasting of assets that are partially the public's.

EQUALITY AND THE DISTRIBUTION OF CHARITABLE GIVING

The potential problems with philanthropy go beyond poor management of philanthropic dollars. When our focus is on public rather than only private morality, our attention moves from the motives and actions of the individual to the effects of the public policies that structure the philanthropic sector. What patterns of philanthropic distribution do public policies bring about?

Social scientists have produced many studies with some interesting, perhaps also disturbing, findings. For example, cur-

rent policies create a regional bias in philanthropy, favoring parts of the country with concentrations of wealthy people.[23] Current policies systematically favor certain kinds of nonprofits, especially those that save money and earn endowment income. Here the very large beneficiaries are private foundations and major private universities.[24] One might ask why public policy should ignore gifts of time and labor and instead reward only gifts of cash or assets.

In keeping with the initial question of this chapter, I focus on whether and how public policies strengthen or weaken the connection between philanthropy and equality. Do public policies governing philanthropy contribute to activities in the form of direct assistance or structural reform that benefits the poor and disadvantaged? Do public policies direct or provide incentives for philanthropic dollars to flow in a redistributive direction, from rich to poor? Can public policy help vindicate the claim of philanthropy to be tightly connected to equality?

On the one hand, public policies in the nonprofit and philanthropic world appear to take account of the likely distributional flow of dollars. Most significantly, in order to qualify for 501(c)(3) status as a nonprofit public charity—the status that permits organizations to receive tax-deductible donations—an organization must serve religious, charitable, scientific, public safety, literary, or educational purposes. Public charities are thereby distinguished from other nonprofit organizations that are primarily mutual benefit societies (e.g., unions, private membership clubs, veterans organizations, etc.). For certain nonprofit organizations that compete with for-profit organizations in the marketplace for business, such as day care centers and hospitals, there are additional rules that the nonprofit organization serve poor or disadvantaged communities. In the world of private foundations, a long history and set of social expectations valorize philanthropic

work to improve society and benefit the least advantaged. In addition, the public policies regulating foundations subject them to more stringent controls than public charities in order to help ensure that foundations produce benefits that are public rather than private. Thus, for instance, since 1969 foundations have been subject to a minimum payout rule, requiring an annual spending rate of at least 5 percent of all endowment assets (via either grant making or administrative costs).[25]

On the other hand, regulations that govern charitable giving seem remarkably indifferent to equality and redistributive outcomes. One of the oldest objections to the provision of tax-deductible donations to qualifying nonprofits is that the policy fails to differentiate between the social benefits produced by various nonprofits. The U.S. government permits a kaleidoscopic array of organizations to qualify as 501(c)(3) public charities, with more than 1.5 million public charities in the United States currently given official recognition. And current law is also remarkably permissive in approving applications for status as a public charity.[26] The tax incentive is a blunt instrument, and it lumps all public charities, no matter their mission, size, impact, or region, into a single category. Thus, from the perspective of the state, assuming we are in the same tax bracket, the $1,000 donation that you make to a contemporary arts museum to underwrite a video installation is worth exactly the same as the $1,000 that I give to a soup kitchen. Are these of equal social value? That social policy should be indifferent between these two kinds of goods and provide equivalent subsidies to their respective donors might seem odd. Yet so long as the recipient organization is a qualifying 501(c)(3), the state grants a tax deduction to the donor.

But let us now consider the obvious question of where philanthropic donations go. What charities do donors favor? When

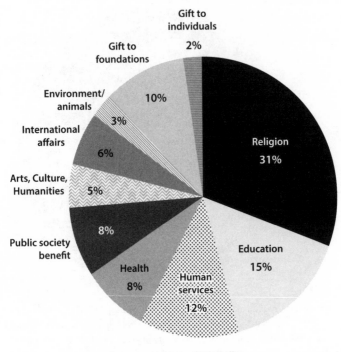

Total = $390 billion

FIGURE 2.5. 2016 Giving by Type of Recipient Organization. *Source*: Giving USA Foundation, "Giving USA 2017."

we move away from the treatment of individual contributions and consider the total distribution of charitable dollars, we find a pattern of giving that is hard to reconcile with expectations of redistributive outcomes. For anyone who believes that charity implies something about almsgiving or assistance for the disadvantaged, the sunny picture of American charitable giving here becomes decidedly cloudy.

Consider first Figure 2.5, a simple chart of the distribution of charitable dollars in 2016 by type of recipient organization. What stands out is that the largest class of recipient organization, by

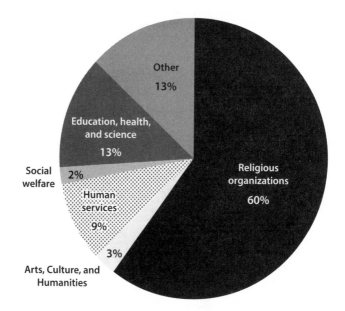

FIGURE 2.6. Distribution of Charitable Dollars Given by Living Individuals by Type of Charity, 1998. *Source*: Independent Sector, *New Nonprofit Almanac and Desk Reference*. *Notes*: For religious organizations, values do not include giving to religious schools or faith-based social services; these dollars are tallied in education and human services, respectively. The "other" category includes giving to international aid and development, private and community foundations, recreation, and other charities.

considerable margin, is religion, meaning giving for the sustenance of religious groups (churches, synagogues, mosques, etc.) for their facilities, operating costs, and clergy salaries. In this sense, religious groups look less like public charities and more like mutual benefit societies.

Some social scientists, like sociologist Robert Wuthnow, argue that at least some of this religious giving should be understood as assisting the needy. But Wuthnow, who writes admiringly of faith-based social services, nevertheless finds that "the amount spent on local service activities is a relatively small proportion of total giving, probably on the order of 5 per-

cent."[27] Moreover, faith-based social service organizations, such as the Salvation Army or Mercy Corps, have been counted in the relevant service provision category. Bottom line: nearly one-third of all charitable giving in the United States—roughly $130 billion—supports religion. If one examines only the charitable preferences of living donors, as in Figure 2.6, the number rises dramatically to 60 percent of all giving.

What of the remaining two-thirds of charitable giving? Education and health care are the next largest recipients. A portion of the donations in these categories provides for basic needs, such as scholarships for the poor and charity health care, but many donations are to higher education to support the donor's alma mater or to a hospital in gratitude for health care received by the donor. Still other categories, such as the arts, do not obviously appear to constitute support for the needy. A simplistic reading of the chart leads to the conclusion that a small percentage, surely less than half of all charitable giving, goes to the needy. Yet let us acknowledge that it is hard to determine what portion of giving in any category constitutes giving to assist the needy.

We have to turn to other studies for a more precise answer. A small number of studies have attempted to measure what portion of charitable giving goes to support the basic needs of individuals. The best recent study, completed in 2007, used multiple datasets and extended generous assumptions about how to count giving that benefits the needy. As shown in Figure 2.7, at most one-third of charity is directed to providing for the needs of the poor.[28]

A closer look at the patterns of giving by living individuals, broken down by income, reveals that the inclination to give to help meet basic needs declines as one rises up the income ladder. According to estimates shown in Figure 2.8, in 2005 millionaires contributed only 4 percent of their giving to basic

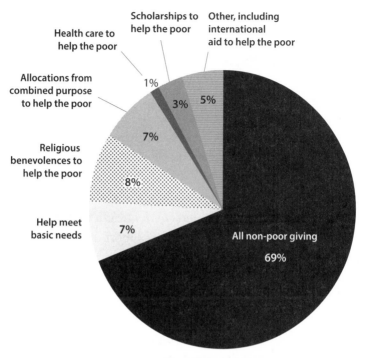

Health care to help the poor

Scholarships to help the poor

Other, including international aid to help the poor

Allocations from combined purpose to help the poor

1%

3% 5%

7%

Religious benevolences to help the poor

8%

Help meet basic needs

7%

All non-poor giving

69%

Total Giving = $252.55B

FIGURE 2.7. Estimates of Giving Focused on the Needs of the Poor, 2005.
Source: Center on Philanthropy at Indiana University, "Patterns of Household Charitable Giving."

needs, contrasted with donors with less than $100,000 of income devoting 10 percent (and a whopping two-thirds of their giving to religion).

The study concludes by making very generous assumptions about what portion of giving in other categories, such as education or health care, might benefit the poor.[29] In the best-case scenario (Figure 2.9), the authors find that at most one-third of all charity goes to assist the poor and that millionaires contribute at most one-fifth of their giving to the needs of the poor.

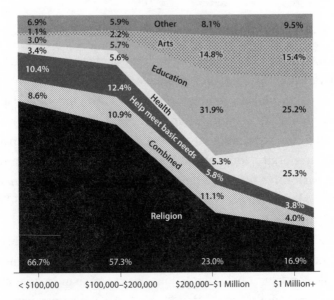

FIGURE 2.8. Estimated Allocation of Charitable Dollars by Income Group, 2005. *Source*: Compiled from data in Center on Philanthropy at Indiana University, "Patterns of Household Charitable Giving."

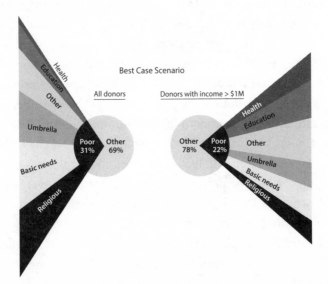

FIGURE 2.9. Best-Case Scenario. *Source*: Compiled from data in Center on Philanthropy at Indiana University, "Patterns of Household Charitable Giving."

Private Foundations

Does the picture change if we limit the analysis to the world of private foundations? Though these constitute a relatively small part of the philanthropic universe (gifts from individuals and their bequests account generally for 80 percent of all private giving, the remaining 20 percent from foundations, private and corporate), foundations might be more straightforwardly redistributive for three reasons. First, the funds that create them almost always come from the very wealthy; it would be difficult for the money to flow upward to the even wealthier. Second, whereas the charitable giving of living individuals is directed very heavily toward religion (60 percent of all charitable contributions), foundations direct less than 5 percent of their grant dollars to religion.[30] Third, at a conceptual level, to the extent that our focus should be on private foundations as a realm of activity separate from ordinary charitable giving, we would have good reason to believe that foundation endeavors, conceived as large-scale interventions with an aim toward social melioration, would be more likely to be redistributive in outcome than the aggregation of charitable contributions to all nonprofit organizations described above. The eye-popping growth of foundations in the past generation also warrants special attention. According to figures produced by the Foundation Center, almost half of the largest foundations in the United States were created after 1989.[31] An even more explosive growth pattern can be seen in family foundations with relatively small endowments. Can foundations lay a greater claim than nonprofits more generally to embrace equality?

Figure 2.10 displays the distribution of foundation dollars in 2014. The grant dollars are certainly distributed more evenly than is the case with the charitable contributions of individuals.

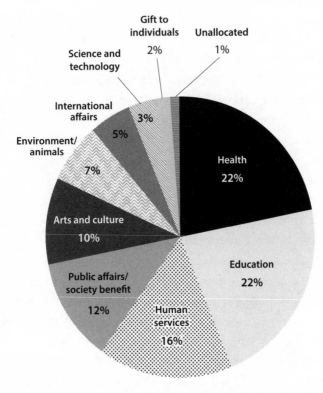

FIGURE 2.10. Distribution of Foundation Dollars by Type of Recipient Organization. *Source*: Foundation Center, "Key Facts on U.S. Foundations."

But the grant categories tell us relatively little about whether the grant dollars are redistributive or not. Consider the education category. Almost half of foundation dollars to education go toward higher education. But we have no way of knowing if these dollars are funding scholarships for the poor, the endowment of a professorial chair, facility improvements, or college athletics. Julian Wolpert's extensive analysis of the redistributional effects of private foundations notes a host of other complex issues, including how to account for the time horizon of foundation activities, which may be directed at long-term rather than short-term

change, and the scope of foundation activities, some of which are very local (community foundations) and others of which are global in reach (e.g., the Gates Foundation). The technical and conceptual issues in trying to measure redistribution notwithstanding, Wolpert concludes that foundations are at best "modestly redistributive," as can be determined with available data.[32]

What can we conclude from these data? The lesson is obvious: if we believe the purpose of philanthropic or charitable giving to be predominantly redistributive, an important mechanism to provide for the basic needs of others, the actually existing distribution of giving in the United States does not meet the test. Not by a long shot.

As an empirical matter, therefore, charity is really not much about caring for the needs of strangers, providing for the poor and disadvantaged. It is not much about almsgiving. It is not an especially significant supplement to the state's efforts to establish a social safety net for citizens.

Other observers reach similar conclusions. Clotfelter examines the distributive benefits of nonprofits and concludes, optimistically I think, that "no overarching conclusions about distributional impact can be made" and that while "in no subsector is there evidence that benefits are dramatically skewed away from the poor and toward the affluent," there is also evidence "that relatively few nonprofit institutions serve the poor as a primary clientele."[33] Based simply on examining the distribution of charitable dollars, then, it is at best very difficult to claim that charitable contributions benefit the poor. Of the alleged redistributive and eleemosynary aims of public charities, Liam Murphy and Thomas Nagel conclude, "The word charity suggests that this deduction is a means of decentralizing the process by which a community discharges its collective responsibility to alleviate the worst aspects of life at the bottom

of the socioeconomic ladder. Since there is disagreement about what the exact nature of that responsibility is, and about which are the most efficient agencies, it is arguably a good idea for the state to subsidize individuals' contributions to agencies of their choice rather than itself making all the decisions about the use of public funds for this purpose. But even if that is so, the existing deduction cannot be defended on those grounds, because many currently deductible 'charitable' contributions go to cultural and educational institutions that have nothing to do with the poor, the sick, or the handicapped. State funding of such institutions may or may not be desirable, but the argument would be very different, and 'charity' is hardly the right word."[34]

The nonprofit sector in the United States is wildly permissive, oversight of the sector is lax, and approval of nonprofit status is trivially easy to obtain. The United States has more than 1.5 million public charities, not counting religious organizations, which receive but do not need to file for nonprofit status, and more than 50,000 new public charities have been created *every year* for the past decade.[35] As a descriptive matter, charitable giving seems to be more frequently about the pursuit of individual projects, a mechanism for the public expression of one's values or preferences, rather than a mechanism for redistribution.

What if public policies actively contribute to inequality, generating *greater* inequalities than would exist absent the public policy? In this case, the extraordinarily generous tax concessions would be even more difficult, perhaps impossible, to justify. Yet in some cases, philanthropy actively exacerbates social inequalities in a way that seems fundamentally at odds with certain egalitarian aims of social policy. Here, public policy does active harm, subsidizing the worsening of inequalities that other policies might reasonably be thought responsible

for diminishing. I turn now to an illustration of exactly this phenomenon.

When Philanthropy Generates Greater Inequality: The Plutocracy of the PTA

In recent years, large private foundations such as the Bill and Melinda Gates Foundation have come under criticism in the United States for funding a wave of controversial efforts to reform poorly performing public schools.[36] In chapter 4 I take up questions about the influence of plutocratic philanthropic voices in public policy and the operation of public institutions such as local schools. Here, I want to examine the more unheralded but no less significant phenomenon of local private fund-raising to supplement the funding of local public schools.

Private funding for public schools is a very old practice. There have long been parent-teacher associations (PTAs) that raise modest amounts of money. Think of bake sales, car washes, and spaghetti dinners. But over the past generation, fund-raising efforts for many local schools and school districts in the United States have become more serious, less a matter of community building or bringing parents into closer connection with the school and more forthrightly and unembarrassedly about maximizing the amount of money raised. What's new is the scale and professional organization of the effort and the total dollars being raised. Where once it was PTAs, with their wide-ranging activities, that were the organizational hub of fund-raising, today many schools and school districts have created independent entities known as local education foundations (LEFs) whose main or sole purpose is to raise private money to supplement public funding of schooling. In some places, the local foundations resemble university fund-raising

offices more than volunteer-driven PTAs. New York City famously hired Caroline Kennedy, the daughter of former president John F. Kennedy, to lead its education foundation, the New York City Fund for Public Schools. LEFs, like PTAs, are almost always 501(c)(3) public charities. Individuals and corporations make tax-deductible contributions to the LEF, which in turn transfers the money, often with strings attached, to the school or district.

School and district policies determine whether private funds can be collected at the school or at the district level (or at both) and whether there are limits on how private funds can be spent (on core academic activities or only on extracurricular activities). Very frequently these donations are earmarked for particular activities—for extracurricular events or materials, for additional school supplies, for field trips—giving the donors a nontrivial amount of input or leverage on how the school or district operates. Although, to the best of my knowledge, parents cannot dictate to the school that a special aide be hired, with their privately donated funds, to shadow their own child around, there are many circumstances that would permit parents collectively to get the district to hire art and music teachers or additional teacher aides, to purchase sophisticated technological equipment, and so on, all of which can be targeted to benefit their own children.

With tight state budgets and a general reluctance in many states to boost education funding, LEFs have grown exponentially in recent years. They exist in almost every large urban district, but they are also increasingly common in smaller and comparatively well-off suburban districts. For most LEFs, but especially those located in suburban districts, the usual donors are parents of the children in the school district or citizens of the town or city in which the district is located. LEFs are

especially common in the region of the country where I live, Northern California. In a nearby town, Hillsborough, parents of schoolchildren receive a letter on the first day of school requesting a charitable contribution to the school, for each child enrolled, in the amount of $2,300.[37]

It is difficult to fault the motives of parents and townspeople who respond to efforts to fund-raise for public schools. Parents seek to do the best by their own children. Townspeople support their local public institutions. Everyone can lay claim to a public spiritedness in contributing to public education (as opposed to sending children to private schools). Yet the distributional consequences of private funding for public schools are not hard to predict. Wealthy schools and school districts can raise substantially more money than can schools that have high concentrations of poor students. The effect is to magnify what Jonathan Kozol memorably described as the savage inequalities of school funding, in which towns with high property wealth spend much more per pupil on education than do poor towns and cities.[38] In short, LEFs worsen existing inequalities in public funding between schools and between school districts. And what's more, they do it with the active support of the state in the familiar form of tax subsidies for charitable contributions.

Private giving to public schools is a nationwide phenomenon, but it is perhaps most prominent in California, a state that has experienced a long decline in public school funding in the wake of the 1971 *Serrano* decision, which mandated much more equal spending across districts in California, and the 1978 passage of Proposition 13, which capped property taxes and thereby severely limited the amount of money that could be raised from property taxes for education. According to the

California Consortium of Education Foundations, more than five hundred LEFs are operating in California. To get a sense of how deeply unequal private funding for public schools is, I collected data on the amount of money raised by LEFs and all other 501(c)(3) school organizations (primarily PTAs) in California. I report some results below.[39]

The overall picture of private dollars for public schools is clear. Most school districts are not raising appreciable amounts of private money per pupil, but a small and growing percentage are, sometimes raising $200 or more per student.

What districts are these, and just how much money are they raising each year? Tables 2.1 and 2.2 give a good illustration of the winners and losers in the private fund-raising campaigns. Table 2.1 lists the top fifteen LEFs in California in 1998, ranked by revenue; Table 2.2 lists the top fifteen LEFs in the Bay Area in 2000, ranked by net assets. Two things immediately stand out. First, these LEFs engage in massive fund-raising campaigns, with each of the top fifteen LEFs in California receiving well over a million dollars in revenue and thirteen of the top fifteen in the Bay Area possessing net assets in excess of a million dollars. Second, we see that when the revenue or assets available to the respective district is calculated on a *per pupil basis*, the list divides sharply into two groups, suburban and urban districts. The italicized rows represent suburban LEFs, each of which raised at least $100 per pupil. The top performer, Woodside Elementary School District, a district with a single elementary school in the backyard of Stanford University, raised more than $7,000 per pupil in 1998. By contrast, the urban districts raise far less. The amount of private money raised in Woodside exceeds, on a per pupil basis, the amount of public money received per pupil in some low-income schools in California.

TABLE 2.1. Top Fifteen California Local Education Foundations, Ranked by Total Revenue, 1998

Foundation	District	Revenue ($)	Revenue per Pupil ($)
BREA Hope, Inc.	*Brea-Olinda Unified*	*5,857,630*	*982*
Project Seed	Oakland Unified	5,671,750	106
LA Educational Partners	Los Angeles Unified	5,258,200	8
Woodside School Foundation	*Woodside Elementary*	*3,384,390*	*7,065*
Manchester Gate	Fresno Unified	2,707,400	35
Irvine Public Schools Foundation	Irvine Unified	1,776,590	77
Ross School Foundation	*Ross Elementary*	*1,700,590*	*4,168*
Cupertino Education Endowment	*Cupertino Union*	*1,672,670*	*111*
Newport-Mesa Schools Foundation	Newport-Mesa Unified	1,603,400	79
New Haven Schools Foundation	*New Haven Unified*	*1,302,190*	*92*
Hillsborough Schools Foundation	*Hillsborough*	*1,240,820*	*932*
Palos Verdes Peninsula Ed.	*Palos Verdes Unified*	*1,234,820*	*133*
Portola Valley Schools Foundation	*Portola Valley Elementary*	*1,111,010*	*1,603*
Berkeley Public Ed. Endowment	Albany City Unified	1,105,970	373
Telacue Education Foundation	Los Angeles Unified	1,057,000	2

Source: Author's dataset.

Note: Suburban districts italicized.

Table 2.3 lists the top fifteen school districts (rather than LEFs) in California in 1998 ranked by the aggregated revenue of all LEFs and other 501(c)(3)s that raise money in the district. The trend seen in Tables 2.1 and 2.2 is here even more pronounced. Wealthy suburban school districts enjoy a massive private fund-raising advantage over urban schools, and the top

TABLE 2.2. The Fifteen Largest Local Education Foundations (LEF) in the
Bay Area, Ranked by Net Assets, 2000

Foundation	Net assets ($)	Net assets per pupil ($)
Woodside School Foundation	*11,308,243*	*24,690*
Cupertino Educational Endowment Foundation	*8,822,870*	*563*
San Francisco Education Fund	8,207,907	137
Hillsborough Schools Foundation	*3,517,164*	*2,510*
Portola Valley Schools Foundation	*2,688,720*	*3,847*
Every Child Can Learn Foundation	2,409,876	40
KIDDO!—Mill Valley Schools Community Foundation	*2,360,500*	*1,019*
Petaluma Educational Foundation	*1,729,572*	*221*
Marcus A. Foster Educational Institute	1,641,393	30
Ross School Foundation	*1,454,616*	*3,637*
Piedmont Educational Foundation	*1,115,254*	*417*
Menlo Park-Atherton Education Foundation	*1,069,295*	*546*
Los Altos Educational Foundation	*932,538*	*237*
Educational Foundation of Orinda	*836,517*	*343*

Source: Author's dataset.
Note: Suburban districts italicized.

performing suburban districts in private fund-raising have an
exponential advantage.

Those who have examined the phenomenon of private fund-
raising have sought to explain it as the effort of parents to avoid
court-mandated or legislative efforts to equalize public school

TABLE 2.3. Top Fifteen California Districts in Private Fund-Raising, Ranked by Total Aggregate Revenue, 1998

District	Total revenue ($)	Pupils	Revenue per pupil ($)
Los Angeles Unified	12,507,000	680,430	18
Oakland Unified	7,377,082	53,564	138
Brea-Olinda Unified	5,983,699	5,965	1,003
Newport-Mesa Unified	3,948,777	20,241	195
Woodside Elementary School	3,384,390	479	7,065
Fresno Unified	3,091,884	78,166	39
San Francisco Unified	3,090,717	61,007	51
Irvine Unified	2,826,291	23,061	122
Palos Verdes Peninsula Unified	2,676,578	9,285	288
Cupertino Union Elementary	2,402,372	15,024	160
San Diego Unified	2,398,120	136,282	17
San Ramon Valley Unified	2,265,910	19,526	116
Los Altos Elementary	1,952,226	3,618	540
Hillsborough City Elementary	1,864,189	1,332	1,400
Ross Elementary	1,841,586	408	4,514

Source: Author's dataset.
Note: Suburban districts italicized.

funding at the state level.[40] Or they have sought to celebrate and expand the practice, seeing it as the virtuous effort of parents and local citizens to support their public schools. The lesson I draw from the phenomenon is not a strictly educational one, however. I see the existence of private fund-raising for public schools as but one illustration of the fact that the public policies that guide philanthropy give much greater deference to liberty than to upholding or promoting equality. And in the school

funding case, we should not at all be surprised. Public policy does much the same thing with respect to parents and their children. We know that parents are a main cause—from their parenting styles to their socioeconomic standing—of inequalities between children when they show up for the first day of kindergarten. Yet liberal democratic states protect a zone of privacy within the family, respecting the liberty of parents to rear their children as they see fit, absent outright abuse or neglect. A democratic society would not countenance a "parenting police force" that would, say, limit the number of bedtime stories that parents read to their children to two. Parental liberty interests have a special place in the domain of the family.[41]

Yet in the phenomenon of private money for public schools, there is no obvious intervention in the family. It is the public institution of the schoolhouse that is the focus of the money and of public policy. The relevant question is not about limits on parental liberty within the family but whether public policy should not merely permit but provide incentives for parents to give money to public schools so that their children can receive a better education than they otherwise would without the private funds. One function of public schools, arguably, and the very reason why society invests so much money in them and compels children to attend them, is to try to *remedy* some of the inequalities that children bring with them into the first day of kindergarten. We would think education policy to be unjust if the systematic and foreseeable effect of public schools was to exacerbate inequalities between children. Yet the institutional structure of philanthropy not only permits charitable giving to exacerbate the vastly different levels of public funding between schools but also *subsidizes the charitable giving* of those who, in seeking to support their own children's or their own town's schools, worsen the inequalities between schools. Rather than

rewarding virtue, public policy rewards what from the perspective of the public must be considered a vice. Tax policy makes federal and state governments complicit in the deepening of existing inequalities that they are ostensibly responsible for diminishing in the first place.

To see the problem more vividly, consider a hypothetical case—let's call it Police Department—that is to my mind analogous to the phenomenon of private giving to public schools. The street on which you live has been beset in recent months by a crime wave. Incidences of break-ins, vandalism, and theft have increased. You and your neighbors attribute the crime wave to lower funding of the police department, which has seen its resources stretched thin as a result of budget cuts. Attempting to come up with a solution, you and your neighbors pool together some money and offer to make a sizable donation to a local police foundation that is set up to provide additional financial support to the local police department. You offer the donation only on the condition, however, that the money be used to hire a new officer whose only patrol will be your block. You expect to take a tax deduction for your donation.

Note that in both the school and the police cases there is an exit option. Parents could choose to send their children to private school, but they would not receive any tax deduction for their tuition payment. Similarly, you and your neighbors could hire a private security officer, but this would not qualify for any deduction either.

Should you be permitted to make the donation to the police department with the strings attached that the money be directed for hiring a police officer to be stationed on your street? I believe intuition runs firmly against any such donation. And public policy tracks this intuition. To the best of my knowledge, not only does local and state public policy forbid anyone

from taking a tax deduction for donations to the operation of police departments,[42] it strictly forbids the donation in the first place. There are some circumstances, it appears, in which philanthropy is simply not welcome. Were my focus on the specific issue of private funding for local public services such as schooling or policing, I would take the opportunity here to draw out several lessons from this hypothetical case—lessons about the importance of public institutions not being directed by the wealthy or deployed in the interest or at the behest of private individuals, lessons about public policy helping to set the incentives for citizens to participate in the messiness of democratic politics rather than seeking private solutions to their problems, and lessons about how the public's interest in schooling has waned in comparison to the public's interest in security. I limit myself however to only one lesson, the one that is germane to the theme of this inquiry. In the police case, the liberty of individuals is constrained in the interest of equality. Private individuals are not permitted to make charitable contributions to a public institution in which all citizens are thought to have an equal stake. Why, then, are they permitted to do so, and with a tax subsidy, in the case of public schools?

Conclusion

A blanket prohibition on private giving to public schools is not necessarily the most justifiable public policy with respect to philanthropy and public education. The aim should be to have policies that shape and structure philanthropy so that it is more egalitarian rather than inegalitarian, perhaps to provide incentives in the case of education for private giving to disadvantaged students, schools, and districts. In other words, the aim should be to make good on the promise of the old story

about philanthropy with which I began—that philanthropy is tightly connected to both liberty and equality.

Such policies are far from utopian. Institutional design here is key, and seeking to justify these institutional arrangements in terms of what advances liberal democratic justice is the aim. It is at this point that an examination of philanthropy becomes an exercise in political philosophy. We need to seek an answer to what norms should inform the institutional design of the laws and policies that shape philanthropy. Public policy creates the institutional context in which philanthropy exists. The public policies designed to create a favorable environment for nonprofits and foundations and to offer incentives for people to make charitable donations represent a wide-scale state action or intervention. Are these institutional arrangements justifiable?

The rocky relationship between philanthropy and equality and the data I have presented about private funding for public schools, I wish to emphasize in conclusion, need not shake the legitimacy of philanthropy or even the justifiability of current tax laws. But we should conclude that the very large tax expenditures of the American public on charitable giving result in subsidies for the activities of individuals that, in the aggregate, bear no tight relationship with equality, construed either as the equal treatment of donors or, distributively, as money directed at the needy. It seems fair to say that public policies governing philanthropy appear to be indifferent to equality, and instead valorize and subsidize the exercise of liberty. What redistribution occurs is more likely the effect of happenstance or the fortunate predilections of individuals rather than the incentive effects of public policy.

Let it be clear: we might still find reasons to justify the institutional arrangements that define the nonprofit sector and

create tax benefits for both nonprofit organizations and their donors. But the justification would have to rest on grounds other than something concerning an egalitarian distributive norm: perhaps on the importance of decentralizing authority, creating a set of mediating institutions in civil society, desiring the production of public goods to be sensitive to local demand, reflecting and generating the pluralism of a diverse democratic society. These are the concerns I take up in the next chapter.

3

A Political Theory
of Philanthropy

We began in the first chapter by observing that the practice of philanthropy is as old as humanity. People have been giving away their money, property, and time to others for millennia.

We also observed, for example in the liturgical system in classical Athens, the institutional design of the waqf in Islam, and the foundations in France and England vigorously criticized by Turgot and Mill, that practices of philanthropy are embedded within social and religious custom, civic norms, and the law. Political and social arrangements facilitate and structure the practice of philanthropy.

The previous chapter provided a descriptive overview of the legal rules in the United States and illustrated tensions between the practice of philanthropy and the value of equality. In the United States and many other countries, the tax code provides incentives, in the form of tax advantages, to people to give away their money and property (though not their time).

The charitable contributions deduction in the United States is barely a century old, created by the U.S. Congress in 1917 shortly after the institution of a system of federal income taxation. Similar incentives built into tax systems exist in most developed and many developing democracies. Most countries, not only democracies, use some kind of deduction scheme, including Australia, Egypt, France, Germany, India, Japan, Mexico, the Netherlands, Russia, South Africa, Spain, and Thailand. To the best of my knowledge, only Sweden provides no subsidy structure at all for charitable giving.[1]

Beyond the tax deduction for charitable giving, legal rules govern the creation of nonprofit organizations and various kinds of endowments, such as private foundations and community trusts. These policies spell out the rules under which these organizations may incorporate and operate, sometimes setting limits on permissible activities (for example, whether nonprofits may engage in electioneering, partisan political communication, or lobbying). Other laws set up special tax exemptions for nonprofit organizations and philanthropic foundations, and they frequently permit tax concessions for individual and corporate donations of money and property. Still other laws protect and enforce donor intent, even beyond death. The effects of these laws are significant: they define and regulate the philanthropic sector, confer the state's imprimatur on what counts as an official charity or foundation, and articulate the range of state-sanctioned charitable purposes. The legal regime promotes and shapes the sector, and in so doing the state and by extension all citizens forgo considerable tax revenue.

Contemporary practice, in which philanthropy is structured by a regulatory framework of incentives, of forgone tax revenue, is not the norm but the historical anomaly. Governments have often respected the liberty of people to make donations

of money and property, and might even have encouraged the practice by providing civic recognition and honor for them to do so, as in classical Athens. Yet I am unaware of cases prior to the twentieth century in which states attempted to stimulate the exercise of a person's liberty to give money away via fiscal incentives such as tax subsidies. Two questions arise: why have such incentives, and what is their justification in a liberal democracy?[2]

The historical practice of philanthropy is littered with instances in which the relevant question that presented itself to the state was how vigorously it should *constrain* the liberty of people to give money away. We have already seen how Turgot and Mill rejected the idea that the law should permit donors to establish foundations that would be harnessed to the donor's intent in perpetuity. The state was entitled to limit the liberty of any person who claimed a right to create a permanent endowment. Donors did not possess something akin to a property right over their charitable assets, neither in life and certainly not after death; the assets belonged, thought Mill, to their intended beneficiaries. For Turgot and Mill, the principle of social utility is what provided the grounds to justify limits on the liberty of would-be philanthropists.

These are not the only grounds, however. Public influence obtained through private wealth might be injurious to the state by, for example, threatening the authority of the ruling class. Aristocratic elites have often been considered public threats, dangerous because they could seek to translate private munificence into political power. In the *Discourses*, Machiavelli tells the following story about ancient Rome:

When the city of Rome was overburdened with hunger, and public provisions were not enough to stop it, one Spurius

Maelius, who was very rich for those times, had the intent to make provision of grain privately, and to feed the plebs with it, gaining its favor for him. Because of this affair he had such a crowd of people in his favor that the Senate, thinking of the inconvenience that could arise from that liberality of his, so as to crush it before it could pick up more strength, created a dictator over him and had him killed. Here it is to be noted that many times works that appear merciful, which cannot be reasonably condemned, become cruel and are very dangerous for a republic if they are not corrected in good time.[3]

The question about constraining the liberty of people to give away money and property remains with us today. We need only consider debates about inheritance taxation and campaign finance contributions to realize that states may have good reasons—reasons founded on justice—to limit the liberty of people to give money away.

We might also point to the U.S. Constitution itself for reasons that in some circumstances individuals should not merely *not* receive a tax concession for a charitable donation but should be entirely blocked from making the donation. The Appropriations Clause of the Constitution—"no money shall be drawn from the Treasury, but in Consequence of Appropriations made by law"[4]—or the so-called power of the purse, can be construed to prohibit private donations to federal agencies. Although the clause is invoked to limit what the executive branch can propose and do without congressional authority, it also appears to limit *any* financing of federal agencies except through congressional authorization. "As a consequence of the appropriations requirement," Kate Stith argues, "all 'production' of government must be pursuant to legislative authority, even where

the additional production is financed with donations and thus appears costless to the Treasury."[5] To the best of my knowledge, this is indeed our current practice: if a U.S. citizen wishes to make a donation to a federal agency, absent congressional authorization to do so (as with the Smithsonian Institution or the Library of Congress), her only option is to write a check, no strings attached, to the U.S. Treasury.[6]

In the United States and elsewhere there have been, and continue to be, reasons to limit the liberty of people to give money away for charitable purposes. I recount these facts simply to show that current practice in the United States and elsewhere is not the historical norm and to convey how unusual, in some sense, tax-subsidized philanthropy actually is.

So here, then, is a simple question of first principle: what attitude should a liberal democratic state have toward the preference of individuals to make donations of money or property for a philanthropic purpose? More generally, what rules should govern philanthropic giving in a liberal democracy? I suggest we consider an answer to the question by starting with a few assumptions that will assist in posing the question in the widest or most general form for liberal democratic theory.

A Simple Framework

Consider this simple framework to motivate the question. Assume first that there is a private property regime of some type and that individuals have duly come into possession of resources over which they have legitimate title. People have property, and they properly own it. Assume second a legitimate tax of some kind on their property, for my purposes here an income tax. To cast my net broadly, I leave open the precise details of the legal regime for property or the scope of taxation.

All the framework requires is a system in which individuals legitimately acquire some property, have possession rights over the property, and are subject to taxation, of some kind, on that property. In short, imagine a liberal democratic society in which individuals have legitimate ownership of private property, in particular some income or wealth, and then they have been subject to whatever counts as legitimate taxation. After being taxed, they have resources that they wish to give away for a charitable purpose. This, I suggest, is a universal phenomenon in any society. What now? How should the state treat the prospective philanthropic donor?

Before proceeding further, two comments about what motivates these assumptions. First, why the assumption about property? I want entirely to set aside for the purposes of this analysis a complaint sometimes made about philanthropy, namely that the money donated by an individual isn't properly or legitimately hers to give in the first place. If, for example, the background distribution of income and wealth is unjust, and some people possess more income or wealth than they would possess under conditions of justice, then the assertion that these people should be free to make donations with their resources might be objectionable. Had a just system of tax and transfer been in place, or if other background conditions of justice had obtained (e.g., equality of opportunity, absence of racial and sex discrimination, inheritance taxes, and so on), then the well-off would-be donor would have less income and wealth and, quite likely, the intended beneficiaries of the donor, if the donor has an eleemosynary aim, would have more. Kant captures the concern aptly: individuals should not deceive themselves that they are practicing praiseworthy beneficence when their wealth is the product of distributional injustice. "Having the resources to practice such beneficence as depends on the goods of fortune

is, for the most part, a result of certain human beings being favored through the injustice of government, which introduces an inequality of wealth that makes others need their beneficence. Under such circumstances, does a rich man's help to the needy, on which he so readily prides himself as something meritorious, really deserve to be called beneficence at all?"[7] Kant's obvious answer is no. The appropriate understanding of philanthropy under these circumstances is that it should serve reparative aims, to redress the background wrongs of the unjust system that produced the unfair distribution of resources in the first place.[8]

A parallel worry I hope to dismiss with the assumption about property is what is sometimes called the problem of dirty money or blood money: wealth obtained through illicit means. Here the problem is not that circumstances of background justice do not hold but that income itself has been generated illegally, via, for example, criminal activity, exploitation, or oppression. When a person whose possessions have been acquired illicitly announces an intention to make philanthropic donations of his wealth, we rightly complain that the money should not be considered his to give at all. If I steal your wallet and announce a plan to donate its contents rather than purchase something for myself, my philanthropic aim does not excuse the initial theft. For the purposes of my motivating framework, I assume lawful and just possession of resources.

Second, why the assumption about taxation? Different theories of justice lead to various views about taxation. In order to consider the case of philanthropy, I avoid taking sides in debates about what system of taxation is best from the point of view of justice. Libertarians might defend low rates of taxation, if any, for the purpose of funding contract enforcement, national defense, and pure public goods. Market democrats such

as John Tomasi might defend modest taxation to fulfill broader equality of opportunity for children.[9] And social democrats or strong egalitarian liberals might defend steeply progressive taxation to fund a large social safety net. Without taking sides in such debates, I want to bring all three along, to the extent possible, in my analysis. So I stipulate only that people have property, that they have been taxed on it in whatever manner is taken to be consistent with justice, and that they have money or property after taxation that they wish to give away. How the state should treat this preference is a question that will now arise for each variant of a liberal democratic theory of justice.

With the framework set up in this manner, here is the question I pose: what attitude should the liberal democratic state have toward the preference of an individual to make a philanthropic donation of her money or property? It is, I think, a fundamental question in that it will arise in any society, liberal democratic or otherwise, and a political theory should provide the resources to answer it.

A liberal democratic state is committed, in virtue of its liberal commitments, to a limited state and robust protection of individual rights and liberties. From the framework I describe, therefore, one plausible starting point in a liberal democratic state regarding philanthropy, it seems to me, is that individuals should possess the liberty to give their money or property away to whomever or whatever they please. Restrictions on that liberty, such as with estate taxation or campaign finance restrictions, stand in need of justification; the state bears the burden of showing why such restrictions are necessary or permissible. In parallel form, I suggest that incentives for people to exercise their liberty to give their money away also stand in need of justification; the state bears the burden of showing why such incentives are desirable and consistent with justice.

Justifications for Tax Incentives

This returns us to my original question: what is the justification for the current practice in the United States and elsewhere of providing tax incentives for citizens to make charitable contributions? Because the tax incentive constitutes a subsidy—the loss of federal tax revenue—it is no exaggeration to say that the United States and other countries currently subsidize the liberty of people to give money away, forgoing tax revenue for an activity that for millennia has gone unsubsidized by the state. As we saw in the previous chapter, the United States has the most generous subsidy structure of any country in the world. What justification for this practice could there be?

The remainder of this chapter lays out and assesses three possible justifications for the existence of tax incentives for charitable giving.[10] I focus special attention on the incentive mechanism currently used in the United States and in many other countries: the charitable contributions deduction, a deduction of charitable gifts from a citizen's taxable income.[11] The first justification is that the deduction is necessary in order to account for the proper base of taxable income; the deduction, in other words, is no subsidy at all. The second justification is that the deduction efficiently stimulates the production of public goods and services that would otherwise be undersupplied by the state. The third justification links the incentive to the desirable effort to decentralize authority, to some degree, in the definition and production of public benefits and, in the process, to support a pluralistic civil society that is itself an important component of a flourishing democracy. My references here are to the practice and regulatory framework of philanthropy in the United States, though I intend my analysis to hold more generally for any liberal democratic state.

TAX BASE RATIONALE

The first justification rejects entirely the claim that the deduction is a subsidy. The deduction constitutes, instead, the fair or appropriate way to treat the donor; deductibility is *intrinsic* to the tax system. First offered by William Andrews, the basic argument is that deducting philanthropic contributions is necessary in order to properly define an individual's taxable income. The reason is that taxable income should be construed as distinct from total income.[12] If taxable income is construed, says Andrews, according to the standard Haig-Simons definition, as personal consumption and wealth accumulation, then charitable donations ought not be included in a person's tax base. The reason is that charity cannot be equated with personal consumption since charitable gifts redirect resources from private and preclusive consumption to public and non-preclusive consumption. Andrews concludes that "a deduction should be allowed whenever money is expended for anything other than personal consumption or accumulation."[13] Tax scholar Boris Bittker offers a similar argument, concluding that charitable donations ought not count as consumption because in making a voluntary donation the donor is made worse off (with respect to others at the same income who do not make a donation), relinquishing use of resources that could have been directed to personal benefit.[14]

Unlike subsidy justifications, the tax base justification focuses on the fair treatment of the donor; it does not inquire into the goods produced with the donation or the efficiency with which these goods are produced. There are four obvious and strong criticisms to make of the tax base rationale.

First, and commonsensically, if a person has legitimate ownership of resources and can rightfully decide how to dispose of those resources, then whatever a person decides to do with

those resources—spend it on luxury goods or give it to charity—is by definition, tautologically, a kind of consumption. Some people have a taste for spending, others for donating; each brings apparent satisfaction to the respective person.

Second, there are obvious benefits that some, perhaps many or even all, donors receive in making a philanthropic contribution. Philanthropy may be motivated by a prosocial or altruistic aim, yet it can simultaneously deliver benefits to the donor. Economists have attempted to model and measure the motivation of receiving a "warm glow" or psychological benefit in acting altruistically.[15] In making a charitable contribution, the donor experiences pleasure in giving and receives in return for the gift a "warm glow," consuming the benefit of her own altruism. A warm glow might be non-preclusive in that purchasing joy through a charitable contribution does not diminish the ability of others to do the same. But a warm glow is undeniably private rather than public. Altruism might also be construed as a scarce resource, anyway. Other economists have demonstrated how much charitable giving, especially to elite institutions such as universities, hospitals, and cultural organizations, is motivated by status signaling.[16] Here the motivation to give is status seeking and self-interested, not altruistic, to maintain position or move up the social hierarchy. Status is zero sum, after all, and only so many names can appear on a donated building. Regardless of motive—altruistic or self-interested—there are returns to the donor that make it impossible to describe donors as engaging in behavior that is public and non-preclusive or that necessarily makes them worse off. We need not be incorrigible cynics to believe that donors are purchasing something for themselves when they make a charitable contribution.[17]

Third, Andrews's theory has perverse implications about the permissible recipients of charity according to current law in the

United States and elsewhere. If for Andrews anything that is not personal consumption or accumulation should be deductible from the donor's tax base, then a billionaire's gift of a million dollars to Walmart, a for-profit company, to encourage its efforts in union busting, ought to be deductible. (Assume the billionaire holds no stock in Walmart.) Similarly, a donation to a foreign country or foreign charity where the donor has no connection and is motivated simply, say, to alleviate poverty ought to be deductible. But U.S. tax law—like the tax regimes of most of other countries— excludes donations of both kinds. In the United States, to qualify for a deduction, philanthropy must be directed to a qualifying public charity, a 501(c)(3) nonprofit organization that has been approved and registered by the Internal Revenue Service.

Finally, and moving from theoretical conceptualization to empirical fact, even the briefest reflection on philanthropy in the real world reveals how donors quite frequently purchase with their charitable dollars rival and excludable material or intangible goods for which they are among the primary consumers. Contributions to one's religious congregation are an obvious example; churches provide something more like club goods than public goods. Or to put it differently, they are more like *mutual benefit* rather than *public benefit* organizations.[18] Donations to arts organizations or university sports teams for which one receives in return premium seats, special access, private tours, and so on are another example. Gifts to construct buildings, fund university chairs, or lay bricks in a public library, school, or park that bear the name of the donor are still another example. And as we saw in the previous chapter, charitable gifts to one's child's public school may also deliver improved educational opportunities or outcomes for one's child, not to mention boosting the value of one's house due to the fact that public school quality and real estate values are correlated.

On top of these criticisms can be added yet another that is more fundamental. I refer to the argument by Liam Murphy and Thomas Nagel that the choice of a tax base cannot be assessed in the absence of the larger normative consideration of what constitutes social and economic justice.[19] The definition of taxable income is strictly instrumental on their view, the tax system just a mechanism for pursuing larger social aims. "Since justice in taxation is not a matter of a fair distribution of tax burdens measured against a pretax baseline, it cannot be important in itself what pretax characteristics of taxpayers determine tax shares."[20] As a result, there is for Murphy and Nagel no such thing as the intrinsic fairness of the tax system or tax base but only taxation that is an instrument in realizing or pursuing the aims of a larger theory of social and economic justice.

Their argument is built on the claim that private property is a convention of the legal system. Property rights are not preinstitutional or prepolitical but rather a consequence of a set of laws that form a part of a broader theory of justice. Consequently, a person's pretax income does not count automatically as a person's own money, though what Murphy and Nagel call everyday libertarianism suggests as much to many people. Without the notion of a pretax baseline of income there can be nothing intrinsic about the selection of a fair tax base. "Since there are no property rights independent of the tax system, taxes cannot violate those rights. There is no prima facie objection to overcome, and the tax structure, which forms part of the definition of property rights, along with laws governing contract, gift, inheritance, and so forth, must be evaluated by reference to its effectiveness in promoting legitimate societal goals, including those of distributive justice."[21] It is nonsense, then, to argue that charitable contributions ought to be deducted from one's

taxable income because such deductions logically belong to the identification of the appropriate tax base.

I accept the Murphy and Nagel thesis but do not attempt here to defend it except to note that, whatever its merits, it locates the argument on the appropriate intellectual terrain: argument about social and economic justice. No one deserves a tax break for a charitable contribution simply in virtue of some account of a person's tax base. Tax incentives for giving, if they are to be justified, find their justification in a larger account of justice for which the tax system is just an instrument.

EFFICIENCY RATIONALE

The more typical defense of the charitable contributions deduction—and one that does, even if sometimes only implicitly, take into account a broader theory of social and economic justice—is that the state accomplishes something of important social value by providing subsidies for citizens to be charitable. The state provides incentives for charity because it is believed that the incentives stimulate the production of something of greater social value than what the state could have produced on its own, had it not offered the incentives.

The subsidy therefore counts as a tax expenditure, the fiscal equivalent of a direct spending program.[22] When the state allows citizens to deduct their charitable contributions from their taxable income, the state forgoes tax revenue, which is to say that all citizens are affected. They are affected in (at least) two important ways. First, they stand to lose some portion of the benefit they would receive from direct governmental expenditures. If every citizen benefits from some fraction of the total revenue of the federal budget, the loss of billions of dollars in tax

revenue through the deduction lowers every citizen's fractional benefit. Second, citizens lose in democratic accountability, for the forgone funds are not accountable, or even traceable, in the way that direct government expenditures are. To give an obvious example, citizens can unelect their representatives if they are dissatisfied with the spending programs of the state; the Gates Foundation also has a domestic and global spending program, partly supported through tax subsidies, but its leaders and trustees cannot be unelected.

Thus the success of the efficiency rationale depends on whether the benefits brought about by the subsidy exceed the costs of the lost tax revenue. Consistent with the Murphy and Nagel thesis, the subsidy is but a mechanism for realizing larger social aims. If these aims are realized, then the subsidy may be defensible.

What's obvious about the efficiency rationale is that it shifts attention from the fair treatment of the donor to the recipient of the donation and the good that is done with the gift. Even so, as we saw in the previous chapter, the particular vehicle used in the United States to provide the subsidy—a deduction from taxable income—is vulnerable to powerful criticisms that keep a focus on fair treatment of the donor. First, the deduction is available only to itemizing taxpayers, and thus the subsidy is capricious, for its availability depends on a characteristic, one's status as an itemizer, that has nothing whatsoever to do with the value of giving. If the subsidy is justified because it produces some social good, then why should two donors who make identical donations to identical organizations, ostensibly producing the identical social good, be treated differently by the tax code?

Second, in a system of progressive taxation the deduction is tied by definition to marginal tax brackets. The richer you are, the less a charitable contribution actually costs you. The deduc-

tion functions as an increasingly greater subsidy and incentive with every higher step in the income tax bracket. Those at the highest tax bracket receive the largest deduction, those in the lowest tax bracket the lowest.

But these concerns do not constitute criticism of the Murphy-Nagel thesis, for these are not criticisms of the efficiency rationale per se. They are criticisms of the mechanism, currently in use in the United States and in many other countries, to deliver the subsidy, the deduction of charitable donations from taxable income. Reform of the subsidy mechanism could eliminate or mitigate the problems. For example, the deduction could be extended to all taxpayers regardless of itemizer status; or the deduction could be eliminated in favor of a partial or total tax credit; or the incentive could come, as in the United Kingdom, in the form of so-called "gift aid," where the state matches some portion of an individual's charitable donation to an eligible organization without reducing the taxes owed by the individual donor.

How then might we assess the efficiency rationale as a whole? One obvious way to evaluate the rationale, rather than just the mechanism currently in use, is to look to the social good the subsidy produces and the efficiency with which it is produced.

Supposing that the goods produced by charitable recipients were of social value, we might ask, for instance, whether the subsidy is so-called treasury efficient. Does the subsidy shake out more in donations than it costs in federal tax revenue? If so, the subsidy is treasury efficient. Economists will then argue about the optimal rate of the subsidy, or how to stimulate the most giving at the least cost to the treasury.

Empirical analyses of the tax deduction in the United States show that the deduction is indeed treasury efficient, though significantly less so than initially was thought.[23] Some evidence shows, however, that the deduction has no effect on giving—is

treasury inefficient—for particular kinds of donations, such as contributions to one's religious congregation (because, it is suggested, such gifts are experienced as religious obligations to be undertaken independent of whether the obligation qualifies as a tax event). Few donors, one might think (or at least hope), are engaging in tax optimization or avoidance strategies when the Sunday basket is passed around in church.[24]

Although treasury efficiency assures us that the subsidy is not a mere reward for charitable giving that would occur even in the absence of the subsidy—a loss of federal tax revenue to produce something that would occur anyway—its success as a justification for tax-subsidized giving depends very much on the initial supposition that the goods produced by charitable recipients are of social value.

When we inquire into the social good produced by charitable donations, rather than focusing squarely on questions of treasury efficiency, three problems present themselves, at least in the U.S. context. We got an initial sense of these problems in the previous chapter's descriptive overview of the distribution of charitable giving. Now we are in a position to analyze this distribution in the context of a particular justification for the institutional arrangements that shape the distribution.

First, U.S. law permits a truly kaleidoscopic landscape of public charities to receive tax-deductible charitable contributions.[25] Some and perhaps many of the social goods produced by charities will be of no value whatsoever to certain citizens. Because churches are eligible to give tax deductions to donors (i.e., congregants) for contributions, atheists are vicarious donors to churches through the tax subsidy. By contrast, Catholics are vicarious donors to Planned Parenthood and its support for abortion rights. Such examples are easily multiplied. The basic

point is that the subsidy cannot be justified as a Pareto improvement, where some benefit and no one is made worse off.[26] At best, the subsidy is a Kaldor-Hicks improvement, where the gains for those who consume the particular social good produced by charity offset the losses to those with no interest in that social good.

But relying on a Kaldor-Hicks improvement as the standard for justifying the efficiency rationale raises a second set of problems. For obvious reasons, as we saw in the previous chapter, the beneficiaries of the deduction are highly skewed toward upper income earners. Wealthier individuals donate more as an absolute amount (but not as a percentage of income) and receive a larger subsidy for giving (the upside-down effect) and claim, as a result, a staggeringly large share of the deduction. Those making $200,000 and above received 70 percent of all deductions for charitable contributions; those making $60,000 and above claim more than 98 percent of all such deductions.[27] The result is a decidedly *plutocratic bias* in the subsidy, where the favored beneficiaries of the wealthy receive the lion's share of the subsidy.

The plutocratic bias is troubling, for systematic overattention in the policy tool itself to the interests and preferences of the wealthy against those of the middle-class and poor seems a strange, indeed unjustifiable, basis for social policy.

This trouble might be undercut if the product of charitable giving were pure public goods, in the economic sense, namely goods that are nonexcludable and nonrivalrous. If wealthy people donate to produce goods that no one can be prevented from enjoying and that no person's consumption reduces the amount available to others, then the plutocratic bias nevertheless redounds to the advantage of all citizens. But the vast

majority of public charities do not produce pure public goods. Hospitals and universities, for instance, together account for more than half of the revenue of all nonprofits organizations in the United States. Both hospitals and universities can easily exclude persons who cannot pay for their services. The same is true for cultural and artistic organizations.

Despite the ability of hospitals, universities, and museums to exclude people who cannot pay for services, a funder of such organizations might point to evidence of positive spillover effects of hospitals in their communities and to the public benefits of basic research and an intellectual and artistic culture that are the products of research universities and museums. It is salutary to see these broader effects, but we should not overstate the benefits in the face of the facts about the generally elite clientele of private hospitals, selective universities, and most cultural organizations.

Leaving aside the strict conditions of pure public goods, the concern about plutocratic bias might be mitigated if the favored beneficiaries of philanthropic donors, and of the wealthy especially, were charities engaged in social welfare or services for the poor. That is, plutocratic bias might be tolerable when charity provides for the basic needs of all citizens and thereby realizes an important aim of distributive justice. At the very least, then, the effect of charitable giving would be to some degree redistributive. Yet this is also not the case, at least in the United States. And this is the third problem with the efficiency rationale. Recall that more than half of all individual giving in the United States goes to religion, and none of this giving goes to the faith-based social-service charities associated with religious groups (e.g., the Salvation Army, Mercy Corps). Those offshoots of religious organizations have been counted in the relevant category of public/social benefit organizations, which receive less than 6 percent

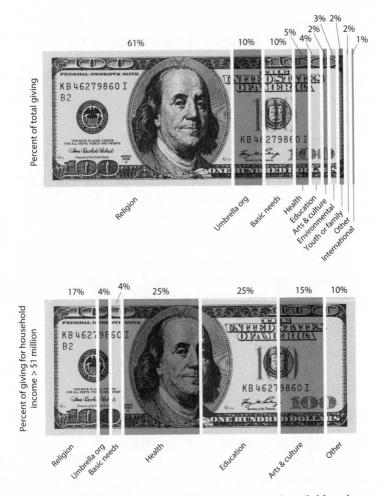

Percent of total giving

61% 10% 10% 5% 4% 3% 2% 2% 2% 1%

Religion Umbrella org Basic needs Health Education Arts & culture Environmental Youth or family Other International

Percent of giving for household income > $1 million

17% 4% 4% 25% 25% 15% 10%

Religion Umbrella org Basic needs Health Education Arts & culture Other

FIGURE 3.1. Donor Allocations by Household Income. *Source*: Compiled from data in Center on Philanthropy at Indiana University, "Patterns of Household Charitable Giving."

of all charitable giving.[28] If we focus squarely on the favored beneficiaries of the wealthy, we see that cultural organizations, hospitals, and universities are the usual recipients. Sometimes these gifts have redistributive benefits (e.g., scholarships for the poor); sometimes not. The best economic analyses of the

redistributional nature of the charitable sector conclude that, at best, no strong conclusions about distributional impact can be made but that plenty of evidence shows "that relatively few nonprofit institutions serve the poor as a primary clientele."[29]

Moreover, as shown in Figure 3.1, the higher up the income ladder, *the less likely donors are to direct their giving to the poor.*

One final and important point. Suppose now that charitable donations were redistributive in the sense that gifts from the relatively wealthy flowed to the relatively poor. Granting this, we may nevertheless not yet conclude that nonprofit organizations and foundations are in fact redistributive all things considered because we must still account for the tax concessions to philanthropy and the counterfactual scenario in which the money flowing into nonprofit organizations and foundations would have been taxed and become public revenue. The relevant question is not merely, "Is philanthropy redistributive?" but rather, "Do philanthropic dollars flow more sharply downward than government spending does?" In order for the return, so to speak, on the public's investment in philanthropy to be worthwhile, philanthropy must do better than the state would do had it taxed the philanthropic assets.

Answering this counterfactual question is difficult. We are forced to speculate about how the state might spend the tax revenue it could have collected if it hadn't extended the tax concessions to philanthropists for their gifts.[30] We are also forced to speculate whether, if denied a tax incentive for giving, donors would or could successfully find alternative mechanisms to shelter their assets from taxation. (Were the latter to occur, it would suggest that a strong, perhaps primary, motivation in charitable giving is not altruism and the desire to direct private assets for other-regarding public benefits, but the desire to diminish one's tax burden. How else to think of someone who,

when denied a tax incentive for giving, elects not to make any donation at all?)[31]

I will not make any such speculation here. Instead, I wish to note that anyone who seeks to ground the special tax treatment of philanthropy in the United States on the sector's redistributive outcomes must confront at least three reasons to be suspicious that any such redistribution actually occurs. There is the first and obvious difficulty that a motley assortment of nonprofit groups all qualify for 501(c)(3) status, puppet theaters and soup kitchens alike. There is the second difficulty that religious groups dominate as the beneficiaries of individual charitable dollars. And there is the third difficulty that the burden on the sector's advocate is to show not merely that philanthropy is redistributive but that it is *more redistributive* than would be government spending. In short, we have some good prima facie reasons to doubt that philanthropy is redistributive in effect or eleemosynary in aim.

These problems once again target the mechanism in the United States and elsewhere to deliver the subsidy: the tax deduction. The plutocratic bias in the subsidy and the lack of redistribution could be altered by both changing the mechanism of the subsidy (change to a capped tax credit, for instance) and limiting the kinds of organizations that are permitted to receive tax-deductible donations (eliminating churches and elite cultural organizations, for instance). Whatever the remedy, the expectation would be that the subsidy must still be *efficient*. To be justified, the subsidy must cost less to the treasury than it produces in social benefits.

I do not explore these sorts of remedies here. Instead, I turn now to an alternative rationale that does not displace the idea of a subsidy but drops the necessity that it be an efficient use of tax dollars in producing certain public benefits.

PLURALISM RATIONALE

The pluralism rationale comes in several stripes and cannot be called a unified theory. The basic idea is that a tax incentive to make charitable donations should not be justified on the basis of assessing the discrete social goods, or outputs, of the various nonprofit organizations funded through these donations. Instead, a tax incentive is justified for its role in stimulating or amplifying the voice of citizens in the production of a diverse, decentralized, and pluralistic associational sector, which is itself normatively desirable because it is considered to be a bedrock of a flourishing liberal democracy. If nonprofit organizations constitute, to a significant degree, the institutional matrix of associational life, then stimulating charitable donations to a wide array of nonprofits might amplify the voice of citizens and enhance civil society to the overall benefit of liberal democracy. Rather than focus on the array of goods produced by charitable organizations, the focus here is on the creation and sustenance of a diverse slate of organizations themselves. The public good or social benefit being produced is civil society itself, not the catalogue of public goods or benefits produced by the roster of organizations that constitute civil society.

Note that this is still a subsidy theory, but there is no necessary demand that the subsidy be treasury efficient. Even if there is a net loss to the treasury in the production of the social goods generated by nonprofit organizations—if the state could more efficiently deliver these goods itself—the pluralism rationale holds that the subsidy is nevertheless worthwhile. Of course, there is no bias against the efficient production of particular goods, but the pluralism rationale does not demand efficiency for the success of the argument. The state might justifiably forgo

tax revenue for the sake of fostering citizens' voices and the sustenance of pluralistic associational life.

Before developing the pluralism rationale in greater detail, consider a few worries. First, vigorous safeguarding of liberty is typically thought to be the institutional guarantee for associational life. Is it really necessary to subsidize the exercise of liberty to produce a vibrant civil society? After all, there was no charitable contributions tax deduction when Tocqueville toured the United States.

Second, the defender of the pluralism rationale has to answer to a disturbing feature of the historical record about associational life over the last century. It is no exaggeration to say that the rise of nonprofit organizations in the United States and the use of the charitable contributions deduction coincides with the *decline* of civic engagement and associational life, at least if the Robert Putnam literature is credible. The post–World War II rise of professionally run nonprofit organizations may have contributed to the calcification of civil society, diminished civic engagement, and a decline in social capital production.[32]

If U.S. taxpayers have spent hundreds of billions of dollars in tax expenditures to support charitable giving over the past generation, we might ask whether this has stimulated an improvement in civil society that would not have happened absent the subsidy. It is hard, perhaps impossible, to answer this counterfactual. Perhaps the decline in civic engagement and associational life is smaller than it would have been in the absence of the subsidy. Whatever the actual fact, the empirical case that the subsidy has improved civil society, or lessened its decline, has to my knowledge not yet been made.

So what, then, is the case for the pluralism rationale in support of subsidizing philanthropy? There are two main and

connected ideas: decentralizing the process of producing social goods and promoting the pluralism of associational life by
diminishing state orthodoxy in defining its contours.

These ideas are given partial expression in a U.S. Supreme
Court opinion from Justice Lewis Powell, where he takes issue
with the notion that the purpose of the nonprofit sector is efficiently to deliver or supplement services or social goods that
the government would otherwise supply through direct expenditures. Powell rejects the view that the primary function of a
tax-exempt organization is to act on behalf of the government
in carrying out governmentally approved policies. "In my opinion, such a view of 501(c)(3) ignores the important role played
by tax exemptions in encouraging diverse, indeed often sharply
conflicting, activities and viewpoints. As Justice Brennan has
observed, private, nonprofit groups receive tax exemptions because 'each group contributes to the diversity of association,
viewpoint, and enterprise essential to a vigorous, pluralistic
society.' Far from representing an effort to reinforce any per-
ceived 'common community conscience,' the provision of tax
exemptions to nonprofit groups is one indispensable means of
limiting the influence of governmental orthodoxy on important
areas of community life."[33]

In a diverse society, there will be heterogeneous preferences
about what kinds of social goods to supply through direct expenditures of tax dollars. Democratic mechanisms for deciding how
to allocate these dollars are of course one fundamental means
of dealing with heterogeneous preferences. The preferences of
the median voter assume a large role here, in theory if not always in practice. But another potentially important means is
to decentralize the authority for deciding what kinds of public
benefits are produced and to permit, indeed to enhance, citizen
voice in this process by providing a stimulus for that voice. Tax

incentives for charitable giving represent, on this view, an effort to stimulate all citizens to cast their own preferences, in the form of dollars, about their favored social goods into civil society, where the resulting funding stream is partly private (from the donor) and partly public (from the tax subsidy).

The result is that citizen groups that cannot muster a majority consensus about a particular public benefit provision through the regular democratic political process will still have a tax-supported means to pursue their minority or eccentric goals. Ordinary associational rights guaranteed by a liberal society protect the liberty of every citizen to join with others to pursue dissenting or conflicting visions of the public good and the production of public benefits; the justification for subsidizing this liberty through tax incentives is to enhance or amplify all citizens' voices, stimulate their contributions to civil society, and assist minorities in overcoming the constraints of majority rule and the median voter. Philanthropy becomes a means of voting for one's favored civil society projects with dollars partially private and partially public.[34]

Note here that concerns about the redistributive nature of charitable dollars recede from view. When the justification for tax incentives for philanthropy runs along the pluralist line, philanthropy is not, at least in the first instance, about assisting the poor or disadvantaged; it is instead about protecting and promoting a flourishing and pluralistic civil society.[35] If citizens should wish to fund nonprofit organizations that provide social services to the poor or disadvantaged, they can certainly do so, but these preferences would not be privileged over, say, preferences for cultural organizations, animal welfare groups, arts institutions, and so forth. Moreover, the tax incentive, now equally available to every citizen, might provide a stimulus for individuals to take a greater interest in social problems, local

organizations, and so on. It might help promote civic agency, association, and engagement.

I believe this pluralism rationale has merit, and it supplies good reason to subsidize the liberty of people to give their money away for philanthropic purposes. But however compelling the pluralism rationale may be, it cannot be said to sit behind the current design of tax-supported giving in most countries. Providing tax deductions for individuals who make charitable gifts does not honor the pluralism rationale but rather undermines and makes a mockery of it.

As described earlier, a tax deduction for charitable contributions, when there is a progressive income tax, establishes a plutocratic element in the public policy. The deduction supplies a greater subsidy to the wealthy, who are, of course, already likely to possess a more powerful voice in associational life and the political arena without any subsidy whatsoever. If the tax incentive for charitable giving is designed as a deduction from taxable income, many people are denied voice entirely (because they do not itemize their deductions) and wealthier citizens claim far more of the subsidized benefit than others. The consequence is a troubling plutocratic bias in the contours of civil society, systematically more organizations favored by the rich and fewer favored by the poor. We get not egalitarian citizen voice in civil society but plutocratic citizen voice, underwritten and promoted by tax policy.[36]

Here, then, in the pluralism rationale is where an egalitarian norm can and should inform the legal rules that structure philanthropy. Many possible mechanisms track the pluralism rationale, but for the sake of illustration, consider two possible designs. First is a flat and capped nonrefundable tax credit for charitable donations. By offering an equivalent tax credit to all donors (say 25 percent of any donation) with the total

annual credit capped at some level (say $1,000), the mechanism avoids the upside-down structure of the deduction, offers an equal credit to all donors, and affords donors the liberty to continue to give money away after the cap has been reached, but no longer with any state subsidy to do so. The policy proposal bears a resemblance to a stakeholding grant or a campaign finance voucher scheme for each citizen, though rather than directing the use of the stakeholding grant for investment in one's own projects or a voucher for expressing political voice, the tax credit could be directed only toward eligible civil society organizations.[37] Call it a civil society stakeholding grant, assigned on an equal basis to every citizen in the form of a nonrefundable tax credit, Bill Gates receiving the same-sized credit as every other citizen. Second, consider the practice of so-called percentage philanthropy, which has arisen recently in several Central and Eastern European countries. In Hungary, for instance, a law passed in 1996 permits citizens to allocate 1 percent of their income taxes to a qualifying nongovernmental organization. This is not a tax credit, as in the previous example, because citizens here do not pay less tax. Citizens redirect what would otherwise be state revenue in the form of income taxes to the civil society organizations of their choice. It must be said, however, that there is nothing in this latter scheme that deserves the description "charity" or "philanthropy," for the scheme redirects only tax dollars, not private dollars. Percentage philanthropy does not require any donation of an individual's own after-tax dollars.

Conclusion

Though people have engaged in philanthropy for millennia, the practice of giving money away has only recently become a

tax-subsidized activity. Philanthropy is now embedded within a framework of public policies, many centered on the tax regime, that structures its practice and alters its shape from what it would otherwise be without the state's intervention. Though nearly all liberal democracies have tax incentives for charitable donations, the justification for this practice is not well understood or theorized. I have canvassed three distinct justifications for providing tax incentives for philanthropy: a tax base rationale, an efficiency rationale, and a pluralism rationale. While I find nothing to recommend the tax base rationale, the efficiency and pluralism rationales do offer potentially good reasons to support subsidies for philanthropy. Neither of these latter two justifications, however, provides support for the actual design of most tax-subsidized giving, where a wide array of eligible recipient organizations and a tax deduction for giving are the favored mechanisms. A political theory of philanthropy might offer a defense, or several distinct defenses, of state incentives for giving money away, but the current practice of state-supported philanthropy, especially in the United States, is indefensible.

Repugnant to the Whole Idea of a Democratic Society?

ON THE ROLE OF FOUNDATIONS

A perpetual charitable foundation is a completely
irresponsible institution, answerable to nobody. . . .
The puzzle for economics is why these foundations are
not total scandals.

—RICHARD POSNER, "CHARITABLE FOUNDATIONS"

In the first chapter, we saw that Turgot and Mill mounted strong
criticism of foundations, or perpetual endowments, in the
seventeenth and eighteenth centuries.[1] Turgot rejected foundations outright, arguing that they were antithetical to social
utility because, among other reasons, honoring donor intent
in perpetuity was to shackle, amid ever-changing social conditions, living and future generations to the ideas of people long
dead. Mill by contrast viewed foundations as potentially useful institutional forms in democratic societies but only when

their existence was time delimited and when government treated endowments as a form of national property, reserving for itself the authority to redirect their purposes when necessary.

At the dawn of the twentieth century in the United States, the wealthiest individuals of the era, such as Andrew Carnegie and John D. Rockefeller, advocated for a modification of the traditional foundation form. The modification was to establish a general-purpose grant-making private foundation whose aim was not the direct provision of services through its own operations but to fund other organizations that would attempt to tackle root causes of social problems. Such foundations have become the standard form, a grant-making rather than operating foundation. In this chapter, I examine the place of private foundations in liberal democratic societies. That private foundations do play a significant role, with enormous resources at their disposal, is incontestable. But what role, if any, ought they play?

I began this book with an account of the controversy surrounding the creation of the Rockefeller Foundation, a largely forgotten historical episode that reveals attitudes and reservations about philanthropy virtually never heard in our contemporary era. I briefly revisit this history before turning to an examination of the legal design of the contemporary private foundation—low accountability, transparency, donor intent protected in perpetuity, and tax-advantaged treatment—that renders it an institutional oddity in democracy. Private foundations are, more or less by definition, the legal sanctioning, or more precisely the legal promotion, of plutocratic voices in democratic societies. Democratic societies involve a commitment to much more than a representative system of government with free and fair elections. Democracy involves a commitment to the equal standing of citizens and an equal re-

spect for their interests. Such equal standing and respect are manifest when citizens are formally equal under the law—there is no second-class citizenship—and when all citizens possess an equal opportunity for political influence and participation.

The existence and growing power of private foundations to influence public policy sits in tension with ordinary democratic expectations of the political equality of citizens. Despite this tension, I make arguments on behalf of foundations that show why, following the ideas of John Stuart Mill in chapter 1, foundations, when accompanied by the right policy structure, can serve as a mechanism for domesticating plutocrats to serve rather than subvert democratic aims.

The Birth of the Private Foundation in the United States

In the early 1900s, John D. Rockefeller wished to convert his mountainous private fortune, derived from his ownership of Standard Oil, into a general-purpose philanthropic foundation with the aim of benefiting all of humankind by stimulating "any and all of the elements of human progress." He and his advisors made plans to incorporate the foundation as a variation of a charitable trust. Incorporation then, as is still true today, was ordinarily a matter for a state legislature. They worried, however, that the scale of his philanthropic resources—well over $1 billion in today's dollars—and the global scope of his ambitions would make the proposed foundation an unwelcome prospect in his home state of New York. State legislatures often imposed caps on the size of a trust and demanded clearly defined, narrow purposes. So Rockefeller in 1909 sought a federal charter to incorporate from the U.S. Congress, hoping for a stamp of approval from the national government.

Skepticism was widespread, and criticism came quickly from many quarters, including the sitting U.S. president, William Taft, and the trustbusting former president, Theodore Roosevelt. As we saw in the introduction, Reverend John Haynes Holmes testified before Congress that, despite admiring the good intentions of Rockefeller, the very idea of the foundation was "repugnant to the whole idea of a democratic society." Senator Frank Walsh described all foundations as "a menace to the welfare of society."[2] Louis Brandeis, the future U.S. Supreme Court justice, said that the Rockefeller Foundation was "inconsistent with our democratic aspirations" and confessed to "grave apprehensions" about the power that was lodged in the hands of a few wealthy men.[3]

Rockefeller was nevertheless determined to obtain the federal charter, and offered a host of amendments intended to limit the power of the foundation. Rockefeller proposed to cap the size of the foundation at $100 million, to require that all investment returns on the initial principal be spent annually, and that the foundation spend out its endowment entirely within fifty years (with a provision to extend its life to one hundred years if two-thirds of Congress were to approve). Most significant of all, Rockefeller proposed that the governance of the foundation be partially public, making the work of the foundation formally accountable to the broader community. This would be accomplished by making members of the board of trustees subject to a veto by a majority of a congressionally appointed board consisting of various political leaders (the president of the United States, the president of the Senate, the Speaker of the House, and the chief justice of the U.S. Supreme Court) and educational leaders (the presidents of Harvard, Yale, Columbia, Johns Hopkins, and the University of Chicago).[4] Growing concern that unchecked power, even when exercised on behalf

of a charitable mission, was a corrupting force in democratic society would be met by creating a new legal template that placed strict limits on the size and life span of the foundation and introduced a measure of public governance.

Yet this was not enough to allay skepticism of Rockefeller's proposed foundation. In 1911, in the midst of antitrust lawsuits against Standard Oil, Attorney General George Wickersham advised President Taft to oppose Rockefeller's proposed federal charter: "The power which, under such bill, would be invested in and exercised by a small body of men, in absolute control of the income of $100,000,000 or more, to be expended for the general indefinite objects described in the bill, might be in the highest degree corrupt in its influence."[5]

Though the U.S. House of Representatives passed a bill to charter the Rockefeller Foundation in 1913, the Senate was stubbornly opposed. And so, after nearly four years of legislative effort, involving serious concessions to skeptical lawmakers, the federal charter failed. Rockefeller and his advisers moved immediately to seek a charter from the New York state legislature. They eliminated all of the concessionary amendments offered to the U.S. Congress. The New York bill was approved in May 1913, officially incorporating the Rockefeller Foundation. An official centennial publication of the Rockefeller Foundation in 2013 recounts this history, noting with some satisfaction that "the people's representatives in Washington had lost their chance to control the world's largest philanthropy."[6]

The fight in the U.S. Congress to charter the foundation reveals a counterfactual history of the general-purpose, grant-making private foundation. Had the U.S. Senate passed the House bill to approve the Rockefeller Foundation, it would have created a legal template for the institutional design of foundations with limits on size and time and provisions for clear public

oversight. The balance between plutocratic voice and democratic voice in the operation of American foundations would have been struck much differently. And of course the Rockefeller Foundation would have closed shop, by spending down its endowment, in either 1963 or 2013. Though one can never be certain with counterfactual histories, it seems likely that the failure to obtain a federal charter and the subsequent decision to incorporate in New York State set in motion an institutional path dependence that led directly to the widespread organization of private foundation activity today with none of the amendments suggested by Rockefeller over one hundred years ago.

Is the operation of such foundations compatible with democracy?

What Is a Foundation For?

In an important sense, foundations have a long history. Analogues of the contemporary philanthropic foundation can be found in antiquity, where endowments funded the creation and sustenance of public monuments and educational institutions, including Plato's Academy. And as we saw in the opening chapter, they are not limited to the Judeo-Christian world. The Islamic waqf is a clear institutional precursor of the modern private foundation, an arrangement designed to structure and elicit private resources to produce public benefits. Waqfs, from as early as the seventh century AD, funded mosques, schools, hospitals, and soup kitchens, much as private foundations undertake similar projects today.

Though rooted in historical traditions, the modern private foundation in the United States is a creation of the age of the Rockefeller controversy. Here were birthed novel features not found in historical antecedents. The idea behind the Rockefeller

Foundation and the similarly minded Carnegie Corporation was to establish an entity with broad and general purposes, intended to support other institutions and indeed to create and fund new organizations, seeking to address root causes of social problems rather than deliver direct services (work "wholesale" rather than "retail"), and designed to be administered by private, self-governing trustees, with paid professional staff, who would act on behalf of a public mission. One other aspect of these foundations was new: their vast resources enabled them to operate on a scale unlike other more ordinary endowments.

For most of the nineteenth century, creating a grant-making foundation at one's private initiative with one's private wealth was not possible; authorization and incorporation by a democratic body were necessary. The prospect that general-purpose foundations might be brought into existence was viewed as a threat to democracy. Even after such foundations were created, they continued to be treated with public scorn and skepticism. In a decision that seems positively unimaginable from today's vantage point, the regents of the University of Wisconsin passed a resolution in 1925 that banned the university from accepting philanthropic donations from foundations.[7]

We have come a long way in one hundred years. Philanthropists are today widely admired, their names trumpeted from buildings and their photos gracing magazine covers. The creation of foundations by the wealthy meets not with public or political skepticism but with widespread gratitude. The permission to create a foundation, moreover, is both free-standing—not requiring approval by a democratically elected body—and, as with ordinary charitable donations, subsidized with tax advantages.

We live today in the second golden age of American philanthropy. In 1930 approximately two hundred private foundations possessed aggregate assets of less than $1 billion. In 1959 there

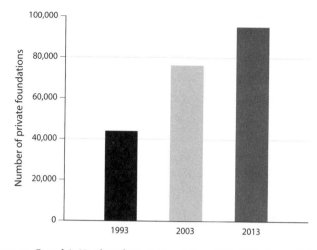

FIGURE 4.1. Growth in Number of Private Foundations, 1993–2013. *Source*: IRS data, "Domestic Private Foundations, 1993–2013."

were more than two thousand, in 1985 just over thirty thousand private foundations. Figure 4.1 shows that the number ballooned to seventy-six thousand in 2004, and as of 2014 the number was nearly one hundred thousand with total capitalization close to $800 billion.[8]

To decide whether this is a healthy development for democracy, we need to ask what philanthropic foundations are for. What role, if any, *ought* foundations play in a democratic society? If they are repugnant to the idea of democracy, as thought Holmes, or inconsistent with democratic aspirations, as thought Brandeis, then perhaps democratic societies ought to abolish them, as Turgot argued, or constrain them to align with democratic purposes, as Mill argued.

Andrew Carnegie thought that the man who dies rich dies disgraced, and the person who opts to distribute private wealth for public purposes should be thanked as a matter of civic gratitude. Conspicuous consumption by the wealthy is hard to see as

preferable to the establishment of a philanthropic foundation. But we should resist this view for two reasons. First, it is to compare philanthropy to the alternative of private consumption, which will nearly always render philanthropy praiseworthy. Instead, we should view philanthropy, especially big philanthropy in the form of private foundations, as an exercise of power and plutocratic voice that warrants democratic scrutiny. The larger the foundation, the greater the potential power. Think here of Bill Gates, whose philanthropy permits him to stride upon the world stage as if he were a head of state. Second, it is to assume that the current laws that define how foundations may be created and structure how they operate are optimal and publicly justifiable. Perhaps foundations could play important roles in democratic societies, despite being an exercise of power and expression of plutocratic voice, if they were subject to different legal arrangements.

Therefore, asking about the purpose of a foundation in a democracy is not an impertinent but an important question. For while foundations of some sort or another have existed for millennia, the modern grant-making foundation in which private assets are set aside in a permanent, donor-directed, tax-advantaged endowment with a fraction of the assets annually to be distributed for a public purpose is, as I have just described, a relatively recent phenomenon, no older than the early twentieth century. Philanthropic foundations in this form are institutional oddities in a democracy, oddities that have considerable power in virtue of their assets.

My argument here is ultimately redemptive. I conclude that despite many antidemocratic features, the modern foundation is not incompatible with democracy. In fact, when foundations function in support of what I will call pluralism and discovery, they can be important contributors to democratic societies.

Foundations as Institutional Oddities

In democratic societies, wrote one prominent twentieth-century philanthropic insider, "there is no more strange or improbable creature than the private foundation."[9] Why are foundations institutional oddities? Foundations represent, by definition, plutocratic voices in a democratic society committed, in principle, to the equality of citizens. But the strangeness of the foundation form goes far beyond this.

The modern philanthropic foundation is perhaps the most unaccountable, nontransparent, peculiar institutional form we have in a democratic society.

FOUNDATIONS LACK ACCOUNTABILITY

In the commercial marketplace, if a company fails to make a profit, because consumers opt not to purchase the goods it sells, the company goes out of business. Companies are driven to please consumers: if consumers don't like or want what a company produces, then they don't buy from it, and if most consumers think this way, the company disappears. Other companies compete for the same consumers. This is the accountability logic internal to the marketplace: meeting consumer demand.

In the public institutions of a democratic state, officials responsible for crafting law and allocating tax dollars must stand for election; if citizens do not approve of the public policies and spending decisions of their representatives, they vote for replacements at the next regularly scheduled election. This is the accountability logic internal to democracy: responsiveness to citizens.

By contrast, foundations have no market accountability; they have neither goods for sale nor marketplace competitors.

Instead of selling anything, foundations give money away to other organizations, whose own livelihood frequently depends on continuing support from foundations. Foundations have no consumers or competitors, only supplicants for their money in the form of grants. If citizens do not like the grant-making decisions of a foundation, there is no recourse because there is nothing to buy and no investors to hold the foundation accountable.

Moreover, foundations have no electoral accountability; no one in a foundation stands for election, regardless of what the public thinks about the distribution of its grants. Suppose a group of people disapprove of what the Gates Foundation, or any other foundation, is doing. What then? There's no mechanism to unelect Bill and Melinda Gates. Referring to the foundation's education grant making, critic Diane Ravitch has called Bill Gates the nation's unelected school superintendent.

Foundations do have certain minimal obligations of procedural accountability. In the United States, a "payout" rule instituted in 1969 requires that foundations disburse at least 5 percent of their assets every year (though administrative costs of running a foundation count toward this payout). There is also a requirement to file an annual tax form with some basic data about foundation trustees, employees and their salaries, and assets. But this is far from substantive accountability. Wealthy people are free to set up foundations, without constituents, consumers, and competitors, for whatever purpose they please, with whatever money they wish, and to continue to hew to this purpose, regardless of the outcome of the foundation's grant making.

To be sure, foundations must direct their grants to officially recognized public charities or, in American tax lingo, 501(c)(3) nonprofit organizations. But in the United States, virtually

any organization can be structured as a nonprofit so long as it promises not to distribute profits to its owners. Moreover, U.S. foundations can distribute grants and fulfill their payout rule by giving to an arcane but increasingly popular vehicle called a donor-advised fund, a charitable investment account that creates no immediate public benefit whatsoever and instead serves to warehouse wealth until the donor decides to distribute it to a public charity.[10] So the public charity requirement is no accountability structure at all.

The lack of any internal accountability is compounded by the difficulty any foundation has in developing mechanisms to generate honest feedback from grantees. As a general matter, people who interact with foundations are deferential and solicitous, pleading for a grant or seeking the next grant. There is little incentive for a potential or actual grantee to offer critical feedback to a foundation. Every person who works in a foundation understands what comes with the territory: people who become foundation officers are transformed overnight into the smartest and best-looking people in a room. The political theorist Harold Laski identified the phenomenon as early as 1930, writing about the *deleterious* effect of foundation grants to universities: "Usually the director gives the impression of considerable complacency and a keen sense of the power at his disposal. He has not often himself been engaged in the serious business of research. He has dipped into an immense number of subjects; he is usually captivated by the latest fashion in each. He travels luxuriously, is amply entertained wherever he goes (he has so much to give), and he speaks always to hearers keenly alert to sense the direction of his own interests in order that they may explain that this is the one thing they are anxious to develop in their own university."[11]

FOUNDATIONS LACK TRANSPARENCY

Apart from a legal requirement that foundations pay out 5 percent of their assets every year and file an annual tax form with some basic data, foundations can, and frequently do, act secretly. They need not have a website, an office, or a telephone number, need not publish an annual or quarterly report or articulate any grant-making strategy. They need not evaluate their grant making; if they do, they need not make such evaluations public. They need not report on trustee decision making.

Some foundations—especially the largest and most professionalized—do operate transparently, providing all of the above information and more. But this is a function of the idiosyncratic preference of a particular foundation, not a legal requirement or professional norm. A great many small family foundations operate with virtually no public trace save their legally required annual tax filing. Thus foundations are often black boxes, stewarding and distributing private assets for public purposes, as identified and defined by the donor, about which the public knows very little and can find out very little.[12]

DONOR-DIRECTED PURPOSE IN PERPETUITY

Foundations are legally designed to enshrine donor intent and protect philanthropic assets in perpetuity.[13] Thus does the dead hand of the donor potentially extend from the beyond the grave to strangle future generations. Foundations must be governed by a board of trustees, but the donors and their family or trusted associates can serve in this role; there is no requirement of community or public governance. Wealth management firms routinely market their services in setting up a family foundation

as vehicles for the intergeneration transmission and sustenance of family values. A founding donor may thereby control the governance and purpose of a foundation forever.

Of such arrangements Richard Posner has observed, "A perpetual charitable foundation . . . is a completely irresponsible institution, answerable to nobody. It competes neither in capital markets nor in product markets . . . and, unlike a hereditary monarch whom such a foundation otherwise resembles, it is subject to no political controls either." He wondered, "the puzzle for economics is why these foundations are not total scandals."[14]

FOUNDATIONS ARE GENEROUSLY TAX-SUBSIDIZED

All of the foregoing might be understandable, if not necessarily justifiable, if foundations were simply one way for the wealthy to exercise their liberty: some choose to consume their wealth; others choose to provide gifts and bequests for heirs; and still others choose to give their money away for a philanthropic purpose. Why demand accountability for the philanthropists?

The answer is by now clear: because foundations represent an exercise of power. And also because foundations—at least in their contemporary incarnation—are not simply exercises of personal liberty.

In his 2001 book *American Foundations*, Mark Dowie relates an amusing and instructive anecdote about the Open Society Institute, one of several foundations set up by financier George Soros. During a meeting to resolve a disagreement about grant-making priorities, Soros is alleged to have announced, "This is my money. We will do it my way." At which point a junior staff member interjected that roughly half of the money in the foundation was not his money, but the public's money,

explaining, "If you hadn't placed that money in OSI . . . about half of it would be in the Treasury."[15] Dowie reports that the junior staffer did not last long in the foundation's employ.

Philanthropy in general, including the creation of foundations, is generously tax-subsidized in the United States and in many other countries. Under current U.S. law, assets transferred to a foundation by a donor are left untaxed in two respects: the donor makes the donation (more or less) tax-free, diminishing the tax burden she would face in the absence of the donation; and the assets that constitute a foundation's endowment, invested (usually to maximize overall return) in the marketplace, are also (more or less) tax-free.[16]

It is worth remembering it was not always thus. Philanthropic activity dates back to antiquity, but tax deductions for donors (as opposed to tax exemptions for asset or property endowments, such as the waqfs we explored in chapter 1) date back only to 1917 and the creation of a federal income tax. Carnegie, Rockefeller, Sage, and their many philanthropic predecessors practiced philanthropy without any federal or state tax incentive for the donation of assets to establish a philanthropic endowment.

Why provide a subsidy for the exercise of a liberty that people already possess, namely to give their money away for a philanthropic purpose? One can imagine various possible justifications for a subsidy, most prominently the idea that a tax incentive will stimulate more philanthropy, more and larger foundations, and therefore more public benefits, than would occur without the subsidy. Supposing the public benefits are of sufficient magnitude and value, the lost treasury revenue might nevertheless be an efficient means of producing these public benefits.

Whether this is true is an empirical question; if it is so, whether this constitutes a good justification for providing a

subsidy is a normative question. I explored the efficiency of the subsidy in the previous chapter and wish here only to emphasize that, today, the existence of foundations is not correctly seen as the product of the exercise of people's liberty to establish a foundation. Foundations *are* created voluntarily and yet they are also the product of public subsidies, the loss of funds that would otherwise be tax revenue, to subsidize their creation.[17] So foundations do not simply express the individual liberty of wealthy people. Citizens pay, in lost tax revenue, for foundations, and, by extension, for giving public expression to the preferences of rich people. Private foundations are not merely plutocratic voices, an observation that would follow from the simple fact that foundations are created by the wealthy. The plutocratic voices of the wealthy are amplified, as it were, by the loss of treasury revenue that would otherwise be expended by democratically elected and accountable representatives.

With few or no formal accountability mechanisms, practically no transparency obligations, a legal framework designed to honor donor intent in perpetuity, and generous tax breaks to subsidize the creation of a foundation, what gives foundations their legitimacy in a democratic society? Why have this institutional form?

As we observed in earlier chapters, we can quickly dismiss one common thought: that foundations exist because they are redistributive, responsive to the needs of the poor or disadvantaged. Foundation giving for basic needs represents a surprisingly small percentage of foundation activity, on the order of 10 percent. And the greater the size of assets in a foundation, the smaller the percentage of grants that go to meet basic needs.[18]

In any case, conceiving of foundations as mechanisms for almsgiving implies that a more just world—a world in which, say, desperate poverty did not exist or in which the basic needs

of individuals were met and did not depend on philanthropic giving—would not need philanthropic foundations. This raises the question whether the justification of and need for philanthropy would disappear if desperate poverty were to be eliminated. I argue that the answer is no. Philanthropy in general and foundations in particular are not just remedial, second-best efforts in democratic societies.

One way of posing the question is to ask whether foundations would be a welcome institutional arrangement, contributory to democratic purposes, if we were starting a democratic society from scratch. Would we want, as a matter of first-best institutional design, foundations in something like the legal form in which they exist today.

The catalogue of the oddities of the foundation form suggests a strong case against. Foundations appear at odds with democracy, for they represent, by definition and by law, the expression of plutocratic voices directed toward the public good. But why, in a democracy, should the size of one's wallet give one a greater say in the public good and public policy? Why should this plutocratic voice be subsidized by the public? And why should democracy allow this voice to extend across generations in the form of tax-protected assets? It would seem that foundations are a misplaced plutocratic, and powerful, element in a democratic society.

Several further arguments lay bare the tensions between philanthropy and democracy and call into doubt several of the institutional arrangements, and ultimately the very legitimacy, of private foundations. Some attack donor discretion and argue that philanthropy is better conceived as reparative justice.[19] Others argue that certain kinds of public good production should not be outsourced to private parties and must be produced and funded collectively, by citizens, if the goods

are to possess the stamp of democratic legitimacy they are said to need.[20] Still others see in the evolution of philanthropy the emergence of a particular kind of high-profile philanthropist, such as Bill Gates, Mark Zuckerberg, and Michael Bloomberg, whose activity supplants the state, subverts public policy processes, and in so doing diminishes democracy.[21]

I find many points of agreement, especially when considering the actual grant-making practices of foundations today. Yet despite all this, I think a role for foundations in democracy can be defended. Against these critics, and against the early skeptics who claimed that foundations are repugnant to democracy or inimical to social utility, I argue that foundations can have important roles to play in democratic societies. We can mount a principled defense of foundations that establishes at the same time a normative standard by which to assess their activity.

The Case for Foundations

The activities of private foundations can be oriented to support rather than subvert democratic aims. The argument is twofold. First, following the claims made in the previous chapter with respect to charitable giving of any kind, foundations can help to overcome problems in public good production by diminishing government orthodoxy and decentralizing the definition and distribution of public goods. Call this the *pluralism argument*. There is a second argument particular to foundations, setting them apart from ordinary charitable giving. Because of their size and longevity, foundations can operate on a different and longer time horizon than can businesses in the marketplace and elected officials in public institutions, taking risks in social policy experimentation and innovation that we should not routinely expect to see in commercial firms or state agencies.

Call this the *discovery argument*. On this basis, we can build the outline of a first-best argument for the existence of foundations that is not at odds with but complementary to democratic governance.

This argument is not intended to justify the full range of legal permissions currently afforded to foundations. I am in particular skeptical that it is possible to defend the legal permission for a foundation to exist in perpetuity. I am also skeptical that the array of tax subsidies attached to philanthropy today is necessary for the creation and sustenance of foundations. I present the general cast of an argument on behalf of foundations that deflects the criticism that they are misplaced in democratic societies and that confers on them a high degree of autonomy and a relative lack of accountability.

To understand what a foundation is for, we cannot and should not, as is commonplace today, ask how foundations can be more effective, have greater impact, be more outcome oriented. The relevant question is not, "How can philanthropic private foundations act more strategically?"[22] Of course foundations should be effective and strategic, but at what? To understand what foundations should be effective at, we first must understand foundations in relation to the market and the state. Only in this manner can we identify the pluralism and discovery arguments.

PLURALISM

It has long been understood that the commercial marketplace does not do well at providing public goods—goods that economists define as nonrivalous and nonexcludable. These are goods that, like a well-lit harbor, are available to everyone if they are available to anyone, and that, like clean air, do not cost more when they are consumed by more people. Beyond the

provision of a lighthouse or clean air, the standard examples of public goods include national defense and basic science. The essential point about public goods is that it is difficult or undesirable to block anyone from consuming them, even if they do not pay. Because private businesses prefer paying customers, public goods are underproduced in the commercial marketplace.

In practice, there are few if any goods that are purely public in the strict nonrivalous, nonexcludable sense. But we needn't rely on a strict definition to see the core idea: goods with a public character will be underproduced by the marketplace, for businesses will not be able to get consumers to pay for goods they cannot be excluded from accessing.

Instead, the state can provide public goods, and such provision is thought to be one of its important functions. In a democratic state, one simple way to predict what public goods will be produced is to recognize that elected representatives tend to vote for the funding of public goods that are favored by a majority of citizens. If a majority of citizens prefer police protection and a minority prefer arts funding, then politicians will vote to fund the police and not the arts. Further, standard models of political behavior in a democracy predict that politicians will fund the public goods preferred by majorities at a level that satisfies the preferences of median voter, who sits in the middle of the political spectrum. Public good production by the state is subject to what might be called a majoritarian constraint and limited by the preference of the median voter. Public goods preferred only by a minority, or levels of public good production above the level preferred the median voter, democratically elected politicians will not (have an incentive structure to) support. So public funding of the arts may generate plenty of Norman Rockwell, but probably not much avant-garde or radical art.

Here enters the pluralism argument on behalf of foundations. A foundation is a corporate structure designed to deploy private assets for public benefit, where what is funded is subject to donor intent. Because donor preferences can be idiosyncratic, foundations can deliver idiosyncratic results. Foundations are thus well, if not uniquely, placed to fund public goods that are underproduced, or not produced at all, by the marketplace or the state. Because donors will have diverse preferences about what goods they wish to fund philanthropically, foundations can be a source of funding for minority public goods or controversial public goods that a democratic state will not or cannot fund.

Expressing the idea less as a response to market failure and a state failure, one core argument on behalf of foundations sees them as an important vehicle for partially decentralizing the process of defining and producing public goods. In a pluralistic democracy, citizens have diverse preferences about what kinds of goods to supply through the direct expenditure of tax dollars. Powered by the idiosyncratic preferences of their donors and free from the accountability logic of the market and democratic state, foundations can help to provide, in the aggregate, a welcome pluralism of public goods that, over time, helps to create an ever evolving, contestatory, and diverse arena of civil society. Such decentralization tempers government orthodoxy in a democracy.

This idea is not novel. It can been seen, for example, in an opinion of Justice Lewis Powell in a 1983 case involving whether Bob Jones University, a religious and nonprofit university that had banned interracial dating, should be permitted to keep its tax-exempt status if it chose to reject a compelling government interest such as ending racial discrimination. Powell joined the majority in conditioning tax-exempt status on nondiscriminatory

racial codes, but rejected the idea that the primary function of a tax-exempt organization is to enact only government-approved policies. For Powell, the provision of tax subsidies for nonprofits, including presumably foundations, "is one indispensable means of limiting the influence of government orthodoxy on important areas of community life."[23] Against the idea of reinforcing aa common community conscience, the funding of nonprofit organizations and their exemption from taxation help constitute the diversity of associational life and viewpoints that are the bedrock of a pluralistic society.

The argument from pluralism turns foundations' autonomy and lack of marketplace and electoral accountability from a defect into an important virtue. Foundations are free, unlike commercial entities, to fund public goods because they need not compete with other firms or exclude people from consuming the goods they fund. And they are free, unlike politicians who face future elections, to fund minority, experimental, or controversial public goods that are not favored by majorities or at levels above the median voter.

Do we need the specific institutional form of the foundation, with the legal privileges that currently attach to it, in order to accomplish the desirable decentralization and curtailing of government orthodoxy? Perhaps not, and certainly not as a logical necessity. Perhaps the charitable behavior of individuals in the simpler form of making donations to favored nonprofit organizations would supply a good portion of the decentralization. Setting up a foundation to carry out this function, especially one that can exist in perpetuity and with minimal payout requirements may be unnecessary.

I worry, for instance, about the massive boom in small foundations. As shown in Figure 4.2, the number of foundations with less than $1 million in assets nearly doubled from 1993 to 2013.

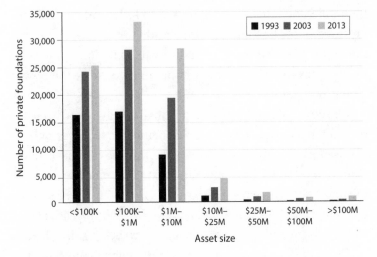

FIGURE 4.2. Growth in Number of Private Foundations by Asset Size, 1993–2013. *Source*: IRS data, "Domestic Private Foundations, 1993–2013."

Foundations with less than $1 million in assets rarely have a paid staff, almost never give away more than $50,000 in a year, and function more or less as a tax shelter and charitable checkbook for wealthy families. These families could accomplish the same outcome, produce the same public benefit, by simply making an ordinary charitable donation, rather than setting up a foundation as the vehicle for their philanthropy, avoiding in the process the overhead expenses that foundations require and that cannot be counted as public benefits. And taxpayers would no longer be subsidizing enormous sums of money that have been committed to a foundation but have not yet been granted to charitable organizations. In 2014, total assets reached nearly $800 billion, stretched across almost 100,000 independent private foundations. More than one-quarter of these assets are held by just the fifty largest foundations. What loss to public benefit would there be with a minimum asset threshold to create a foundation, say

$10 million or $50 million? I think very little, and quite possibly there would be some gain, for wealthy individuals under the minimum asset threshold might be inclined to donate more of their money to public charities rather than to create their own family foundations.[24]

Moreover, even if foundations of all endowment sizes do partially decentralize the definition and provision of public goods, the resulting pluralism of philanthropic voices will have a plutocratic not fully democratic cast. The minority, experimental, or controversial public goods funded by foundations will represent the diverse preferences of the wealthy, not of the wider citizenry. There is no good reason to believe that the diversity of preferences among the wealthy mirrors the diversity of preferences among all citizens. Indeed, there is empirical evidence to suggest that, at least in the United States, the very wealthy (both the top quarter and the top 1 percent of wealth holders, the latter of which account for the lion's share of private foundations) have significantly more politically conservative preferences than average citizens.[25] Thus, the activity of foundations, even when it decentralizes the production of public goods, retains a plutocratic character. I see no way to avoid this conclusion, for while wealthy and poor people tend to give the same percentage of their incomes to charity, in absolute terms the wealthy have much more to give.

Does this mean that we should eliminate foundations? I do not think so. What follows, I believe, tells not against foundations as such but against the tax-subsidized aspect of foundation activity. If foundations create a plutocratic pluralism, public subsidies that stimulate more such activity are harder to justify. Perhaps a plutocratic tempering of government orthodoxy is better than no tempering at all. And if this is true, then perhaps some tax subsidy for foundations could still be justified

if it turned out that subsidies were essential to stimulate the creation of foundations. History, however, suggests otherwise.

I conclude that the decentralization argument provides a plausible but not definitive case for foundations as a democracy-supporting institutional design in a democratic society.

DISCOVERY

Foundations can supply more than the financial fuel for a pluralistic associational life. They can also stimulate innovation. Here the idea is that foundations serve as a democratic society's "risk capital," a potent discovery mechanism for experimentation in social policy with uncertain results over a long time horizon.[26]

Begin with an uncontroversial supposition: a democratic state wishes to advance general welfare or to pursue the aims of justice, however understood. But democratic representatives do not know the best means for achieving such aims, either at any given moment or, especially, with an eye toward changing social conditions in the future. What kinds of policies and programs, for instance, will best promote educational opportunity and achievement? Some believe universal preschool is the answer, others a better school finance system, others better and more pervasive opportunities for online learning. Examples easily multiply. What kinds of policies will best reduce recidivism rates in prisons or in substance abuse programs? Or what kinds of changes will reduce carbon emissions with the lowest cost to economic growth?

To answer these questions, a democratic society, recognizing its elected leaders are not all-knowing, that reasonable disagreement on the best means to pursue just ends is likely, and that social conditions are always evolving, might wish to stimulate and decentralize experimentation in social policy so that better

and more effective policies at realizing democratically agreed upon aims can be identified and adopted. Moreover, this need for experimentation is never-ending. In light of constant change in economic, cultural, technological, and generational conditions, the discovery process is, in ideal circumstances, cumulative, in contributing to society a storehouse of best, or simply very effective, practices for different contexts and shifting priorities.

To be sure, the government can stimulate some measure of experimentation and risk-taking innovation on its own. It can, for example, invest in basic research with uncertain outcomes. (The most common approach would be to direct public funding to research universities, whether they be public or private; research universities are perhaps quintessential institutional mechanisms for discovery.) It can develop federal structures of government that treat jurisdictional subunits as sites of policy experimentation. Hence Justice Louis Brandeis's famous description of American states as laboratories of democracy. Democratic government has good reason to be experimentalist, to approach policy and institutional design as a form of problem solving. I adopt here the stance in a growing literature in democratic theory that defends the arrangement of democratic institutions so as to promote a problem-solving, experimentalist mode of governance.[27]

Such approaches notwithstanding, political leaders would also be right to harbor some skepticism that democratic government would be ideally suited to carry out such experimentation itself. For one thing, citizens in a system of democratic governance tend to expect and prize tested and reliable outcomes in public policy. Elected representatives who allocate public funds to highly risky strategies to social problems—in the sense that the selected policy may fail in delivering any benefits at all—also

run the risk of being punished at the ballot box. Furthermore, wasteful government spending tends to be deplored, and yet experimentation requires that some experiments fail if the approach is to deserve the label experimentation in the first place.

What extragovernmental mechanisms, then, could be designed to carry out decentralized experimentation? My claim is that foundations can be one mechanism among others, such as federalism, for this important work of discovery and experimentation.

And foundations have a structural advantage over market and state actors in this discovery effort: a longer time horizon. Once more, the lack of accountability may be a surprising advantage. An essential feature of the discovery argument focuses on the *time horizons* involved with innovation and risk taking in the marketplace and public institutions of the democratic state. Unlike profit-driven businesses, foundations are not subject to quarterly or annual earnings reports, bottom-line balance sheets, or impatient investors or stockholders. Commercial entities in the marketplace do not have an incentive structure that systematically rewards high-risk, long-time-horizon experimentation; they need to show results in order to stay in business. Similarly, public officials in a democracy do not have an incentive structure that rewards high-risk, long-time-horizon experimentation; they must show short-term results quickly from the expenditure of public dollars to stand a strong chance of reelection.

Dennis Thompson casts the issue a bit differently by identifying one of the built-in problems of democratic societies as a structural difficulty in representing the interests of future generations. He calls this the problem of "presentism": democracy's systematic and pervasive bias in favor of the present.[28] Democratic government is ill-suited, in his view, to tackle long-term

problems. (In chapter 5, I examine the case for philanthropy as a mechanism to provide for the interests of future generations.) Thompson identifies several sources of this presentist bias, including the considerable body of social scientific evidence that shows how humans tend to favor the present and short term over the distant and long term. And democratic governments are meant to be responsive to citizens' preferences, so we can expect government policies in democratic societies to favor the present and short term. In the face of undeniable problems, such as climate change, that will confront future generations, democracy's presentism is a major liability.

Thompson's preferred solution to combat democracy's presentism is democratic trusteeship, the idea that present generations can represent the interests of future generations by acting to protect the democratic process itself over time. I agree with Thompson's diagnosis of presentism, and have no argument against democratic trusteeship. Thompson neglects other institutional solutions, however. The private philanthropic foundation is also a worthy institutional design to combat presentism. Precisely because of their lack of ordinary democratic accountability and legal permission to persist for decades, foundations can fund experiments and innovation where the payoff, if it comes, is over the long haul, benefitting future rather than present generations. Moreover, because the universe of private foundations is diverse and donor-driven, different foundations are likely to experiment with different approaches, improving the chance that effective or simply better social policies or solutions to social problems will be found.

In sum, foundations, free of both marketplace or electoral accountability regimes, answerable to the diverse preferences and ideas of their donors, with an endowment designed to last decades or more, are especially well, perhaps uniquely, situated

to engage in the sort of high-risk, long-run policy innovation and experimentation that is healthy in a democratic society and that addresses the interests of future generations.

How is philanthropic discovery to be evaluated? And what is the uptake mechanism that could disseminate or bring to scale successful experiments that are the product of foundation-fueled innovation? Failed innovations die, though society has presumably learned something from the failure. Other foundations may take up and modify the experiment and later generate positive results. Still other foundation projects succeed in showing positive effects. Ideally, foundation-funded experiments would be subject to demanding social science review, not anecdotal reports from the field. What's essential to recognize, however, is that from the perspective of a foundation, success in its philanthropic giving consists not in funding innovative and risky social policy experiments and then sustaining the most successful of them forever. Because the assets of even the largest foundations are dwarfed by the assets of the marketplace and the state, success consists in seeing the successful or proven policy innovations brought to scale by the commercial marketplace or by the state. That is to say, a successful innovation reaches a broader population not because the foundation that funded the initial experiment now pays for its distribution or adoption across a much larger group of people. The hoped-for outcome is that the marketplace or the government plays this role. In the case of the marketplace, foundation-funded projects can be demonstrations that a revenue-generating, if not profit-maximizing, market for some social goods exists. At which point it is reasonable to expect that capital investments and the ordinary operation of the marketplace economy will kick in. In the case of the government, the foundation's social policy innovation can be presented, as it were, to citizens for

incorporation as a public undertaking or responsibility. Foundations, in this model, provide funding for policy experiments that, to use Eric Beerbohm's apt term, "audition" for the stamp of approval by a democratic public.[29] A foundation project that was initially privately funded and democratically unaccountable auditions for adoption as a publicly funded and democratically accountable government responsibility.

Some of the greatest accomplishments of American foundations do seem to fit this model. Consider the quintessential example of successful foundation activity, Andrew Carnegie's promotion of public libraries. Carnegie provided significant funding for the construction of libraries, but conditioned his grants to municipalities on modest matching public dollars (usually 10 percent annually). Between 1911 and 1917, Carnegie's philanthropy contributed to the creation of more than fifteen hundred public libraries. The library grant program was discontinued shortly thereafter, yet citizens found the libraries important enough that they demanded that they become the full responsibility of the local municipality. The privately financed public libraries successfully auditioned for inclusion in public budgets. Similar accounts could be given for other foundation successes, such as the Green Revolution, the development of Pell Grants in higher education, the coordination of a national 911 emergency response system, and the emergence of microlending—all the result of foundation-funded innovations brought to scale by either the marketplace or the state.

The institutional design of foundations permits them to operate on a different time horizon than the marketplace and the government. Because their endowments are designed to last, foundations can fund higher risk social policy experiments. Foundations can use their resources to identify and address

potential social problems decades away or innovations whose success might be apparent only after a longer time horizon. In short, unlike business and the state, foundations can "go long." They can be the seed capital behind one important discovery procedure for innovations in effective social policy in a democratic society. This, I believe, is the stronger argument on behalf of foundations.

Notice, however, that the foundations capable of providing sufficient risk capital for discovery have significant assets and likely have a professional staff able to manage and disseminate its learning. The small family foundation that gives away less than $50,000 a year is not in a strong position to carry out such a task. Here is another reason for concern about the growth in small foundations and another reason for considering a high floor of assets for foundation establishment.

This is an argument, of course, in favor of not mass philanthropy but professionalized and elite philanthropy. It is an argument not that philanthropy supplants or supplements what government does but that foundations perform a distinct role. It is an argument not that plutocratic voices stand in ineliminable tension with democracy but that such voices can be directed, through policy and social norms, to serve the aim of democratic experimentalism.

Need the endowments that fuel foundation grant making be perpetual? If so, need the founder's intent be honored in perpetuity? On this matter, I side with Mill in believing that perpetuity is unnecessary and even potentially injurious to the social utility of a foundation. The famous dictum of Thomas Jefferson expresses the principle well: "That our creator made the earth for the use of the living, and not of the dead; that those who exist not can have no use nor rights in it, no authority or

power over it."[30] No argument from principle could specify the optimal life span of a foundation; the relevant consideration here is that a foundation have an incentive structure that permits, or indeed encourages, work on a longer time horizon than other social institutions. What Rockefeller's advisors proposed to Congress in 1911, that the life span of a foundation be capped at a hundred years, or five generations, seems to me an adequately long horizon in which to engage in the important, democracy-supporting work of discovery.

More to the point, how might public policy or the creation of philanthropic norms guide private foundations and orient them more reliably toward longer time horizons and the work of discovery? I offer some brief speculations. One possibility would be to expect in their annual public reporting a long-term or intergenerational impact statement. Another possibility would be to introduce, especially among the largest foundations, a voluntary peer review in which the philanthropic strategies and investments were subject to periodic evaluation by expert peers, be they other foundation leaders or the beneficiaries of grants. Peer review could in principle foster norms that, without the need for formal legal regulation, help to hold private foundations to a discovery mode. I have in mind the norms that have arisen in the world of academia, where professors with tenure enjoy an unaccountability for their scholarly productivity that is in many respects quite similar to the unaccountability of the assets in a private foundation. Tenure may help to guide scholars toward longer-time-horizon projects than they undertook when they were untenured, and the practice of peer-reviewed scholarship helps to sort better from worse research and creates a forum for reputational competition. Perhaps something similar in the world of philanthropic foundations would be salutary.

Conclusion

One wants to know, of course, how well actual foundations perform in the United States and elsewhere when measured against the vision articulated and defended here. Are foundations fulfilling the specified role in a democratic society I have outlined? Are they good at fostering pluralism and discovery? A rigorous assessment is beyond the scope of my argument, but it is worth noting in conclusion that skepticism is certainly warranted.

Many prominent foundation observers, including many who are friends of foundations, believe that foundations are underperforming when measured on almost any yardstick of success.[31] And they are certainly underperforming if measured by the standards of pluralism and discovery. In 1949, a prominent foundation leader, Edwin Embree, wrote an article called "Timid Billions," concluding that despite obvious social problems and ample philanthropic assets, there was "an ominous absence of that social pioneering that is the essential business of foundations."[32] More recently, Gara LaMarche, who spent more than fifteen years at two of the world's largest foundations, concluded that foundations tend to be risk averse rather than risk taking. "Courageous risk-taking is not what most people associate with foundations," he writes, "whose boards and senior leadership are often dominated by establishment types. If tax preference is meant primarily to encourage boldness, it doesn't seem to be working."[33] Joel Fleishman, the former director of Atlantic Philanthropies and author of *The Foundation: A Great American Secret*, thinks that foundations would do their work better if they were more transparent and risk taking. Others, such as Waldemar Nielsen, a prominent author on the subject of philanthropy, have challenged foundations'

support for innovation, arguing that foundations are more frequently on the "trailing edge, not the cutting edge, of change." A more recent review of foundation activity suggests that only a small fraction of grant making should count as investing boldly in social change.[34]

Perhaps these critics are correct. If so, then so much the worse for foundations, and so much the worse for the distinctive institutional privileges that currently attach to them. My aim here is not to defend the existing behavior and performance of foundations but to identify the right standard by which to assess their performance and confer a certain amount of legitimacy on their distinctive and considerable institutional privileges. I have provided an argument about what foundations are for in a democratic society, about why a democracy would opt to create something as odd as the institutional form of a foundation. I have countered the idea that foundations are essentially repugnant to democracy. My point is that in spite of their plutocratic power, the peculiar institutional form of the foundation can have an important role in a democracy.

Are foundations democratically required? I am not prepared to answer this question affirmatively, for a democratic government has multiple mechanisms to cultivate pluralism and foster discovery. But I have shown that foundations are certainly democratically permissible, and that it is possible to defend a role for foundations, in something like the form they exist today, that would make them supportive of rather than injurious to democracy.

5

Philanthropy in Time

FUTURE GENERATIONS AND INTERGENERATIONAL JUSTICE

With Chiara Cordelli

In the previous chapter I examined the case for private philanthropic foundations. Such foundations are growing in number and in wealth, and they play an increasingly consequential role in political, social, religious, and cultural life in many different countries, not merely funding a wide array of public benefits but also seeking quite purposefully to alter public policies. There is good reason for skepticism that foundations should be welcome in liberal democratic societies, for they represent more or less paradigmatic examples of plutocratic voices in a democratic setting that prizes egalitarian relationships between citizens, especially in the political arena. The chapter's conclusion, however, was that private foundations could be supportive, not corrosive, of democratic aims provided that they operate in the mode of "discovery": a vehicle for social

policy innovations and experiments that neither a democratic government nor the market is likely to undertake.

In this chapter, I extend the analysis of private foundations and explore their potential significance as an institutional design in democratic societies to register and incorporate the interests of future generations. I explore the idea of philanthropy as a transfer of private wealth from one generation to the public interests of future generations and as a vehicle to support intergenerational justice.[1]

Liberal democratic political philosophy usually regards the intergenerational transmission of private wealth with suspicion. The long-standing practice of family inheritance is routinely decried. It violates the idea of meritocracy, that wealth should be earned on the basis of work and achievement, not via lucky inheritance; and it sits in tension with equality of opportunity, which provides the state with reasons of justice at least to tax, if not to prohibit, inheritance. These are principles of *intragenerational* justice.

Some add that a just state has also reasons of *intergenerational* justice to offset, beyond taxing, transfers of wealth from parents to children. Gaspart and Gosseries, for example, argue that a society committed to justice should not allow the present generation to transfer to the next generation more wealth than the present generation itself inherited on the grounds that this would be unfair toward the worst-off members of the current generation.[2] They suggest that a just society compensate for the aggregate positive savings derived from *private* transfers by reducing *public* transfers to the next generation. Although liberal democratic states do not generally endorse such offsetting policies, many adopt constraining policies on private familial transfers, such as estate or inheritance taxes.[3]

Yet, unlike family transfers, other types of intergenerational private transfers of wealth are neither limited nor merely permitted by states. They are actively *encouraged* or subsidized. The United States and many other liberal democracies do not merely tolerate but promote *intergenerational charitable private transfers* by granting substantial tax incentives to individuals who set up or donate to private foundations; these foundations are designed, if not required, to exist in perpetuity.[4]

Private foundations are nongovernmental, nonprofit corporate entities endowed with private funds whose main role is to support financially, in the form of grants, other charitable and civil society organizations. As we saw in the previous chapter, these philanthropic corporations took form in the United States with the creation of the Carnegie and Rockefeller foundations in the early twentieth century and remain robust today. Nearly a hundred thousand private foundations currently operate in the United States. Their aggregate assets exceed $800 billion.[5] Private philanthropic foundations, as a corporate form, are legally designed to outlive their donors into the indefinite future, permitted in principle to last in perpetuity. Since 1969, they have been required by law to spend down at least 5 percent of their assets each year. We refer on occasion in what follows to "perpetual foundations" because legal regimes permit perpetual existence. For our purposes, however, what is important is multigenerational existence, the capacity to act on behalf of future generations, not the capacity to exist in perpetuity.[6] For the reasons articulated in the previous chapter, there are good grounds to reject perpetuity as a defensible time horizon for philanthropy.

Unlike family inheritance, which is generally taxed, private charitable donations to foundations are given advantageous tax treatment. In the United States, for example, although family

inheritance can be taxed at a 40 percent rate, transfers to private philanthropic foundations pass entirely free of tax. Private foundations are also largely not subject to income taxes. Moreover, some who argue in favor of inheritance taxes do so because they believe such taxation creates an incentive for wealthy individuals to create and fund private philanthropic foundations.[7] Foundations are not quite an invention of the tax code (as we have seen, similar entities, such as the charitable trust and the waqf, have existed for centuries across many different societies), but in their current form they are clearly an artifact of the state's public policies, which confer on them a certain form and a considerable set of privileges.

Private foundations, in their current mode of operation, are sometimes criticized for being unaccountable and for helping the rich to shelter their wealth from taxation. In this chapter we avoid such debates. Neither do we aim to assess whether the particular tax treatment or governance structure of foundations in contemporary democracies is justified. Do the tax concessions produce greater flows of assets into foundations than would occur in the absence of the foundations? Does the 5 percent payout rule increase total grant making, and presumably social benefit production, than would occur without such a rule? These questions require a complex balancing of both empirical and normative factors beyond the scope of our purpose here.

Instead, we answer the *normative* question of whether a just state may have principled reasons not only to permit but also to encourage (e.g., through tax incentives) intergenerational charitable transfers of private wealth. We use the private foundations as the most prominent example of already-existing institutions through which such transfers can happen (though other institutional arrangements, such as charitable trusts,

might also be used). In particular, we ask whether a liberal democracy may have good reasons, *derived from a principle of intergenerational justice*, to encourage private charitable transfers (while, by assumption, also having good reasons to limit or forbid transfers of wealth from parents to children).

We argue that there are three main reasons why an intergenerational principle of just savings, such as that found in John Rawls's work, may support policies aimed at encouraging private intergenerational charitable transfers.[8] The first reason relates to the distinctive role that long-enduring philanthropic institutions can play to support the reproduction of a particular form of capital—social capital—over time. Since (1) the reproduction of this form of capital, at each generational stage is, we will argue, required by an intergenerational just savings principle, and since (2) private philanthropic entities may be better placed than other actors to support this reproductive function, we argue that (3) a state may have justice-based reasons to encourage private intergenerational charitable transfers through philanthropic entities, like foundations or alternative independent bodies (*instead of* transferring public funds to the next generation through centralized public funds).

The second reason a state may have for encouraging intergenerational private charitable transfers results from the fact that, in some circumstances, public transfers may not be sufficient to fulfill the requirements of intergenerational justice and should thus be *supplemented* by private transfers. The need for supplementing public transfers with private transfers may occur, for example, when the present generation can foresee that serious, but highly unlikely, events could compromise the stability of the next generation's institutions. We have in mind low-probability events such as natural disasters like earthquakes or human-caused disasters such as terrorist attacks. In

such cases, we will argue, the *low probability* that a catastrophic event will happen may provide the current generation with sufficient reason not to impose a sacrifice on the worst-off members of the current generation by transferring (public) funds designated for their support to the next generation in order to preserve the stability of that next generation's institutions. Yet, in such hard cases a *remainder* is left. The very purpose of the just savings principle is left unfulfilled. We thus argue that intergenerational private charity can and should be encouraged to play a supplementary role toward fulfilling this purpose.

Finally, a state has a third reason to encourage private transfers of wealth to philanthropic foundations on grounds of intergenerational justice. Even in reasonably well-ordered societies, the democratic process, where public officials are subject to short-time-horizon forms of accountability, such as periodic elections, may fail to act on the long-time-horizon interests of the society, or put differently, in the interest of future generations. This is due, in part, to the short-termism and presentism built in to the democratic process itself.[9] Philanthropic institutions, given their *long time horizon* and their position as private, *nonstate*, and *nonmarket* institutions, can play a salutary and perhaps essential role in counteracting these tendencies. Following on and building upon the analysis in chapter 4, philanthropic foundations can engage in discovery, a form of long-time-horizon experimentation designed to produce discoveries or innovations in public policies that are unlikely to be brought about via public or commercial marketplace institutions. For example, philanthropic foundations are well suited to undertake long-term and risky investments in green technologies that may take more than a generation to develop and that have high expected benefits but a very high risk of failure or a radically uncertain chance of success.

We began by noting the general skepticism of liberal political philosophers concerning the justice of intergenerational
private transfers of wealth. When such transfers are to provide
for heirs, we share the skepticism. But we also think that there
are underappreciated reasons for not merely tolerating but
encouraging intergenerational charitable transfers of private
wealth. We emphasize that none of these arguments, alone or in
combination, is intended to show that the promotion of intergenerational private transfers of wealth, through tax incentives
or other mechanisms, is required by justice. Here we provide
three independent arguments, specifically from the standpoint
of intergenerational justice, that should be taken into consideration when assessing the all-things-considered case for such
promotion, that, in other words, render the state-supported
encouragement of private foundations *compatible* with justice.

John Rawls's conception of intergenerational justice forms
the background of our discussion, and so, before moving to
substantive arguments, we give a brief overview of it.

Just Savings and Intergenerational Assistance

Rawls's theory of intergenerational justice involves two stages.[10]
Until (reasonably) just institutions are established in a society,
each generation has a duty of justice to transfer to the next
one more capital than the amount inherited from the previous generation. This is *the accumulation stage*. Once just basic
institutions are in place and basic liberties are effectively protected, the obligation to save (to add extra capital to the inherited stock) ceases. At this stage, the already existing stock of
capital only needs to be preserved or substituted. The current
generation can save if it wishes, but it is not required to do so.
This is *the steady-state stage*.

Much could be said about this principle, its derivation and justification in Rawls's theory.[11] Here, however, we clarify those aspects of the principle necessary for our discussion.

First, Rawls clearly states that the point and purpose of the just savings principle is "to establish" *and preserve* "(reasonably) just institutions for a free constitutional democratic society (or any well-ordered society) and to secure a social world that makes possible a worthwhile life for all its citizens."[12] In this respect, he argues, "the duty of assistance and the duty of just savings express the same underlying idea."[13] Both are necessary to the ultimate goal of creating and preserving a peaceful and stable global social order, constituted by internally well-ordered societies, over time.

Second, Rawls clarifies that *what* needs to be saved or preserved is not reducible to economic and material forms of capital. It includes cultural capital as well as technological assets. Indeed, it includes "real capital of all kinds."[14] More generally, the criterion to identify what kind of capital ought to be saved or preserved is provided by the very purpose of the just savings principle—whatever kind of capital is necessary to establish and preserve just institutions that effectively secure and protect the basic liberties of citizens. In this respect, Rawls emphasizes how informal norms and attitudes, as well as the political and social culture of a society, are "all-important" in explaining why some societies have institutions that are more just than others.[15]

Third, Rawls specifies that "*how much* is needed" in order to secure and preserve just institutions, and thus to guarantee the effective exercise of basic liberties, "will depend on a society's particular history" and circumstances.[16] This is clear in the case of assisting burdened societies. Different levels and kinds of assistance will be needed to bring other countries to the point at which they can attain and then maintain just institutions,

depending on the causes of their being burdened. Similarly, it seems reasonable to assume that even the same society, at different generational stages, may need more or fewer resources in order to maintain the justice of its institutional arrangements. All else equal, if generation G2 is hit by a meteor strike, it will need more capital than G1 to maintain its well-orderedness. So, if the point of the just savings principle is, like the point of the duty of assistance, to preserve stability and the effective protection of basic liberties over time, we may have cases, even *after* the accumulation stage formally ends, in which some generations will have to provide the next generations with more resources than they actually received, assuming they are able to foresee, with a reasonable degree of certainty, that the next generation will face a serious risk of falling back into a *burdened* state. Rawls does not directly consider these cases of "regress" in his discussion of the just savings principle. He simply argues that, under favorable circumstances, once the accumulation stage ends, each generation should leave to the next roughly the same amount of capital as it inherited from the previous one. However, if we have a duty to assist *external* burdened societies, with which we do not share any relationship of cooperation, so that they can bring about and preserve just or decent institutions (even if we are not the cause of their being burdened), it seems that, *a fortiori*, we have a duty to do the same for the next generation with which we do share a cooperative scheme. In cases of foreseeable regress to a burdened status, we find it reasonable to supplement the just savings principle with a *principle of intergenerational assistance*, which kicks in when well-ordered societies are at high risk of becoming unstable due to external factors.

Finally, it is important to note where the just savings principle stands in relation to other principles of justice. The just savings principle is constrained by the liberty principle and, in

turn, constrains the difference principle.[17] The upshot is that, for Rawls, securing the stability of just institutions over time, and thus securing the effective exercise of basic liberties for the next generation, has priority over the socioeconomic condition of the worst-off here and now (albeit not over their basic liberties).[18]

After this brief overview of the intergenerational principle of just savings, we can return to our original question: are there any reasons, based upon this principle, for a state actively to encourage intergenerational charitable transfers of private wealth through long-enduring philanthropic foundations or similar entities? In order to answer affirmatively, we demonstrate not only that such transfers are *compatible* with the just savings principle but also that private transfers of this kind may be sometimes *necessary* to fulfill the just savings principle or, less demandingly, at least better placed to fulfill it than alternative public mechanisms. In what follows we consider a society at the steady-state stage, the obligation of which is (unless special circumstances of foreseeable regress arise) to leave to the next generation the same amount of capital it received from the previous one.

The Reproduction of Social Capital Argument

Sociologists, political scientists, and political philosophers, from Alexis de Tocqueville to Robert Putnam, have studied and celebrated social capital as an important, perhaps essential, determinant of the stability and effectiveness of a constitutional democratic order.[19] It is a multifaceted concept. Here we understand social capital to refer to individual or collective attitudes of generalized trust, civicness, and reciprocity that are generated by and embedded in cooperative activities and networks. In this respect, the concept of social capital includes

both an account of the political virtues and informal norms that contribute to securing the stability of basic political, social, and economic institutions, assist in overcoming collective action problems, and help to ensure citizens' compliance with just institutions, as well as an account of how these virtues and norms are generated and supported through participation in cooperative activities, here emphasizing activities above the family and beneath the state. The idea of social capital bears close resemblance to Rawls's own account of how the morality of association, which includes modes of participation in voluntary associations beyond the family, plays a fundamental role in the development of a sense of justice.[20]

Although many democratic theorists would agree that "the well-working of the formal institutions of a liberal constitutional order depends on the health of informal social institutions and associations" because of the social capital these associations produce,[21] discussions of intergenerational justice tend to neglect this form of capital.

Perhaps this is so because social capital, unlike natural and economic forms of capital, cannot be stockpiled, reserved, or transferred, and unlike cultural capital, it does not accumulate over time. Indeed, unlike other forms of capital, social capital is embedded in, and constituted by, *social relationships* (as well as by the immaterial norms and virtues these relationships produce).

Yet, if we assume that social capital is important for the stability of a constitutional democratic order, in addition to other more familiar forms of capital, the just savings principle— whose purpose is to secure that stability over time—demands that current generations secure or preserve the conditions for the intergenerational *reproduction* of social capital so that the next generation can generate an amount of this capital sufficient to support the stability of its own institutions.

How can social capital be reproduced and sustained across generations? The answer is to be found in a complex and sometimes contentious social science literature. We cannot provide a full discussion here. For our purposes it suffices to note that the nuclear family, to which Rawls assigns the role of reproducing culture over time, would not seem to be the ideal or natural candidate (or at least not sufficient) for the reproduction of social capital over time. This is because families tend to be inward-looking and to reproduce exclusive and particularistic bonds rather than more generalized forms of trust.

By contrast, associational life in civil society—voluntary and mediating associations different from family, market, and governmental institutions—is one of the primary sources, or the primary source, of social capital.[22] Associations generate social capital especially when they exhibit a cooperative, participatory, and inclusive character. Tocqueville was probably the first to identify a close connection between the presence of a vibrant associational life and the democratic nature of institutions.[23] More recently, the enormous literature building upon Robert Putnam and Theda Skocpol has added considerable social scientific evidence for the connection between certain forms of associational life—those that facilitate face-to-face interaction especially—and the production of social capital. We therefore have reason to believe that, although different generations may need different institutions to produce social capital depending on their circumstances, cooperative forms of association, whether they be face-to-face or digital, amateur or professional, large or small, single or federated, are likely to remain important in the reproduction of this kind of capital.

The intergenerational reproduction of social capital thus plausibly requires the reproduction of a vibrant and participa-

tory civil society over time. This, of course, does not mean that the identical array of associations, either in kind or in number, that constitute any current civil society must endure across generations. This way of reproducing civil society would unfairly impose the present generation's conceptions of the good, as expressed by and embedded in their current associations, on the next generation. What needs to be sustained over time, instead, is not just the essential and basic liberty of association but the social infrastructure—the financial and organizational capacity—needed for civil society to reproduce and adapt. This demands, we think, a certain stability. Civil society thus needs reliable sources of funding and a stable, although flexible, organizational infrastructure.

The most reliable source of funding would seem to be public funding via the state. However, relying exclusively on public funding for associational life is not ideal. One reason is the need to maintain some financial and thus political *independence* between the state and associational life. Independence is necessary for civil society associations to be able to act as a "buffer" or a countervailing force to state power. Independence is also necessary if associations are to act as alternative or complementary governance mechanisms to public ones.[24]

A second reason is provided by *pluralism*. It is often feared that state funding can freeze civil society.[25] Public money frequently comes with strings attached, and direct public expenditures permit the majority to shape civil society according to its preferences, whereas what makes civil society associations distinct from governmental entities is precisely their capacity to pursue and represent minority interests and unrepresented voices. Associational life is a site of pluralism, and making the funding of civil society entirely dependent on the median voter or majority preferences may curtail pluralism.

Finally, a funding system for associations that relies entirely on the state may have the negative effect of crowding out *altruism* and solidarity since it would make charitable donations to associations superfluous.

In order to overcome these shortcomings, while securing civil society with a sustained capacity to operate effectively and to reproduce and adapt itself over time, a private funding system (e.g., charitable donations) supported by public incentives has much to recommend it.

Further, in order to ensure that the next generation's civil society has sufficient support to reproduce itself, a part of these tax-incentivized charitable donations should be stored in funds specifically to support that reproduction. Among existing corporate forms, philanthropic foundations, permitted to exist across generations, would seem to be well suited for this role. We should not make this conclusion, however, with too certain a conviction that philanthropic financing of civil society associations in their current form will automatically generate social capital. As described in chapter 2, Putnam and others document a decline in civic engagement at the same time that the number of formal nonprofit organizations has skyrocketed.[26] To get the social capital a democratic society needs to sustain itself across generations, we may need more informal, face-to-face, or federated associations rather than professionally managed and national nonprofit organizations. If this is so, then private funders should prefer—and public policy should provide them incentives to prefer—the particular associational forms that generate social capital.

An important question is how much philanthropic foundations should, in their capacity as "intergenerational funds for the reproduction of social capital," be expected, on grounds of justice, to transfer to future generations, through their

endowments. If we follow Rawls's just savings principle, we may conclude that each generation should transfer to the next (as a matter of duty) as many philanthropic assets (in aggregate) as it received from the previous one (assuming that both the population and the level of public transfers remain constant). Political institutions should, at any given generational stage, require each foundation to comply with "an intergenerational endowment requirement" (a percentage of their total philanthropic assets) established in light of that principle.

Importantly, funds in an endowment should have one string attached. By this we mean that the foundation's next-generation trustees should be required to distribute those resources to civil society groups (or alternative sources of social capital) with the purpose of reproducing the infrastructure of a civil society able to maintain just institutions. The next generation would not be allowed to spend the relevant portion of the endowment for causes unrelated to that goal. At the same time, current donors ought not to expect future generations to use those funds to foster their *own* legacy (the legacy of the current donors) and conceptions of the good. In this respect, funds should be transferred without any strings attached. This is the price that donors and foundations, properly motivated by a sense of justice, would need to pay in exchange for tax advantages.[27]

We leave open the question of what foundations should be required to do, once their intergenerational requirement is met. Should foundations be permitted to transfer the rest of their resources to future generations, or should they be required to comply with an "intragenerational distribution requirement" that would impose on them an obligation to spend the rest of their funds so as to promote current social causes?

The answer depends on whether we think that Rawls's difference principle should apply intergenerationally.[28] If the

worst-off members of each generation should be better off than they would be under any alternative regimes, then once the threshold established by the just savings principle is met, the rest should be directed to improve the conditions of the current generation's worst-off members. In which case, although donors may not be prohibited, on grounds of liberty, to transfer their charitable donations to the next generation, they could be actively discouraged by the state, such as through a tax on intergenerational charitable transfers similar to a tax on family inheritance.

Alternatively, following the orthodox Rawlsian view, which denies the application of the difference principle at the intergenerational level, the conclusion is that intergenerational transfers, beyond the just savings threshold, should be neither prohibited nor discouraged, *yet also not encouraged*. They should be simply permitted, where individuals can exercise their liberty, or not, to make intergenerational charitable transfers.[29]

In summary, we have argued that justice not only permits but gives reason to encourage, via subsidies and incentives, intergenerational charitable private transfers of wealth as an important, possibly the best, means of securing an adequate reproduction of social capital over time. Yet, beyond this threshold, these transfers should be either limited or, at least, not encouraged, unless exceptional circumstances arise. In the next section we examine one such circumstance.

The Precaution against Remote Risks Argument

Intergenerational public transfers of wealth are essential to the fulfillment of the just savings principle. But encouraging intergenerational private transfers can, in some situations, be an essential *supplement* to public transfers—essential to fully

realize the purpose of the just savings principle. To make this argument, we first discuss the importance of probabilities in determining what opportunity costs current generations can be expected to incur to protect the basic liberties of future generations.

Consider the following situation: For any current generation, the institutions of which are reasonably just, there is a *very low* probability that the *next* generation will be affected by an event, say a natural disaster such as a meteor strike or a massive volcanic eruption or an event caused by humans, such as a terror attack, that will seriously compromise the stability of its institutions and cause a regress of the society to a burdened state.[30] Scientists are able to determine, in statistical terms, the probability of the catastrophic event. Suppose the probability is one in one million. What should the current generation do? Does it have a duty of justice to transfer to the next generation more capital than it would have to transfer were that probability absent?

Recall that, at the steady-state stage, a current generation is obliged to transfer only what it received from the previous generation, no more and no less. However, in this case, we confront the possibility of a *regress* to the accumulation stage, since the next generation could become a burdened society. If this is correct, then the current generation would have a duty to save. Put differently, the current generation may be under a duty of intergenerational assistance to help the next generation prevent that destabilizing catastrophe or preserve the stability of its institutions, for example by saving resources so as to facilitate adaptation to the consequences of the catastrophic event (even if the present generation bears no causal responsibility for that event).

Indeed, if we look at the *magnitude*, rather than at the probability, of the expected burdens that the worst-off members of the current generation would have to face in order to help

the next generation, compared to the expected burdens the next generation would have to face, were the event to occur, we may conclude that the present generation should save and transfer to the future generation (rather than use for the current generation). This is not because more people will be seriously harmed by the catastrophic event than by restrictions on current consumption. It is rather because, given the equal moral status of present and future generations, securing the basic liberties of future people may enjoy priority over the socioeconomic interests of present ones. This priority is confirmed by the very rationale behind the just savings principle—securing and preserving stable liberty-protecting institutions—and by the fact that this principle constrains the difference principle.[31]

Focusing on the magnitude, not probability, of expected burdens when deciding whether the current generation should save appears in line with standard contractualist approaches. Thomas Scanlon, for example, argues that "the grounds for rejecting a principle [or policy] are based simply on the burdens it involves for those who experience them, *without discounting them by the probability that there will be anyone who actually does so.*"[32] The contractualist approach is that a principle must be acceptable from the perspective of the individual or generation who would end up suffering the worst burden, and on this basis we can conclude that a principle or policy permitting the present generation to consume rather than save could be reasonably rejected from the perspective of the next generation. Indeed, the (risk of) burdens this policy would involve (by failing to prevent them) for the future generation are more severe than the burdens the opposite policy would impose on the present generation—the former burdens are more severe, given that they concern something more fundamental than socioeconomic distributive justice, namely the protection of basic liberties.

Supposing we should care about only the magnitude of burdens, then it would follow that the current generation would be required to save, perhaps at very high rates, at the expense of the worst-off members of the current generation. A state would, for example, be required by justice to impose extra taxes on the current generation so as to work on predictive and preventative technologies or to set aside sufficient funds for rebuilding after a catastrophic event.

But probabilities do count. Indeed, if probabilities did not count in determining what burdens we can be reasonably expected to bear in order to prevent risk of harm in the future, we would end up with overburdensome directives. For example, we would be required to ban air travel because of the remote risk that some people will be killed by falling planes (because the burden of being killed would always outweigh the burden of being prevented from traveling). And in fact contractualists do recognize the importance of probabilities. Scanlon, for example, qualifies his position by arguing that while the *ex ante* probability that harm will occur cannot diminish the complaint of the affected parties, it is relevant to determining the *reasonable precautions* that the agent has to take to avoid causing harm.[33] A prohibition on air travel, Scanlon adds, could be reasonably rejected because, given how remote the risk of harm is, it would impose unreasonable burdens—it would be "too confining."[34] Were the risk of harm dramatically higher, prohibition may no longer be unreasonable.

Similar considerations may apply to the *prevention* of foreseeable harm. Given the low probability that the next generation will be suffering a catastrophic earthquake or terrorist attack, it would be "an unreasonable precaution" for a state to impose extra costs on the worst-off members of the current generation in order to protect the next generation and its

institutions from that unlikely threat. The current generation should not be required by its state to incur that sacrifice, since this level of precaution could be reasonably rejected by the current generation (e.g., it would not pass a test of public justification). And yet, a *remainder* is left. The probability, albeit very low, that the next generation will regress into a burdened state still remains, and this calls for *supplementary* action.

In such "hard cases," it seems plausible to argue that philanthropy should supplement what is strictly required by justice in order for the purpose of the just savings principle to be *fully* secured. Although it might be unreasonable for a state coercively to impose restrictions on use by the current generation, we believe it is not unreasonable for a state, precisely in light of its commitment to the purpose of the just savings principle, to encourage its citizens to make voluntary, private transfers to philanthropic foundations, the assets of which are designed to endure across generations and where one purpose of philanthropic investment is to fund the development of precautionary strategies and technologies aimed at protecting the future generation from regressing to a burdened state. For example, a state could reasonably encourage individuals collectively to save private wealth so that the next generation could use that extra capital to cope with those events, would they occur. State-subsidized donations to philanthropic entities can here be understood as "intergenerational saving funds for emergencies" or "rainy-day funds for low-probability catastrophes." In this case, the next generation would not be at liberty to use these savings for any purpose but could use them only in line with the purpose for which those donations have been encouraged. These savings would supplement the private charitable intergenerational transfers needed to secure the reproduction of social capital over time.

It's essential that the policies meant to stimulate intergenerational charitable transfers provide clear incentives for donors to direct their funding toward precautionary strategies for future generations. If the dead hand control of past donors has locked up charitable assets for opera, religion, provisions for animals, and so on, a future generation facing an unexpected but grave risk and threatened with regress to a burdened state will be stuck with potentially useless charitable savings. In the case of especially grave threats, if they should come to pass, a democratic society might need to adopt Mill's conclusion, as described in chapter 1, that the state be permitted, if necessary to prevent regress, to abrogate the terms of a charitable bequest.

So far the case on behalf of intergenerational charitable transfers has been made on the basis of intergenerational justice within any particular society. If we adopt a global perspective, however, and incorporate all of humanity into our concern, we can identify a related argument on behalf of deploying philanthropic entities to develop precautionary strategies. Several recently created philanthropic entities provide an illustration of what we have in mind here. The Future of Humanity Institute at Oxford University and the Open Philanthropy Project in California devote considerable resources to research on so-called existential risks to humanity, risks that could cause human extinction or vastly reduce the number of future generations. These include global catastrophic risks from climate change, bioterrorism, pandemic preparedness, and the possible evolution of malicious artificial intelligence.[35] Support for such important research—what could be more essential than staving off human extinction?—might be provided from public sources. But the just savings principle, as we have seen, also places weight on the interests of the worst off in the current

generation against the interests of the as yet unborn. Thus, there is good reason for a state to stimulate philanthropic contributions with the aim of reducing global catastrophic risk. There are additional reasons, in any case, why a democratic state is likely significantly to *underinvest* public funds on behalf of low-probability and long-time-horizon undertakings. These reasons are the subject of the next section.

This time, long-term philanthropic institutions play a counteracting rather than a complementary or supplementary role.

The Discovery Argument

Dennis Thompson argues that "democracy is partial toward the present."[36] By this he means that the policies and laws produced by the democratic process tend to neglect the interests of future generations. This bias toward the present, which Thompson calls "presentism," is purposeful, due in part to the fact that public officials in a democracy need to be both responsive and accountable to the electorate, united with the fact that the electorate tends to both want and fear more what is immediate than what is far off. Further, public officials in democracies are held accountable by periodic elections. In order to build a case for reelection, politicians have strong incentives to show their constituencies actual results during their term in office, not promises of long-term results, the effects of which cannot (yet) be seen. The dynamic privileges short-term over long-term results and public expenditures with low risk of failure.

Both factors, presentism and short-termism, explain why the democratic process tends to disregard or underweight the interests of future generations, by discouraging the adoption of policies aimed at preventing long-term risks, as well as poli-

cies or public expenditures whose expected benefits could be great but whose risk of failure is very high.

Unlike elected leaders in democratic governments, philanthropic foundations can be long-enduring, multigenerational entities. In the United States, for example, private foundations are legally designed to outlive their donors and each generation of trustees. Further, as discussed in the previous chapter, their leadership is not accountable to the public through elections. They are not subject to investor pressure to show short-term gains and maximize profit; indeed, there is no expectation of profit at all. Foundations lack both electoral and marketplace accountability.

These features of the governance of private foundations put their leaders in a fundamentally different position, with a fundamentally different incentive structure for behavior, than government officials or corporate leaders and shareholders. Private philanthropic foundations are insulated from any structural accountability to short-time horizon success. Foundations have time to develop, adopt, and revise strategies that are experimental, pursuing low-probability but very high social value projects. These are projects whose results might not be apparent for many years. Because of these distinctive features, foundations can *in principle* be regarded as a desirable means of counteracting both the presentism and short-termism of the democratic process as well as of the commercial marketplace.

Democratic societies are in constant need of experimentation when it comes to public policy, and they especially suffer a dearth of such experimentation when it comes to acting in conditions of uncertainty. In light of constant change in economic, cultural, technological, and generational conditions, the discovery process is never-ending but also cumulative. In

keeping with the language of the previous chapter, we can call this the need for discovery.

When it comes to work of discovery, foundations have an incentive structure, unlike state and market institutions, that rewards high-risk, long-time-horizon experimentation. Foundations can provide risk capital for the future that both public and commercial institutions fail to provide. They can, for example, make long-term and risky investments in green technologies that may take more than a generation to develop and that have high expected benefits but a very high risk of failure or a radically uncertain chance of success.

One defense of the philanthropic foundation, and public subsidies designed to support them, is that foundations, answerable not to the median voter but only to the diverse preferences of their donors, with an endowment permitted to exist across many generations, may be strongly, if not uniquely, positioned to engage in the important work of risky, intergenerational policy innovation and experimentation. Such work, we posit, is essential to the intergenerational sustenance of just institutions.

This vision would require a sharp departure from the way many foundations currently operate. Indeed, in current societies, many foundations are often regarded as a threat to democratic values rather than as a desirable means of compensating for certain built-in shortcomings of the democratic process. Recall Richard Posner's skeptical observation that "a perpetual charitable foundation . . . is a completely irresponsible institution, answerable to nobody . . . and, unlike a hereditary monarch whom such a foundation otherwise resembles, it is subject to no political controls either."[37]

Posner and earlier such critics, such as Turgot and Mill, are right that the perpetual charitable foundation, as it actually functions in current societies, stands in tension with democratic

values. Our contention is simply that, unlike the perpetuity of a hereditary monarch, both the long-termism of foundations and the absence of elective mechanisms of accountability could *in principle* be justified in light of future generations' interests, supposing foundations harnessed their potential in order to compensate for the presentism and short-termism of the democratic process.

Foundations should take advantage of their combined non-elective and potential permanence to do what democratic governments routinely fail to do: *think long*. They can be the seed capital behind high-risk, long-time-horizon discoveries that benefit and protect future generations.

In sum, the role that foundations are distinctively placed to play in counteracting both the presentism and the short-termism of the democratic process (as well as the commercial marketplace) provides a potential third reason for securing the continuity of philanthropic foundations over time, by encouraging private transfers of wealth, namely donations, to foundations. Incentives should however be conditional on the operation of foundations in this discovery mode.

Conclusion

There are three reasons why intergenerational *charitable* transfers of private wealth may be treated differently from intergenerational *family* transfers of private wealth. Although the latter should be limited or prohibited, the former may be in some cases encouraged. Our argument is based on the view that philanthropic institutions, unlike the nuclear family, can play three important roles in helping a society fulfill its intergenerational obligations and thereby honoring the just savings principle. First, they can *complement* political institutions in securing a

reproduction of social capital over time. Second, they can *supplement* political institutions in fulfilling the ultimate purpose of the just savings principle, in circumstances where a regression from the steady-state stage to the accumulation stage is possible, although unlikely. Third, they can *counteract* the short-termism and presentism of the democratic process in a way that promotes the long-term interests of future generations.

CONCLUSION

Should we understand philanthropy as an individual act or a social practice? When one thinks about philanthropy as an individual act, or the sum of all individual philanthropic actions, its contrast is private spending or personal saving. This first-person, agential perspective leads us to questions of personal morality. When one thinks about philanthropy as an organized social practice that directs private resources for the production of some public benefit, one gains a view on philanthropy that is less agential. Here philanthropy is defined by a set of norms, structured by policy choices and embedded within a larger political economy. Its contrast here is public finance via taxation and the broad set of rules that define exchanges in the marketplace. This structural perspective leads us to questions of political morality.

My intent is to have framed the topic in such a way that the place of philanthropy in a liberal democratic society becomes an unavoidable and fundamental question: given the ubiquity and universality of philanthropy, what attitude should a state have toward the preference of people to give money away for some prosocial or public purpose?

When I began thinking about philanthropy, I found no shortage of reasons, drawn from history and my own reflections, to criticize the actual role of philanthropy in democratic societies. Sometimes philanthropic assets are wasted, and that seemed bad. Other times philanthropic assets have enormous effects

in steering or changing public policies, and that also seemed worrisome. In a democratic society marked by enormous income and wealth inequality, and with large numbers of people living in poverty, that only a modest percentage of total philanthropic giving is directed at the relief of poverty or toward assistance for the disadvantaged seemed both surprising and problematic. Tax subsidies for philanthropic giving, I learned, cost U.S. citizens well more than $50 billion annually, and that seemed peculiar, since individuals already possess the liberty to give money away. What was the purpose of the subsidy? Private foundations occasionally appear like tax shelters, vanity projects, or public projections of the eccentric preferences of the wealthy, and sometimes all three at once. Why did this strange institutional form exist in democratic societies?

I wanted to form a clearer understanding of my reactions, to understand better the basis of such questions and skepticism, and I went looking in the scholarly literature with which I am most familiar: philosophy and political science. Philanthropy is a time-immemorial activity that raises questions of first principle for social theorists, and I would find many efforts to understand and evaluate it. I was especially interested in how to understand the role of philanthropy in liberal democratic societies. Yet in political philosophy I found very little that addressed my initial untutored reactions and questions.

This book is the result. I have emphasized the public over the private morality of philanthropy, seeking a framework for understanding what role philanthropy should play in a society committed to liberal democratic values. My hope is to have demonstrated that the practice of philanthropy raises important and unavoidable questions for political philosophy. To answer these questions, we need a political theory of philanthropy. And this theory has given me more confidence in some of my early

and more unconsidered criticisms; much of my criticism persists and now rests, I think, on a more solid foundation. At the same time, some of my earlier criticisms have diminished or disappeared; I am no longer as troubled as I once was, for example, by the frequency of policy instruments, such as tax concessions for giving, that are indifferent between poverty alleviation and support for cultural and educational organizations.

The theory I develop has given me powerful reasons to defend a variety of important roles that philanthropy can and should play in liberal democratic societies. The arguments I've presented here carve out a role for philanthropy that involves, for ordinary donors, pluralism and, for private foundations, discovery. It is an important contribution that individual giving can make to pluralism and the limitation of governmental orthodoxy on associational life and the definition and production of public goods. It is an important contribution that private philanthropic foundations can make in taking an experimentalist long-time-horizon approach to policy innovation that state agencies and marketplace firms are structurally unlikely to undertake. It is an important contribution that philanthropy can make to the project of promoting and securing justice across generations.

It has not been a fully exhaustive analysis, and many important questions remain about the public morality of philanthropy. For example, the practice of donor discretion, which permits donors not merely to choose the cause they will support but also to attach strings to their gift, introduces potentially worrisome *forms of paternalism* in the donor-beneficiary relationship. In attaching strings, philanthropists can (and do) sometimes seek to impose their own vision of the good on other people, thereby undermining the autonomy of recipients. Or consider that philanthropy, especially when the poor rely on the largesse of donors, can also form troubling *forms*

of dependence, leading to the subservience or subordination of the recipient to the donor. Philanthropy calls out for an analysis through republican political theory, alert to questions of domination by philanthropists.[1] Finally, consider the rise of effective altruism, a movement inspired largely by philosophers that seeks to move donors to maximize the good they do with their donations (and career choices). Effective altruists have a powerful private morality for informing giving—fund proven and highly effective charitable organizations that maximize human or animal welfare—but they have ignored the implications for public morality.[2]

In addition to questions concerning paternalism, dependence, and effective altruism, a host of recent developments in the institutional patterns of philanthropy cry out for the attention of political theorists, social scientists, and investigative journalists. Two particular developments come to mind.

First is the stunning rise in the United States of the donor-advised fund or DAF. Such funds were created by community foundations as a place for ordinary citizens to contribute modest sums to a charitable investment account: a place to make a philanthropic contribution but not yet distribute the money to a charitable organization. Funds are legally conferred to a separate entity—the fund managers—who possess the authority to make distributions from the fund while the initial donor advises on how to direct the assets. In practice, the donor retains full control over the distributions. This structure introduces a time asymmetry between the moment the donor receives the full tax benefit of a charitable contribution—at the time of transfer to the DAF—and the moment at which some social benefit is produced—at the time of transfer from the DAF to a charitable nonprofit. DAFs represent an opportunity to warehouse phil-

anthropic assets with no legal requirement to make allocations from the fund.

For many decades, DAFs were minor entities in the philanthropic universe. In the past generation, however, they have become a kind of kudzu that is eating the U.S. charitable sector. Most people have never heard of DAFs, and so they would be surprised to learn that the largest recipient of charitable contributions in the United States for the past few years is not the United Way, the Salvation Army, or Stanford University, but the Fidelity Charitable Gift Fund. In 2017, six of the top ten recipients of charitable contributions were DAFs.[3] In light of these facts, how should public policy treat DAFs?

Second is the increasing number of especially wealthy philanthropists who are rejecting the standard philanthropic form—the private philanthropic foundation—and creating instead a for-profit entity, a limited liability company (LLC), as their preferred vehicle for social change. Mark Zuckerberg and his wife Priscilla Chan announced in 2015 that they would commit 99 percent of their wealth to advance human potential. Their announcement came not with the establishment of a tax-advantaged private foundation but with a for-profit LLC. In adopting the LLC form, the Chan Zuckerberg Initiative avoids the already modest regulatory requirements concerning annual reporting of grant making and prohibitions on political giving that attach to private foundations. Without any disclosure requirements at all, LLCs can engage in charitable grant making, invest in start-up companies, and direct their funds toward political advocacy and electioneering.[4]

Zuckerberg is not the only big donor to opt for the LLC form over the private foundation. Other prominent examples, each with many billions of dollars, include the Emerson Collective

(founded by Laurene Powell Jobs), the Omidyar Network (created by Pierre and Pam Omidyar), and Good Ventures (Dustin Moskovitz and Cari Tuna).

For-profit philanthropy in the form of an LLC threatens to unleash the power of wealthy elites in an especially nontransparent and unaccountable manner. It permits, in Jane Mayer's memorable phrase, the weaponization of philanthropy through the dissemination of dark money.[5] How should a democratic society regard for-profit philanthropy?

To answer questions about paternalism, dependence, effective altruism, DAFs, and LLCs, we need a framework for evaluating what the role of philanthropy should be in a liberal democratic society. We need more attention paid by scholars and journalists to the phenomenon of philanthropy.

Regardless of my particular conclusions, or for that matter of the approach to the political theory of philanthropy I develop and defend, I will count my efforts a success if this book shows why we need to think about philanthropy more seriously in philosophy and in society more generally. Philanthropy presents questions far beyond how much and to whom we should give money. It is not just a matter of private morality, it is a matter of public morality. We need political *theories* of philanthropy. This book I offer as but one such contribution.

NOTES

Introduction

1. Quoted in Ron Chernow, *Titan: The Life of John D. Rockefeller, Sr.* (New York: Vintage, 2004), 563.

2. Frederick Taylor Gates and Robert Swain Morison, *Chapters in My Life* (New York: Free Press, 1977), 161.

3. According to Rockefeller Foundation documents, Rockefeller's wealth was estimated to be 1.5 percent of the U.S. economy. An equivalent percentage of the U.S. gross domestic product would peg Rockefeller's wealth in 2016 dollars at nearly $280 billion, almost four times the wealth of Bill Gates.

4. Eric Abrahamson, Sam Hurst, and Barbara Shubinski, *Democracy and Philanthropy: The Rockefeller Foundation and the American Experiment* (New York: Rockefeller Foundation, 2013), 35.

5. Gates and Morison, *Chapters in My Life*, 209.

6. Quoted in Peter Dobkin Hall, "Philanthropy, the Nonprofit Sector & the Democratic Dilemma," *Daedalus* 142 (2013): 147–148.

7. U.S. Congress, Commission on Industrial Relations, "Report of the Commission on Industrial Relations: Final Report and Testimony" (1912), 7916–7917.

8. Frank P. Walsh, "Perilous Philanthropy," *Independent* 83 (1915): 262–264.

9. The Rockefeller Foundation possesses well-maintained archives and has published considerable materials that document the history of the foundation, including this early and contentious founding period. Discussion of the charter bill and its revisions was found in Abrahamson, Hurst, and Shubinski, *Democracy and Philanthropy*, 35; Eric Abrahamson, *Beyond Charity: A Century of Philanthropic Innovation* (New York: Rockefeller Foundation, 2013), 58; and Hall, "Philanthropy."

10. Frederick P. Keppel, *The Foundation: Its Place in American Life* (London: Macmillan, 1930) for the 1930 figure; other figures from author calculations of IRS data.

11. Aristotle, *Nicomachean Ethics*, in *The Basic Works of Aristotle*, ed. Richard McKeon (New York: Random House, 1941), 935–1126, bk. 2, sec. 9.

12. Singer introduced his basic argument in 1972 in his "Famine, Affluence, and Morality," *Philosophy and Public Affairs* 1 (1972): 229–243, and to the extent philosophers have written about philanthropy or charity, Singer's argument has dominated discussion. In recent years Singer has made efforts to popularize his view, e.g., *The*

Life You Can Save: How to Do Your Part to End World Poverty (New York: Random House, 2010); *The Most Good You Can Do: How Effective Altruism Is Changing Ideas about Living Ethically* (New Haven, CT: Yale University Press, 2015). For another philosopher's defense of effective altruism, see William MacAskill, *Doing Good Better* (New York: Gotham Books, 2015).

13. Robert D. Putnam, *Bowling Alone: The Collapse and Revival of American Community* (New York: Simon & Shuster, 2000); Theda Skocpol, *Diminished Democracy: From Membership to Management in American Civic Life* (Norman: University of Oklahoma Press, 2003); Theda Skocpol and Morris Fiorina, eds., *Civic Engagement in American Democracy* (Washington, DC: Brookings Institution Press, 1999); Nancy Rosenblum and Robert Post, eds., *Civil Society and Government* (Princeton, NJ: Princeton University Press, 2002); Simone Chambers and Will Kymlicka, eds., *Alternative Conceptions of Civil Society* (Princeton, NJ: Princeton University Press, 2002); Mark Warren, *Democracy and Association* (Princeton, NJ: Princeton University Press, 2001); Victor M. Muniz-Fraticelli, *The Structure of Pluralism: On the Authority of Associations* (Oxford: Oxford University Press, 2014); Nancy L. Rosenblum, *Membership and Morals: The Personal Uses of Pluralism in America* (Princeton, NJ: Princeton University Press, 1998).

14. Will Kymlicka, "Altruism in Philosophical and Ethical Traditions: Two Views," in *Between State and Market: Essays on Charity Law and Policy in Canada*, ed. Jim Phillips, Bruce Chapman, and David Stevens (Toronto: McGill-Queen's University Press, 2001), 87–126. Kymlicka operates, it should be said, with a limited definition of charity—gifts of money to other people in need—and he specifically separates donations to organizations that promote activities enjoyed by the donor (e.g., cultural groups) and causes preferred by the donor (e.g., environmental groups or gun lobbies). Nevertheless, Kymlicka's argument is set to undermine any account of philanthropy or charity whose aim or justification is redistributive or eleemosynary (115).

15. For an analysis of the content and historical trajectory of these left-wing critiques in the U.S. setting, see Barry D. Karl and Stanley N. Katz, "Foundations and Ruling Class Elites," *Daedelus* 116 (1987): 1–40. For a classic exposition of the Gramscian critique, see Donald Fisher, "The Role of Philanthropic Foundations in the Reproduction and Production of Hegemony: Rockefeller Foundations and the Social Sciences," *Sociology* 17 (1983): 206–233.

Chapter 1: Philanthropy as an Artifact of the State

1. For a modern example, think of status-seeking competition to occupy seats on prestigious nonprofit boards of trustees, such as museums, or the arms race in naming rights on college campuses for buildings, classrooms, and more. Several universities, including Harvard and Berkeley, have offered up naming rights for bathrooms.

2. Marcel Mauss, *The Gift: Forms and Functions of Exchange in Archaic Societies*, trans. Wilfred Douglas Halls (London: Routledge, 1990), 18. For a related argument

about the distinctively modern tradition of distributive justice as distinct from an earlier tradition of charity, see Samuel Fleischacker, *A Short History of Distributive Justice* (Cambridge, MA: Harvard University Press, 2004).

3. For a marvelous history, see Jonathan Levy's "Altruism and the Origins of Nonprofit Philanthropy," in *Philanthropy in Democratic Societies: History, Institutions, Values*, ed. Rob Reich, Chiara Cordelli, and Lucy Bernholz (Chicago: University of Chicago Press, 2016). Also see Levy's "From Fiscal Triangle to Passing Through: Rise of the Nonprofit Corporation," in *Corporations and American Democracy*, ed. Naomi Lamoreaux and William Novak (Cambridge: Cambridge University Press, 2017), and Norman I. Silber, *A Corporate Form of Freedom: The Emergence of the Nonprofit Sector* (Boulder, CO: Westview, 2001).

4. In this section, I draw on the excellent accounts offered by Paul Veyne, *Bread and Circuses: Historical Sociology and Political Pluralism* (London: Penguin, 1992); Josiah Ober, *Mass and Elite in Democratic Athens: Rhetoric, Ideology, and the Power of the People* (Princeton, NJ: Princeton University Press, 1991); Vincent Gabrielsen, *Financing the Athenian Fleet: Public Taxation and Social Relations* (Baltimore: Johns Hopkins University Press, 1994); Matthew R. Christ, *The Bad Citizen in Classical Athens* (Cambridge: Cambridge University Press, 2006); Matthew R. Christ, "Liturgy Avoidance and Antidosis in Classical Athens," *Transactions of the American Philological Association* 120 (1990): 147–169; Marc Domingo Gygax, *Benefaction and Rewards in the Ancient Greek City: The Origins of Euergetism* (Cambridge: Cambridge University Press, 2016); and Brooks A. Kaiser, "The Athenian Trierarchy: Mechanism Design for the Private Provision of Public Goods," *Journal of Economic History* 67 (2007): 445–480. See also Peter Wilson, *The Athenian Institution of the Khoregia: The Chorus, the City and the Stage* (Cambridge: Cambridge University Press, 2003); John Ma, *Statues and Cities: Honorific Portraits and Civic Identity in the Hellenistic World* (Oxford: Oxford University Press, 2013); Marc Domingo Gygax, "Gift-Giving and Power Relationships in Greek Social Praxis and Public Discourse," in *The Gift in Antiquity*, ed. Michael Satlow (Hoboken, NJ: John Wiley, 2013); and Ian Morris, "Gift and Commodity in Archaic Greece," *Man* 21 (1986): 1–17.

5. "At a certain time in the fourth century, liturgical contributions in a year equaled more than half (about 59 to 67 percent) of the amount of total national revenue, which was derived from other sources. And even when the public finances improved shortly thereafter, the annual expenditure of liturgists was still equal to one fifth (about 19 to 21 percent) of the revenue coming into the state coffers." Gabrielsen, *Financing the Athenian Fleet*, 226.

6. Christ, "Liturgy Avoidance," 155.

7. Ober, *Mass and Elite*, 229.

8. Gabrielsen, *Financing the Athenian Fleet*, 7.

9. Ibid., 35.

10. Ober, *Mass and Elite*, 199.

11. On the matter of punishment, Gabrielsen writes, "Refusal to discharge any liturgy entailed punishment. Trierarchs, in particular, were persecuted if declining

to perform their duty, unless they resorted to supplication or sought asylum in the sanctuary of Artemis in Mounichia" (Gabrielsen, *Financing the Athenian Fleet*, 92).

12. Ibid., 92.

13. Reflecting the dual elements of voluntarism and obligations, some scholars describe the trierarchy as a form of public finance and taxation (e.g., Gabrielsen) and others as a mechanism for private provision of public goods (e.g., Kaiser). The more familiar term among classicists is "euergetism," defined as private liberality for public benefit in Paul Veyne's classic formulation in *Bread and Circuses*.

14. Ober, *Mass and Elite*, 241–242.

15. Gabrielsen, *Financing the Athenian Fleet*, 220. Also, "The diversion of the naval command into the liturgical orbit placed munificence in this area under the regulatory mechanisms of democratic statutes that generally but unequivocally spelled out the obligation incumbent upon wealthy citizens to serve the state (or the people) with their 'body and property'" (219).

16. Although no exact modern analogue exists, one can find a related procedure in real estate regimes, where self-assessed property values determine the property taxes that are owed but also set the sales price for one's property. In *Radical Markets* Eric Posner and Glen Weyl have invoked the Athenian antidosis as a potent mechanism to reimagine a property regime that, they believe, would have powerful justice-promoting effects. Eric A. Posner and E. Glen Weyl, *Radical Markets: Uprooting Capitalism and Democracy for a Just Society* (Princeton, NJ: Princeton University Press, 2018), 55–57.

17. When the iconic Washington Monument in was structurally damaged by an earthquake in 2011, for example, wealthy financier David Rubenstein volunteered to pay for half of the repair job. Rubenstein, who also donated the Magna Carta to the National Archives and donated millions for the restoration of Monticello, Jefferson's home in Virginia, claimed to be motivated by nothing more than his love for the country. See Jennifer Steinhauer, "A Billionaire Philanthropist in Washington Who's Big on Patriotic Giving," *New York Times*, February 20, 2014.

18. See Kevin C. Robbins, "The Nonprofit Sector in Historical Perspective: Traditions of Philanthropy in the West," in *The Nonprofit Sector: A Research Handbook*, 2nd ed., ed. Walter W. Powell and Richard Steinberg (New Haven, CT: Yale University Press, 2006). Similarly, exploring only the Western tradition, see Jerome B. Schneewind, ed., *Giving: Western Ideas of Philanthropy* (Bloomington: Indiana University Press, 1996). For a more general overview, see Ian Morris, *Why the West Rules—for Now: The Patterns of History and What They Reveal about the Future* (London: Profile Books, 2010).

19. In this section I draw on the following sources: Marshall Hodgson, *The Venture of Islam*, 3 vols. (Chicago: University of Chicago Press, 1974); Amy Singer, *Charity in Islamic Societies* (Cambridge: Cambridge University Press, 2008); Amy Singer, "Soup and Sadaqa: Charity in Islamic Societies," *Historical Research* 79 (2006): 306–324; Amy Singer, "The Persistence of Philanthropy," *Comparative Studies of South Asia, Africa and the Middle East* 31 (2011): 557–568; Moshe Gil, "The Earliest Waqf

Foundations," *Journal of Near Eastern Studies* 57 (1998): 125–140; Timur Kuran, "Institutional Roots of Authoritarian Rule in the Middle East: Civic Legacies of the Islamic Waqf" (Economic Research Initiatives at Duke Working Paper 171, 2014), http://ssrn.com/abstract=2449569; Timur Kuran, "The Provision of Public Goods under Islamic Law: Origins, Impact, and Limitations of the Waqf System," *Law and Society Review* (2001): 841–898; Timur Kuran, "The Political Consequences of Islam's Economic Legacy," *Philosophy and Social Criticism* 39 (2013): 395–405; David Powers, "Orientalism, Colonialism, and Legal History: The Attack on Muslim Family Endowments in Algeria and India," *Comparative Studies in Society and History* 31 (1989): 535–571; Yaacov Lev, *Charity, Endowments, and Charitable Institutions in Medieval Islam* (Gainesville: University Press of Florida, 2005); and Nicholas Terpstra, "Charity, Civil Society, and Social Capital in Islamic and Christian Societies, 1200–1700: Models and Hypotheses for Comparative Research," in *Philanthropy and Civic Engagement in Arab Societies*, ed. B. Ibrahim et al. (Cairo: American University of Cairo, 2012).

20. One observes a connection between Islam and Judaism in the tight relationship between Muslim *sadaqa* and Jewish *tzedakah*.

21. Kuran, "Provision of Public Goods," 849–850; Singer, *Charity in Islamic Societies*, 91, citing Hodgson, *Venture of Islam*, 2:124.

22. Powers, "Orientalism, Colonialism, and Legal History," 537–538; Kuran, "Provision of Public Goods," 849; Singer, *Charity in Islamic Societies*, 186.

23. Kuran describes the sacrality of waqfs as creating a "credible commitment device" that insulated them from political upheavals and the prospect of any political intervention to claim their assets or redirect their purposes (Kuran, "Provision of Public Goods," 847; Kuran, "Political Consequences," 400).

24. Kuran, "Institutional Roots," 11; Kuran, "Provision of Public Goods," 856; and Singer, *Charity in Islamic Societies*, 100–109.

25. See Terpstra, "Charity, Civil Society, and Social Capital," for some speculation on how the institution of the waqf influenced the endowed foundation in Europe.

26. Kuran, "Provision of Public Goods," 853–854, notes that such efforts persisted even through tumultuous political changes: "Half a century after the abolition of the Turkish monarchy and the relocation of Turkey's capital to Ankara, congregational services at certain Anatolian mosques still ended, in keeping with their deeds, with prayers for the health of the reigning sultan in Istanbul."

27. Much of Kuran's work over the past decade has been devoted to explaining why Islam and the Middle East did not develop democracy, and chief among his explanations is the waqf system. For the most recent and comprehensive statement, see his "Institutional Roots."

28. Robbins, "Nonprofit Sector in Historical Perspective," 27. For an excellent cross-national historical study of social attitudes and policies concerning inheritance, see Jens Beckert, *Inherited Wealth* (Princeton, NJ: Princeton University Press, 2004).

29. In this section, I draw upon Anne-Robert Turgot and his 1756 article "Fondation," in Diderot's *Encyclopaedie*, reprinted in *The Turgot Collection*, ed. David Gordon (Auburn, AL: Mises Institute, 2011), 461–469; Jack A. Clarke, "Turgot's Critique

of Perpetual Endowments," *French Historical Studies* 3 (1964): 495–506; Peter Groenewegen, *Eighteenth-Century Economics: Turgot, Beccaria and Smith and Their Contemporaries* (London: Routledge, 2002); Frank Edward Manuel, *The Prophets of Paris* (Cambridge, MA: Harvard University Press, 1962); Keith Baker, *Condorcet: From Natural Philosophy to Social Mathematics* (Chicago: University of Chicago 1975); Jesse Brundage Sears, "Philanthropy in the History of American Higher Education" (U.S. Department of the Interior, Bureau of Education, Bulletin 26, 1922); Harry Rudman, "Mill on Perpetual Endowments," *History of Ideas Newsletter* 3 (1957): 70–72.

30. See Groenewegen's *Eighteenth-Century Economics*. Groenewegen notes here that Schumpeter considered Turgot one of the first economic theorists, one of the main contributors to establishing economics as an independent and scientific field of study (49).

31. "Fondation" is sometimes translated as "Foundations," sometimes as "Endowments."

32. Turgot, "Fondation," 461, 463.

33. Ibid., 462.

34. Alexis de Tocqueville, *Memoir on Pauperism*, trans. Seymour Drescher (London: Ivan R. Dee, 1997), 30. Tocqueville was mostly concerned with government-provided relief, though his view also impugns formally organized charitable organizations. Thoreau, "Walden," in *Political Writings*, ed. Nancy Rosenblum (Cambridge: Cambridge University Press, 1996), 77.

35. Turgot, "Fondation," 461, 465.

36. Becker: "There is surely a tendency for foundations to become more liberal over time. Examples of foundations that started out conservative and became much more liberal with time include the Ford, Pew, and Packard Foundations—the Packard Foundation shifted rapidly after the death of its conservative founder David Packard. I do not know of any large foundations that moved from being very liberal to becoming conservative. The two main reasons for this shift in philosophy are 1) that the children of successful conservative self-made businessmen tend to be more liberal than their parents. There are several reasons for this, but one is simply "regression to the mean": conservative parents have less conservative children, although one might expect this to produce some foundations that go from liberal to conservative. 2) Over time foundations come under the management of professional foundation personnel instead of the founders and people they trust. Professional managers tend to be highly educated and liberal, just like the majority of journalists at major newspapers." See http://www.becker-posner-blog.com/2007/01/charitable-foundations-and-their-effects—becker.html.

The most colorful example of such founder regret comes from Henry Ford II, the grandson of Henry Ford who had established the Ford Foundation in 1936. Henry Ford II observed in a 1973 interview, "The Foundation's been a fiasco from my point of view from day one. And it got out of control and it got in the control of a lot of liberals. . . . I've tried to break up the Foundation several times and have been unsuccessful. . . . I didn't have enough confidence in myself at that stage to push and scream

and yell and tell them to go fuck themselves, you know, which I should have done." Quoted in Larissa MacFarquhar, "What Money Can Buy," *New Yorker*, January 6, 2016.

37. Turgot, "Fondation," 464.

38. Ibid., 469.

39. Clarke, "Turgot's Critique," 497.

40. Turgot, "Fondation," 469.

41. For an illuminating exploration of the history of the corporate body, see David Ciepley, "Beyond Public and Private: Toward a Political Theory of the Corporation," *American Political Science Review* 107 (2013): 139–158.

42. Immanuel Kant, "The Metaphysics of Morals," in *Practical Philosophy: The Cambridge Edition of the Works of Immanuel Kant*, ed. Allen Wood, trans. Mary Gregor (Cambridge: Cambridge University Press, 1996), 503.

43. In the United States, the law not merely permits charitable trusts to be perpetual but also, in recent years, against long-standing adherence to the "Rule Against Perpetuities," allows private trusts, intended for private benefit, to be perpetual. See Steven J. Horowitz and Robert H. Sitkoff, "Unconstitutional Perpetual Trusts," *Vanderbilt Law Review* 67 (2014): 1769–1822.

44. In this paragraph I follow the analysis of Clarke, "Turgot's Critique," 495.

45. Baron de Montesquieu, *The Complete Works of M. de Montesquieu*, vol. 2 (London: T. Evans, 1777), http://oll.libertyfund.org/titles/838#Montesquieu_0171 -02_632.

46. J. S. Mill, "Corporation and Church Property," in *The Collected Works of John Stuart Mill*, vol. 4IV, ed. J. M. Robson (Toronto: University of Toronto Press, 1963–1991), http://oll.libertyfund.org/titles/165; J. S. Mill, "Educational Endowments," in "Report of Commissioners on Education in Schools in England, Not Comprised within Her Majesty's Two Recent Commissions on Popular Education and Public Schools," *Parliamentary Papers* 28, pt. 2 (1867–1868): 67–72; J. S. Mill, "Endowments," *Fortnightly Review*, April 1869, 377–390.

47. J. S. Mill, *Autobiography* (London: Longmans, Green, Reader, and Dyer, 1873), 128.

48. Mill, "Corporation and Church Property," 199.

49. Ibid., 200.

50. Ibid., 188–189.

51. Ibid., 189.

52. Ibid., 190.

53. Ibid., 191.

54. Ibid., 191.

55. Ibid., 191.

56. Ibid., 198.

57. Ibid., 203.

58. Ibid., 204.

59. Mill, "Endowments," 377.

Chapter 2: Philanthropy and Its Uneasy Relation to Equality

1. This chapter draws upon Reich, "Philanthropy and Its Uneasy Relation to Equality," in *Taking Philanthropy Seriously: Beyond Noble Intentions to Responsible Giving*, ed. William Damon and Susan Verducci (Bloomington: Indiana University Press, 2006), 27–49, and Reich, "Philanthropy and Caring for the Needs of Strangers," *Social Research* 80 (2013): 517–538.

2. For debates about ideal and nonideal theory, see John Rawls, *The Law of Peoples* (Cambridge, MA: Harvard University Press, 1999); A. John Simmons, "Ideal and Nonideal Theory," *Philosophy & Public Affairs* 38, no. 1 (2010): 5–36; Zofia Stemplowska, "What's Ideal about Ideal Theory?," *Social Theory and Practice* 34, no. 3 (2008): 319–340; and Zofia Stemplowska and Adam Swift, "Rawls on Ideal and Nonideal Theory," in *A Companion to Rawls*, ed. Jon Mandle and David A. Reidy, (Chichester, West Sussex: John Wiley, 2014), 112–127.

3. See Amartya Sen, *The Idea of Justice* (Cambridge, MA: Harvard University Press, 2009), Jacob T. Levy, "There's No Such Thing as Ideal Theory," *Social Philosophy and Policy* 33, nos. 1–2 (2016): 312–333; William A. Galston, "Realism in Political Theory," *European Journal of Political Theory* 9 (2010): 385–411; David Miller, *Justice for Earthlings* (Cambridge: Cambridge University Press, 2013).

4. Emma Saunders-Hastings similarly takes no side, arguing that reaching conclusions about philanthropy drawn from ideal theory but applied to circumstances in the real world of actually existing philanthropy can lead us astray. "If we stipulate, in the background, a fully just distribution of influence over political decisions, then any subsequent philanthropic influence on those decisions or their application will look undemocratic. It could only distort what is (ex hypothesi) the appropriate distribution of influence over a decision. But if the distribution of influence over political decision making is not democratic, it is harder to evaluate interventions that influence or weaken the efficacy of political decisions" (Saunders-Hastings, "Plutocratic Philanthropy" *Journal of Politics* 80, no. 1 (2018): 149–161.

5. The justly famous passage reads, "Americans of all ages, all conditions, and all minds are constantly joining together in groups. In addition to commercial and industrial associations in which everyone takes part, there are associations of a thousand other kinds: some religious, some moral, some grave, some trivial, some quite general and others quite particular, some huge and others tiny. Americans associate to give fêtes, to found seminaries, to build inns, to erect churches, to distribute books, to send missionaries to the antipodes. This is how they create hospitals, prisons, and schools. If, finally, they wish to publicize a truth or foster a sentiment with the help of a great example, they associate. Wherever there is a new undertaking, at the head of which you would expect to see in France the government and in England some great lord, in the United States you are sure to find an association." Alexis de Tocqueville, *Democracy in America*, trans. Henry Reeve and Francis Bowen (New York: Vintage, 1945), 595.

6. "Eleemosynary" means "of or relating to charity."

7. Robert Nozick, *Anarchy, State, and Utopia* (New York: Basic Books, 1974), 305.

8. Isaiah Berlin, "The Pursuit of the Ideal," in *The Crooked Timber of Humanity: Chapters in the History of Ideas* (Princeton, NJ: Princeton University Press, 2015), 1–16.

9. For one economist's perspective on how tax policy creates "distortions" in the philanthropic sector, see Charles T. Clotfelter, "Tax-Induced Distortions in the Voluntary Sector," *Case Western Reserve Law Review* 39 (1988): 663–694.

10. Giving USA Foundation, "Giving USA 2017: The Annual Report on Philanthropy for the Year 2016" (Chicago: Giving USA Foundation, 2017). The number of hours volunteered is another frequent measure of giving, and U.S. citizens also rank highly here in cross-national comparisons. For one study, see Charities Aid Foundation, "World Giving Index 2014," https://www.cafonline.org/pdf/CAF_WGI2014 _Report_1555AWEBFinal.pdf.

11. For a general overview, see Rob Reich, Christopher Wimer, Shazad Mohamed, and Sharada Jambulapati, "Has the Great Recession Made Americans Stingier?" in *The Great Recession*, ed. David B. Grusky, Bruce Western, and Christopher Wimer (New York: Russell Sage Foundation, 2011), 294–313. See also Suzanne Perry, "The Stubborn 2% Giving Rate," *Chronicle of Philanthropy*, July 17, 2013.

12. John J. Havens, Mary A. O'Herlihy, and Paul G. Schervish, "Charitable Giving: How Much, by Whom, to What, and How?," in Powell and Steinberg, *Nonprofit Sector*, 543.

13. For a detailed overview of the tax treatment of individual donors and nonprofit organizations, see John Simon, Harvey Dale, and Laura Chisolm, "The Federal Tax Treatment of Nonprofit Organizations," in Powell and Steinberg, *Nonprofit Sector*, 267–306.

14. The "tax expenditure" concept was pioneered by Stanley Surrey in the late 1960s and applied to every tax concession in the tax code. Surrey equated tax expenditures with direct spending programs in terms of their respective impact on the federal treasury. The concept has had practical effects: the U.S. federal government and many state governments now publish an annual list of actual and estimated tax expenditures in their annual budgets. For a comprehensive overview, see Stanley S. Surrey and Paul R. McDaniel, *Tax Expenditures* (Cambridge, MA: Harvard University Press, 1985). For criticism on democratic grounds about the increasing use of tax expenditures as hidden spending programs, see Suzanne Mettler, *The Submerged State: How Invisible Government Policies Undermine American Democracy* (Chicago: University of Chicago Press, 2011). Oddly, Mettler barely discusses charitable tax expenditures, despite the fact that they constitute among the largest tax expenditures overall. For a cross-national comparison of charitable tax expenditures, see Lilian V. Faulhaber, "Charitable Giving, Tax Expenditures, and Direct Spending in the United States and the European Union," *Yale Journal of International Law* 39 (2014): 87.

15. Mettler, *Submerged State*.

16. Clotfelter, "Tax-Induced Distortions," 663; Burton A. Weisbrod, "The Pitfalls of Profits," *Stanford Social Innovation Review*, Winter 2004, https://ssir.org/articles/entry/the_pitfalls_of_profits.

17. Calculated from the Internal Revenue Service, "Statistics of Income Bulletin," Table 1 (Individual Income Tax Returns: Selected Income and Tax Items, 2015), https://www.irs.gov/statistics/soi-tax-stats-individual-income-tax-returns. The late 2017 passage of new tax legislation doubled the standard deduction, putting itemization further out of reach of most taxpayers and thereby giving even fewer people a financial incentive to donate money. Economists predict that the share of households claiming a charitable deduction will fall to 9 percent, meaning that the policy instrument intended to stimulate charitable giving will not be available to more than 90 percent of taxpayers.

18. This perhaps surprising fact—that, in terms of percentage of income given away, poor people are more generous than rich people, and both poor and rich are more generous than the middle class—accounts for the U-shaped curve of giving. See Russell N. James and Deanna L. Sharpe, "The Nature and Causes of the U-Shaped Charitable Giving Profile," *Nonprofit and Voluntary Sector Quarterly* 36 (2007): 218–238.

19. Richard A. Musgrave and Peggy B. Musgrave, *Public Finance in Theory and Practice*, 4th ed. (New York: McGraw-Hill, 1984), 348.

20. I mean that in a progressive system of income taxation, by mathematical logic, a tax deduction is necessarily regressive. One other interesting implication: the higher the rates of taxation, the lower the cost of charitable giving. A 50 percent rate of tax on income converts a $1,000 charitable donation to a price of $500 ($500 in forgone taxes); a 75 percent rate of tax on income converts a $1,000 charitable donation to a price of just $250 ($750 in forgone taxes). With tax deductions as the subsidy structure for charitable giving, raising tax rates simultaneously increases the incentive to give money away.

21. Congressional Budget Office, "The Distribution of Major Tax Expenditures in the Individual Income Tax System" (No. 43768, 2013), https://EconPapers.repec.org/RePEc:cbo:report:437680.

22. For a review of various proposed reforms, see Evelyn Brody, "Charities in Tax Reform: Threats to Subsidies Overt and Covert," *Tennessee Law Review* 66 (1998): 687–763; C. Eugene Steuerle and A. M. Sullivan, "Toward More Simple and Effective Giving: Reforming the Tax Rules for Charitable Contributions and Charitable Organizations," *American Journal of Tax Policy* 12 (1995): 1–46; Roger Colinvaux, Brian Galle, and Eugene Steuerle, "Evaluating the Charitable Deduction and Proposed Reforms" (Urban Institute, June 2012).

23. Clotfelter, "Tax-Induced Distortions."

24. See Brody, "Charities in Tax Reform," 696.

25. The purpose of the payout rule is to ensure that donors to foundations do not take advantage of tax benefits while warehousing their philanthropic assets. The ability to satisfy the payout rule via administrative expenses or payments to donor-advised funds constitutes an evasion of the rule's purpose.

26. Every year the IRS approves more than fifty thousand new public charities, with an approval rate of over 99 percent (of applications on which a decision was rendered). For more detail, see Rob Reich, Lacey Dorn, and Stefanie Sutton, "Anything Goes: Approval of Nonprofit Status by the IRS" (Stanford, CA: Stanford University Center on Philanthropy and Civil Society, 2009)

27. Robert Wuthnow, *Saving America? Faith-Based Services and the Future of Civil Society* (Princeton: Princeton University Press, 2004), 49.

28. Center on Philanthropy at Indiana University, "Patterns of Household Charitable Giving by Income Group 2005" (2007), www.philanthropy.iupui.edu/files/research/giving_focused_on_meeting_needs_of_the_poor_july_2007.pdf.

29. In examining giving to health, for example, "contributions intended to benefit people living in poverty were approximated by looking at the purpose for which the recipient organization was founded. Thus, half of the amount going to charities helping terminally ill children was considered 'to benefit people living in poverty' (in part because families with such ill children have few financial resources, even if they are not strictly living in poverty—this is an example of always trying to 'err on the high side'). Half of the amount donated to hospice programs and services for the aging were considered to be focused on the needs of the poor. Contributions to health care clinics, even ones that do not primarily serve the poor (e.g., Cleveland Clinic) were counted as 'focused on the poor' for the purposes of this study" (ibid., 23).

30. Foundation Center, "Key Facts on U.S. Foundations" (2014), http://foundationcenter.org/gainknowledge/research/nationaltrends.html; Giving USA Foundation, "Giving USA 2017."

31. Author calculations from Foundation Center data.

32. Julian Wolpert, "Redistributional Effects of America's Private Foundations," in *The Legitimacy of Philanthropic Foundations: United States and European Perspectives*, ed. Kenneth Prewitt, Mattei Dogan, Steven Heydemann, and Stefan Toepler (New York: Russell Sage Foundation, 2006), 144.

33. Clotfelter, "Tax-Induced Distortions," 22.

34. Liam Murphy and Thomas Nagel, *The Myth of Ownership: Taxes and Justice* (Oxford: Oxford University Press, 2002), 127.

35. See Reich, Dorn, and Sutton, "Anything Goes."

36. See Diane Ravitch, *The Death and Life of the Great American School System* (New York: Basic Books, 2011); Sarah Reckhow, *Follow the Money: How Foundation Dollars Change Public School Politics* (Oxford: Oxford University Press, 2013); Megan E. Tompkins-Stange, *Policy Patrons: Philanthropy, Education Reform, and the Politics of Influence* (Cambridge, MA: Harvard Education Press, 2016).

37. Rob Reich, "Not Very Giving," *New York Times*, September 4, 2013.

38. Jonathan Kozol, *Savage Inequalities: Children in America's Schools* (New York: Broadway Books, 2012).

39. Eric Brunner and Jon Sonstelie have undertaken similar research and were kind enough to share with me their database of 501(c)(3) school organizations in California. For their own conclusions, see Brunner and Sonstelie, "School Finance

Reform and Voluntary Fiscal Federalism," *Journal of Public Economics* 87 (2003): 2157–2185. See also Catherine Brown, Scott Sargrad, and Meg Benner, "Hidden Money: The Outsized Role of Parent Contributions in School Finance" (Center for American Progress, April 2017), https://perma.cc/BUB6-UF4L.

40. Brunner and Sonstelie, "School Finance Reform."

41. For an important analysis of parents' interests in rearing children, including a discussion of bedtime stories, see Harry Brighouse and Adam Swift, *Family Values: The Ethics of Parent-Child Relationships* (Princeton, NJ: Princeton University Press, 2014).

42. Donations are often permitted to local police foundations that fund scholarships for the children of police or provide grants to families of officers killed in the line of duty; funds do not go to support regular department operations. In addition, individuals can sometimes make tax-deductible gifts to municipal and state governments.

Chapter 3: A Political Theory of Philanthropy

1. For an overview of tax incentives for charitable giving across twenty-one countries, see Lester M. Salamon and Stefan Toepler, *The International Guide to Nonprofit Law* (New York: John Wiley, 1997).

2. Ruth W. Grant's *Strings Attached: Untangling the Ethics of Incentives* (Princeton, NJ: Princeton University Press, 2011) provides an excellent analysis of the ethical dimensions of the general use of incentives. She views them as an exercise of power that stands in need of political and moral justification. She neglects, however, a golden opportunity to employ her framework to analyze philanthropy, and this in two respects: first, in the use of tax incentives for charitable contributions and, second, in the strings that donors routinely attach to their contributions. For more, see my review of the book in *Perspectives on Politics* 12 (2014): 223–224.

3. Niccolo Machiavelli, *Discourses on Livy*, trans. Harvey C. Mansfield and Nathan Tarcov (Chicago: University of Chicago Press, 1996), III.28, 276.

4. U.S. Constitution, article I, section 9, clause 7.

5. Kate Stith, "Congress' Power of the Purse," *Yale Law Journal* 97 (1988): 1357. Stith notes that Congress has passed legislation to permit some federal agencies to receive private donations, among them the National Park Service, the National Archive, the Library of Congress, and the Smithsonian. Despite the congressional authorization, Stith argues that this private funding is of questionable constitutionality: "Where broad executive discretion is inherent in our constitutional scheme, the most questionable form of spending authority is open-ended authority to receive and spend donations and gifts. As long as the executive agency is prepared to accept the donation, Congress loses effective control over the contours of authorized government activity. Where a donor conditions a gift broadly—for instance, for the defense of the United States—the recipient federal agency is able to direct the supplemental funds to activities that might not have garnered congressional approval. Where the donor specifically conditions the gift—for instance, for defense in the Persian Gulf—

the donor may effectively specify the objects of government expenditure. In either event, where Congress cannot significantly circumscribe an agency's purposes and powers, to allow the agency to spend all contributions would be to permit private power, subject only to executive discretion, to influence the contours of government and government policy" (1384–1385).

6. The history of the Smithsonian Institution is fascinating. James Smithson, a ne'er-do-well Scotsman who had never set foot in the country, bequeathed his considerable fortune in 1838 to the United States to establish, he prescribed in his will, the Smithsonian Institution to increase the diffusion of knowledge among men. Many in Congress were opposed to accepting the gift, worried about the corrupting influence of private, especially foreign, money in democratic politics. Senator James Calhoun argued that "it was beneath the dignity of the United States to receive presents of this kind from *anyone*." See William Rhees, ed., *The Smithsonian Institution: Documents Relative to Its Origin and History* (Washington, DC: Smithsonian Institution, 1879).

7. Kant, "Metaphysics of Morals," 573.

8. This is the argument of Chiara Cordelli, "Reparative Justice and the Moral Limits of Discretionary Philanthropy," in Reich, Cordelli, and Bernholz, *Philanthropy in Democratic Societies*.

9. For an elaboration of the market democratic theory, see John Tomasi, *Free Market Fairness* (Princeton, NJ: Princeton University Press, 2012). Tomasi regrettably does not discuss the role of philanthropy, though one might expect it to play a large role. For more, see Rob Reich, "Gift Giving and Philanthropy in Market Democracy," *Critical Review* 26 (2014): 408–422.

10. In this chapter I draw from a modest literature on the charitable deduction, which is unwieldy and narrow, resting almost entirely within tax law and, to a lesser extent, economics journals. What's remarkable about this literature is how little it engages with normative argument. Most theories about the deductions, comments David Pozen, "lack a coherent normative basis" (Pozen, "Remapping the Charitable Deduction," *Connecticut Law Review* 39 [2006]: 547). For one normatively grounded argument, see Miranda Perry Fleischer, "Equality of Opportunity and the Charitable Tax Subsidies," *Boston University Law Review* 91 (2011): 601–663.

11. As explained earlier, the mechanism of an income tax deduction for a charitable donation works by creating a subsidy at the rate at which the donor is taxed. So a person who occupies the top tax bracket—currently 39 percent in the United States—would find that a $1,000 donation actually "cost" her only $610. The government effectively pays $390 of her donation, subtracting this amount from her tax burden. Similar incentives exist for the creation of private and family foundations and for contributions to community foundations, where donations and bequests to a foundation are deducted from estate and gift taxation. In permitting these tax incentives, federal and state treasuries forgo tax revenue. Had there been no tax deduction on the $1,000 contribution, the state would have collected another $390 in tax revenue.

12. William D. Andrews, "Personal Deductions in an Ideal Income Tax," *Harvard Law Review* 86 (1972): 309–385.

13. Ibid., 325.

14. Boris I. Bittker, "Charitable Contributions: Tax Deductions or Matching Grants?" *Tax Law Review* 28 (1972): 37.

15. James Andreoni, "Impure Altruism and Donations to Public Goods: A Theory of Warm-Glow Giving," *Economic Journal* 100 (1990): 464–477.

16. Amihai Glazer and Kai A. Konrad, "A Signaling Explanation for Charity," *American Economic Review* 86 (1996): 1019–1028; William T. Harbaugh, "The Prestige Motive for Making Charitable Transfers," *American Economic Review* 88 (1998): 277–282; William T. Harbaugh, "What Do Donations Buy? A Model of Philanthropy Based on Prestige and Warm Glow," *Journal of Public Economics* 67 (1998): 269–284.

17. Recent studies in neuroscience claim to show that helping others boosts happiness in the giver. Philanthropy is allegedly a win-win: good for the recipient, good for the donor.

18. Some people mistakenly believe that gifts to religious organizations do in fact provide public goods because many congregations are thought to provide extensive social services. The best available evidence about the use of donations to churches does not bear this out. Sociologist Robert Wuthnow, who writes admiringly of faith-based social service providers, observes that "the amount spent on local service activities is a relatively small proportion of total giving, probably on the order of 5 percent" (Wuthnow, *Saving America?*, 49). It might nevertheless be the case that giving to religion is a means to provide a variety of social services to fellow congregants, and therefore wealthier congregants support, through their religious donations, poorer congregants. Of course, if this is so, the social services are limited to fellow believers only, a limitation that serves as a peculiar and unfair basis, from the standpoint of justice, for the provision of such services if they are genuinely needed.

19. Murphy and Nagel, *Myth of Ownership*.

20. Ibid., 98.

21. Ibid., 58–59.

22. On the concept of a tax expenditure, see Surrey and McDaniel, *Tax Expenditures*. On the ubiquity and scope of their use in official state policy, see Mettler, *Submerged State*, and Christopher Howard, *The Hidden Welfare State: Tax Expenditures and Social Policy in the United States* (Princeton, NJ: Princeton University Press, 1997). Howard examines nearly all the major tax expenditures, the home mortgage interest deduction, employer pensions, the earned income tax credit, and targeted jobs tax credits, and his book is framed as an examination of the hidden welfare state, but he curiously provides no discussion of the charitable contributions deduction, one of the costliest of all tax expenditures.

23. Newer studies that take long-term effects into account generally find lower price elasticities than earlier studies, ranging from −0.47 to −1.26 rather than −1.09 to −2.54. The decision to make a charitable donation is not made solely with reference to the availability of a deduction in any given year; people are likely to look to the year ahead and the year behind in deciding how much to give. Because previous studies have focused on short-term effects of changes in tax incentives, they have often exag-

gerated the impact of incentives. When tax benefits for charitable contributions decreased one year, short-term studies documented a significant decrease in giving for that year. But these studies missed the longer term reactions of donors, who would eventually increase their giving again once they became accustomed to the changes in tax incentives. Another development in recent studies is the use of panel studies as opposed to cross-sectional or time series samples. Panel data provide information from the same group of individuals at successive points in time. See, for instance, Gerald E. Auten, Holger Sieg, and Charles T. Clotfelter, "Charitable Giving, Income, and Taxes: An Analysis of Panel Data," *American Economic Review* 92 (2002): 371–382. See also Jon Bakija and Bradley Heim, "How Does Charitable Giving Respond to Incentives and Income?" (National Bureau of Economic Research working paper, 2008) and Michelle H. Yetman and Robert J. Yetman, "How does the Incentive Effect of the Charitable Deduction Vary across Charities?," *Accounting Review* 88 (2012): 1069–1094. The overall picture is that incentives are significantly less important than was initially thought. In explaining why people make charitable contributions, Evelyn Brody concludes, "Apparently tax considerations are not paramount. After all, philanthropy long preceded the enactment of the federal income tax, and no income-tax subsidy is available to the 70% of individual taxpayers who claim the standard deduction" (Brody, "Charities in Tax Reform," 714).

24. Fack and Landais argue that wealthy donors across many countries frequently use philanthropy as a tax cheating strategy. Their results show, for example, that in the United States "a very significant fraction (around 30%) of contributions reported by the very wealthy before 1969 were driven by tax avoidance or tax cheating purposes." See Gabrielle Fack and Camille Landais, "Philanthropy, Tax Policy, and Tax Cheating: A Long-Run Perspective on US Data," in *Charitable Giving and Tax Policy: A Historical and Comparative Perspective*, ed. Fack and Landais (Oxford: Oxford University Press, 2016), 61–114.

25. U.S. law permits tax-deductible donations to organizations "operated exclusively for religious, charitable, scientific, testing for public safety, literary, or educational purposes, to foster national or international amateur sports competition, or for the prevention of cruelty to children or animals" (Internal Revenue Code sec. 501(c)(3)). In 2012, not including churches or religious groups, these numbered in excess of 1.3 million organizations. Counting churches and religious groups, which do not need to register as nonprofit organizations with the state but receive all the tax benefits that attach to the legal status of a public charity, the number of tax-exempt organizations balloons quickly to nearly 2 million. The IRS also approves more than 50,000 new 501(c)(3) nonprofits every year, with an approval rate of applicants (those for which a decision is rendered) at over 99 percent. See Reich, Dorn, Sutton, "Anything Goes."

26. This is Mark Gergen's argument in "The Case for a Charitable Contributions Deduction," *Virginia Law Review* 74 (1988): 1393–1450.

27. Calculations based on Congressional Budget Office data in "Distribution of Major Tax Expenditures."

28. Giving USA publishes an annual data book on charitable giving, from which I have drawn these figures. Recall here that donations to religion (i.e., to one's own congregation) do not fund more than trivial amounts of service provision; these donations predominantly fund operating expenses of the congregation (e.g., utilities, salaries, facilities, etc.).

29. Charles T. Clotfelter, ed., *Who Benefits from the Nonprofit Sector?* (Chicago: University of Chicago Press, 1992), 22.

30. Western European governments have been historically more redistributive than the United States. The counterfactual question presented here has correspondingly greater bite the more redistributive a government is with its taxpayers' money.

31. Fack and Landais provide some evidence that the wealthiest Americans have indeed been motivated by tax avoidance. Using the natural experiment of the 1969 law that significantly changed enforcement rules for contributions to private foundations, they develop a model to estimate cheating behaviors. They note that annual creation of private foundations dropped by more than 80 percent between 1968 and 1970, "suggesting that private foundations were largely used as tax sheltering vehicles." See Fack and Landais, "Philanthropy, Tax Policy, and Tax Cheating," 64.

32. See Putnam, *Bowling Alone*, and Skocpol, *Diminished Democracy*, on the rise of bureaucratic civil society.

33. *Bob Jones University v. United States*, 461 U.S. 574 (1983). The majority decision in this case argued that the IRS could revoke the tax-exempt status of an organization at odds with established public policy or that fails to meet a public interest requirement in the statute that regulates nonprofit, tax-exempt 501(c)(3) organizations. Bob Jones University, a 501(c)(3) organization, had a policy that denied admission to applicants who were in interracial marriages or who advocated interracial dating or marriage. Powell's opinion concurred with the majority holding but disagreed with the rationale for revoking tax-exempt status as articulated by his fellow justices, that tax-exempt organizations must "demonstrably serve and be in harmony with the public interest."

34. Saul Levmore nicely articulates this view, adding that the mechanism might also encourage volunteering for and oversight of nonprofits by "develop[ing] a sense of commitment to chosen charities". See Levmore, "Taxes as Ballots," *University of Chicago Law Review* 65 (1998): 406. For a similar proposal in the domain of campaign finance, see Bruce Ackerman and Ian Ayres, *Voting with Dollars* (New Haven, CT: Yale University Press, 2002).

35. Liam Murphy and Thomas Nagel write, "The word charity suggests that [the charitable contribution] deduction is a means of decentralizing the process by which a community discharges its collective responsibility to alleviate the worst aspects of life at the bottom of the socioeconomic ladder. Since there is disagreement about what the exact nature of that responsibility is, and about which are the most efficient agencies, it is arguably a good idea for the state to subsidize individuals' contributions to agencies of their choice rather than itself making all the decisions about the use of public funds for this purpose. But even if that is so, the existing deduction cannot be defended on those grounds, because many currently deductible 'charitable' con-

tributions go to cultural and educational institutions that have nothing to do with the poor, the sick, or the handicapped. State funding of such institutions may or may not be desirable, but the argument would be very different, and 'charity' is hardly the right word" (*Myth of Ownership*, 127). The pluralism rationale is an attempt to supply this "very different" argument.

36. For a similar argument, see Saunders-Hastings, "Plutocratic Philanthropy."

37. See Bruce Ackerman and Anne Alstott, *The Stakeholder Society* (New Haven, CT: Yale University Press, 2000) and Ackerman and Ayres, *Voting with Dollars*. For a similar proposal in the charitable sector, see Ryan Pevnick, "Democratizing the Nonprofit Sector," *Journal of Political Philosophy* 21 (2013): 260–282.

Chapter 4: Repugnant to the Whole Idea of a Democratic Society?

1. This chapter draws on my "What Are Foundations For?," *Boston Review* 38 (2013): 10–15 and "Repugnant to the Whole Idea of Democracy: On the Role of Foundations in Democratic Societies," *PS: Political Science and Politics* 49 (2016): 466–471. The epigraph is from Richard Posner, "Charitable Foundations," *Becker-Posner Blog*, January 1, 2007, http://www.becker-posner-blog.com/2007/01/chari table-foun.html.

2. U.S. Congress, Commission on Industrial Relations, "Report of the Commission on Industrial Relations," 7916–7917. Walsh, "Perilous Philanthropy," 262–264.

3. U.S. Congress, Commission on Industrial Relations, "Report of the Commission on Industrial Relations," 7663–7664.

4. Abrahamson, Hurst, and Shubinski, *Democracy and Philanthropy*, 35; and Hall, "Philanthropy."

5. Abrahamson, Hurst, and Shubinski, *Democracy and Philanthropy*, 40–41.

6. Ibid., 44.

7. The resolution was rescinded in 1929. See Keppel, *The Foundation*, 25. Today, the University of Wisconsin is working to raise as much philanthropic money as possible and, like virtually every major public university, maintains its own private, nonprofit corporation, established in 1945, to encourage individuals and philanthropic foundations to make gifts and grants to the university.

8. See Keppel, *The Foundation*, for the 1930 figure; other figures are from my calculations of IRS data.

9. Waldemar A. Nielsen, *The Big Foundations* (New York: Columbia University Press, 1972), 3.

10. See Ray Madoff, "When Is Philanthropy? How the Tax Code's Answer to This Question Has Given Rise to the Growth of Donor-Advised Funds and Why It's a Problem," in Reich, Cordelli, and Bernholz, *Philanthropy in Democratic Societies*, 158–177.

11. Harold J. Laski, "Foundations, Universities and Research," in *The Dangers of Obedience and Other Essays* (New York: Harper, 1930), 169–170. Or consider this

representative observation in the annual report of the William T. Grant Foundation. Its president, Robert Granger, writes, "Paul LeMahieu, senior vice president at the Carnegie Foundation for the Advancement of Teaching, once joked to me, 'Foundations don't have any natural predators.' He's right. Like most foundation presidents, I spent my career on the other side of my current desk, where many people were willing to tell me when my bad ideas were bad. But, when I joined the Foundation in 2000 as senior vice president for program, I seemed to get a bit smarter."

12. It's not just small family foundations that seek to avoid transparency. It was revealed in 2017 that James Simons, a billionaire hedge fund manager and long-standing donor to the Institute for Advanced Study in Princeton, New Jersey, had created the Simons Foundation International with an estimated $8 billion endowment. Incorporated in Bermuda, making its assets entirely tax-free, the foundation has, according to a 2017 profile of Simons in the *New Yorker*, no web page or public presence at all. D. T. Max, "Jim Simons, the Numbers King," *New Yorker*, December 18 and 25, 2017.

13. Protecting donor intent in perpetuity was not always given robust legal recognition. See Ray D. Madoff, *Immortality and the Law: The Rising Power of the American Dead* (New Haven, CT: Yale University Press, 2010), 91.

14. Posner, "Charitable Foundations."

15. Mark Dowie, *American Foundations: An Investigative History* (Cambridge, MA: MIT Press, 2001), 247.

16. I say "more or less" in each case because there are sometimes modest limits on tax-free donations to foundations and modest limits on tax-free investment returns on a foundation's endowment.

17. Tax subsidies for charitable giving cost the U.S. Treasury more than $50 billion in 2014.

18. See chapter 2; see also Reich, "Philanthropy and Caring."

19. See, for instance, Cordelli, "Reparative Justice."

20. See, for instance, Eric Beerbohm, "The Free Provider Problem: Private Provision of Public Responsibilities," in Reich, Cordelli, and Bernholz, *Philanthropy in Democratic Societies*.

21. Aaron Horvath and Walter Powell, "Contributory or Disruptive: Do New Forms of Philanthropy Erode Democracy?," in Reich, Cordelli, and Bernholz, *Philanthropy in Democratic Societies*; Saunders-Hastings, "Plutocratic Philanthropy," 149–161. See also Reckhow, *Follow the Money*; Tompkins-Stange, *Policy Patrons*.

22. A small library of books and reports have been written over the past decade about "strategic giving" and outcome-oriented, results-driven philanthropy. For two prominent examples, see Paul Brest and Hal Harvey, *Money Well Spent: A Strategic Plan for Smart Philanthropy* (New York: Bloomberg Press, 2008); Peter Frumkin, *Strategic Giving: The Art and Science of Philanthropy* (Chicago: University of Chicago Press, 2006).

23. *Bob Jones University v. United States*, 461 U.S. 574 (1983). A version of the argument can also be seen in remarks made by an early president of the Carnegie Corporation, Frederick Keppel, who wrote in 1930, "Clearly, there is the greatest variety

alike in the size, the purpose, the organization, the program, and the geographical range of American foundations; we are far from agreement as to the most useful form or organization or as to the most fruitful type of program. But all this is, of course, as it should be, since the ultimate basis of the utility of the foundation as an instrument of progress will probably rest upon this very diversity" (Keppel, *The Foundation*, 12).

24. Donor-advised funds have experienced a boom over the past decade. They are sometimes called private foundations for regular people. Their rising popularity should worry observers of philanthropy in the United States. See Madoff, *Immortality and the Law* for arguments against donor-advised funds.

25. See Benjamin I. Page, Larry M. Bartels, and Jason Seawright, "Democracy and the Policy Preferences of Wealthy Americans," *Perspectives on Politics* 11 (2013): 51–73; Martin Gilens, *Affluence and Influence: Economic Inequality and Political Power in America* (Princeton, NJ: Princeton University Press, 2012).

26. To the best of my knowledge, the first use of the phrase "foundations are society's risk capital" is in Arnold J. Zurcher's "Foundations: How They Operate as Society's Risk Capital," *Challenge* 4 (1955): 16–19.

27. The Brandeis phrase is found in his opinion in *New State Ice Co. v. Liebmann*, 285 U.S. 262 (1932). See also Christopher Ansell, *Pragmatist Democracy: Evolutionary Learning as Public Philosophy* (Oxford: Oxford University Press, 2011); Joshua Cohen and Charles Sabel, "Directly Deliberative Polyarchy," in Joshua Cohen, *Philosophy, Politics, Democracy* (Cambridge, MA: Harvard University Press, 2009), 181–222; Charles Sabel, "Dewey, Democracy, and Democratic Experimentalism," *Contemporary Pragmatism* 9, no. 2 (2012): 35–55; and Michael Dorf and Charles Sabel, "A Constitution of Democratic Experimentalism," *Columbia Law Review* 98 (1998): 267–473. We also see a version of a problem-solving approach to democracy in Josiah Ober's interpretation of classical Athens, *Democracy and Knowledge: Innovation and Learning in Classical Athens* (Princeton, NJ: Princeton University Press, 2008).

28. Dennis F. Thompson, "Representing Future Generations: Political Presentism and Democratic Trusteeship," *Critical Review of International Social and Political Philosophy* 13 (2010): 17–37. See also the excellent set of essays in Iñigo González-Ricoy and Axel Gosseries, eds., *Institutions for Future Generations* (Oxford: Oxford University Press, 2017).

29. Beerbohm, "Free Provider Problem."

30. Thomas Jefferson to Thomas Earle, September 24, 1823. In a separate letter to James Madison, Jefferson was equally emphatic. It is self-evident, Jefferson wrote, "'that the earth belongs in usufruct to the living'; that the dead have neither powers nor rights over it" and that "one generation is to another as one independent nation to another." Thomas Jefferson, "Letter to James Madison," September 6, 1789, in *The Papers of Thomas Jefferson, Federal Edition*, vol. 15 (Princeton, NJ: Princeton University Press, 1958), 384–391.

31. Foundation leaders and observers have long invoked experimentalism as one of their chief responsibilities, even if the record of living up to this responsibility is spotty. Consider David Owen's discussion of private foundations in Britain.

"Foundation executives think of their greatest single function as that of operating a 'first-run experiment station'" (Owen, *English Philanthropy, 1660–1960* [Cambridge, MA: Harvard University Press, 1964], 557).

32. Edwin R. Embree, "Timid Billions: Are the Foundations Doing Their Job?," *Harper's Magazine* 198 (1949): 28–37.

33. Gara LaMarche, "Democracy and the Donor Class," *Democracy* 34 (2014): 55.

34. William Foster, Gail Perreault, Alison Powell, and Chris Addy, "Making Big Bets for Social Change," *Stanford Social Innovation Review*, Winter 2016, 26–35.

Chapter 5: Philanthropy in Time

1. This chapter is the product of joint work with Chiara Cordelli. An earlier version of the chapter appears as "Philanthropy and Intergenerational Justice," in González-Ricoy and Gosseries, *Institutions for Future Generations*. I have made some unilateral revisions, but I retain the collective "we" rather than the singular "I" to mark the collaborative nature of the work. Where the text and argument depart from what appears in *Institutions for Future Generations*, I alone bear responsibility for errors or mistakes.

2. This argument is based on the view that Rawls's difference principle applies intergenerationally. See Frédéric Gaspart and Axel Gosseries, "Are Generational Savings Unjust?," *Politics, Philosophy & Economics* 6 (2007): 193–217, 204.

3. Beckert, *Inherited Wealth*.

4. For an overview of U.S. policies, see Madoff, *Immortality and the Law*; Reich, "What Are Foundations For?"

5. Foundation Center, "Key Facts."

6. On debates about spending down or "sun-setting" philanthropic endowments, see Michael Klausner, "When Time Isn't Money: Foundation Payouts and the Time Value of Money," *Stanford Social Innovation Review* 1 (2003): 51–59.

7. Jens Beckert, "Why Is the Estate Tax So Controversial?," *Society* 45 (2008): 521–528.

8. As in previous chapters, the terms "charitable" and "philanthropic" are used interchangeably here to indicate private transfers of money whose ultimate goal is to support some kind of public benefit.

9. See Thompson, "Representing Future Generations."

10. See John Rawls, *The Law of Peoples* (Cambridge, MA: Harvard University Press, 1999), 106–107.

11. See John Rawls, *A Theory of Justice* (Cambridge, MA: Harvard University Press, 1971), 252–256, 288–292; John Rawls, *Political Liberalism* (New York: Columbia University Press, 2005), 274; Rawls, *Law of Peoples*, 170.

12. Rawls, *Law of Peoples*, 107.

13. Ibid., 107.

14. Ibid., 107.

15. Ibid., 108.

16. Ibid., 107.

17. Rawls, *Theory of Justice*, 258.

18. See Gaspart and Gosseries, "Are Generational Savings Unjust?," 196–200.

19. Obviously Tocqueville did not use the term "social capital." See Tocqueville, *Democracy in America*. For a contemporary moral theory of social capital, see Stephen Macedo, "The Constitution, Civic Virtue, and Civil Society: Social Capital as Substantive Morality," *Fordham Law Review* 69 (2001): 1573–1593. For a sociological account, see Robert Putnam, Robert Leonardi, and Raffaella Y. Nanetti, *Making Democracy Work: Civic Traditions in Modern Italy* (Princeton, NJ: Princeton University Press, 1993); Putnam, *Bowling Alone*; Alejandro Portes, "Social Capital: Its Origins and Applications in Modern Sociology," *Annual Review of Sociology* 24 (1998): 1–24. For an overview of contemporary debates on social capital within different disciplines, see Dario Castiglione, Jan W. Van Deth, and Guglielmo Wolleb, eds., *The Handbook of Social Capital* (Oxford: Oxford University Press, 2008).

20. Rawls, *Theory of Justice*, sec. 71. See also Chiara Cordelli, "Justice as Fairness and Relational Resources," *Journal of Political Philosophy* 23 (2015): 86–110.

21. Macedo, "Constitution, Civic Virtue, and Civil Society," 1593.

22. Elisabeth S. Clemens, "The Constitution of Citizens: Political Theories of Nonprofit Organizations," in Powell and Steinberg, *Nonprofit Sector*.

23. Tocqueville, *Democracy in America*.

24. Joshua Cohen and Joel Rogers, *Associations and Democracy* (London: Verso, 1993).

25. Rosenblum, *Membership and Morals*.

26. See Putnam, *Bowling Alone* and Skocpol, *Diminished Democracy*.

27. Although principles of justice may not directly guide the action of individuals, they do apply to the tax code and constrain the justification of tax incentives.

28. For a reason why it should, see Gaspart and Gosseries, "Are Generational Savings Unjust?"

29. Even here, however, transfers to future generations, beyond the threshold required by just savings, could be arguably discouraged on grounds of special obligations toward existing fellow citizens. Whether such obligations can be justified is a complicated matter, which we do not resolve here.

30. The types of threats we have in mind are different from natural catastrophes due to anthropogenic climate change, which are both high-probability catastrophes and caused by past and present generations' emissions. In the case of climate change, we believe that coordinated state action at the international level is needed. Yet some aspects of work on climate change might plausibly be addressed by foundations: basic research into technological approaches for which there is no obvious market, efforts to shift public opinion, discovery of particular mechanisms to overcome collection action problems, and convening and funding NGOs working at the global level.

31. See Gaspart and Gosseries, "Are Generational Savings Unjust?," 196–200.

32. Thomas Scanlon, *What We Owe to Each Other* (Cambridge, MA: Harvard University Press, 1998), 208, italics added.

33. Scanlon, *What We Owe to Each Other*, 209.

34. Scanlon, *What We Owe to Each Other*, 209.

35. See Nick Bostrom, "Existential Risk Prevention as Global Priority," *Global Policy* 4 (2013): 15–31. Bostrom mentions other potential existential risks, including asteroid strikes, supervolcanoes, and earthquakes.

36. Thompson, "Representing Future Generations."

37. Posner, "Charitable Foundations."

Conclusion

1. For a discussion of charity through a lens of freedom as nondomination, see Philip Pettit, *Just Freedom* (New York: Norton, 2014) and Robert S. Taylor, "Donation without Domination: Private Charity and Republican Liberty," *Journal of Political Philosophy* (forthcoming).

2. For the two most important books on effective altruism, see Singer, *Most Good You Can Do*, and MacAskill, *Doing Good Better*.

3. For an overview of donor-advised funds, see Madoff, "When Is Philanthropy?"; for an overview of giving patterns in 2017, see Giving USA Foundation, "Giving USA 2017."

4. For an overview of LLCs, see Dana Brakman Reiser, "Is the Chan Zuckerberg Initiative the Future of Philanthropy?," *Stanford Social Innovation Review*, Summer 2018.

5. See Jane Mayer, *Dark Money: The Hidden History of the Billionaires behind the Rise of the Radical Right* (New York: Anchor Books, 2017).

BIBLIOGRAPHY

Abrahamson, Eric John. *Beyond Charity: A Century of Philanthropic Innovation*. New York: Rockefeller Foundation, 2013.

Abrahamson, Eric John, Sam Hurst, and Barbara Shubinski. *Democracy and Philanthropy: The Rockefeller Foundation and the American Experiment*. New York: Rockefeller Foundation, 2013.

Ackerman, Bruce, and Anne Alstott. *The Stakeholder Society*. New Haven, CT: Yale University Press, 2000.

Ackerman, Bruce, and Ian Ayres. *Voting with Dollars*. New Haven, CT: Yale University Press, 2002.

Andreoni, James. "Impure Altruism and Donations to Public Goods: A Theory of Warm-Glow Giving." *Economic Journal* 100 (1990): 464–477.

Andrews, William D. "Personal Deductions in an Ideal Income Tax." *Harvard Law Review* 86 (1972): 309–385.

Ansell, Christopher. *Pragmatist Democracy: Evolutionary Learning as Public Philosophy*. Oxford: Oxford University Press, 2011.

Aristotle. *Nicomachean Ethics*. In *The Basic Works of Aristotle*, edited by Richard McKeon, 935–1126. New York: Random House, 1941.

Auten, Gerald E., Holger Sieg, and Charles T. Clotfelter. "Charitable Giving, Income, and Taxes: An Analysis of Panel Data." *American Economic Review* 92 (2002): 371–382.

Baker, Keith. *Condorcet: From Natural Philosophy to Social Mathematics*. Chicago: University of Chicago Press, 1975.

Bakija, Jon, and Bradley Heim. "How Does Charitable Giving Respond to Incentives and Income?" National Bureau of Economic Research working paper, 2008.

Beckert, Jens. *Inherited Wealth*. Princeton, NJ: Princeton University Press, 2004.

———. "Why Is the Estate Tax So Controversial?" *Society* 45 (2008): 521–528.

Berlin, Isaiah. "The Pursuit of the Ideal." In *The Crooked Timber of Humanity: Chapters in the History of Ideas*, 1–16. Princeton, NJ: Princeton University Press, 2015.

Bittker, Boris I. "Charitable Contributions: Tax Deductions or Matching Grants?" *Tax Law Review* 28 (1972): 37–63.

Bob Jones University v. United States, 461 U.S. 574 (1983).

Bostrom, Nick. "Existential Risk Prevention as Global Priority." *Global Policy* 4 (2013): 15–31.

Brest, Paul, and Hal Harvey. *Money Well Spent: A Strategic Plan for Smart Philanthropy.* New York: Bloomberg, 2009.

Brighouse, Harry, and Adam Swift. *Family Values: The Ethics of Parent-Child Relationships.* Princeton, NJ: Princeton University Press, 2014.

Brody, Evelyn. "Charities in Tax Reform: Threats to Subsidies Overt and Covert." *Tennessee Law Review* 66 (1998): 687–763.

Brown, Catherine, Scott Sargrad, and Meg Benner. "Hidden Money: The Outsized Role of Parent Contributions in School Finance." Center for American Progress, April 2017. https://perma.cc/BUB6-UF4L.

Brunner, Eric, and Jon Sonstelie. "School Finance Reform and Voluntary Fiscal Federalism." *Journal of Public Economics* 87 (2003): 2157–2185.

Castiglione, Dario, Jan W. Van Deth, and Guglielmo Wolleb, eds. *The Handbook of Social Capital.* Oxford: Oxford University Press, 2008.

Center on Philanthropy at Indiana University. "Patterns of Household Charitable Giving by Income Group 2005." 2007. www.philanthropy.iupui.edu/files/research/giving_focused_on_meeting_needs_of_the_poor_july_2007.pdf.

Chambers, Simone, and Will Kymlicka, eds. *Alternative Conceptions of Civil Society.* Princeton, NJ: Princeton University Press, 2002.

Charities Aid Foundation. "World Giving Index 2014." https://www.cafonline.org/pdf/CAF_WGI2014_Report_1555AWEBFinal.pdf.

Chernow, Ron. *Titan: The Life of John D. Rockefeller, Sr.* New York: Vintage, 2007.

Christ, Matthew R. *The Bad Citizen in Classical Athens.* Cambridge: Cambridge University Press, 2006.

———. "Liturgy Avoidance and Antidosis in Classical Athens." *Transactions of the American Philological Association* 120 (1990): 147–169.

Ciepley, David. "Beyond Public and Private: Toward a Political Theory of the Corporation." *American Political Science Review* 107 (2013): 139–158.

Clarke, Jack A. "Turgot's Critique of Perpetual Endowments." *French Historical Studies* 3 (1964): 495–506.

Clemens, Elisabeth S. "The Constitution of Citizens: Political Theories of Nonprofit Organizations." In Powell and Steinberg, *Nonprofit Sector*, 207–220.

Clotfelter, Charles T. "Tax-Induced Distortions in the Voluntary Sector." *Case Western Reserve Law Review* 39 (1988): 663–694.

———, ed. *Who Benefits from the Nonprofit Sector?* Chicago: University of Chicago Press, 1992.

Cohen, Joshua, and Joel Rogers. *Associations and Democracy.* London: Verso, 1993.

Cohen, Joshua, and Charles Sabel. "Directly Deliberative Polyarchy." In Joshua Cohen, *Philosophy, Politics, Democracy*, 181–222. Cambridge, MA: Harvard University Press, 2009.

Colinvaux, Roger. "The Importance of a Participatory Charitable Giving Incentive." *Tax Notes* 154 (2017): 605–614.

Colinvaux, Roger, Brian Galle, and Eugene Steuerle. "Evaluating the Charitable Deduction and Proposed Reforms." Urban Institute, June 2012.

Congressional Budget Office. "The Distribution of Major Tax Expenditures in the Individual Income Tax System." No. 43768, 2013. https://EconPapers.repec.org /RePEc:cbo:report:437680.

Cordelli, Chiara. "Justice as Fairness and Relational Resources." *Journal of Political Philosophy* 23 (2015): 86–110.

Dorf, Michael, and Charles Sabel. "A Constitution of Democratic Experimentalism." *Columbia Law Review* 98 (1998): 267–473.

Dowie, Mark. *American Foundations: An Investigative History*. Cambridge, MA: MIT Press, 2001.

Embree, Edwin R. "Timid Billions: Are the Foundations Doing Their Job?" *Harper's Magazine* 198 (1949): 28–37.

Fack, Gabrielle, and Camille Landais. "Philanthropy, Tax Policy, and Tax Cheating: A Long-Run Perspective on US Data." In *Charitable Giving and Tax Policy: A Historical and Comparative Perspective*, edited by Gabrielle Fack and Camille Landais, 61–114. Oxford: Oxford University Press, 2016.

Faulhaber, Lilian V. "Charitable Giving, Tax Expenditures, and Direct Spending in the United States and the European Union." *Yale Journal International Law* 39 (2014): 87–129.

Fisher, Donald. "The Role of Philanthropic Foundations in the Reproduction and Production of Hegemony: Rockefeller Foundations and the Social Sciences." *Sociology* 17 (1983): 206–233.

Fleischacker, Samuel. *A Short History of Distributive Justice*. Cambridge, MA: Harvard University Press, 2005.

Fleischer, Miranda Perry. "Equality of Opportunity and the Charitable Tax Subsidies." *Boston University Law Review* 91 (2011): 601–663.

Fleishman, Joel. *The Foundation: A Great American Secret*. New York: Public Affairs, 2007.

Foley, John P., ed. *The Jefferson Cyclopedia*. New York: Funk and Wag nalls, 1900.

Foster, William, Gail Perreault, Alison Powell, and Chris Addy, "Making Big Bets for Social Change," *Stanford Social Innovation Review*, Winter 2016, 26–35.

Foundation Center. "Key Facts on U.S. Foundations." 2014. http://foundationcenter .org/gainknowledge/research/nationaltrends.html.

Frumkin, Peter. *Strategic Giving: The Art and Science of Philanthropy*. Chicago: University of Chicago Press, 2008.

Gabrielsen, Vincent. *Financing the Athenian Fleet: Public Taxation and Social Relations*. Baltimore: Johns Hopkins University Press, 1994.

Galston, William A. "Realism in Political Theory." *European Journal of Political Theory* 9 (2010): 385–411.

Gaspart, Frédéric, and Axel Gosseries. "Are Generational Savings Unjust?" *Politics, Philosophy & Economics* 6 (2007): 193–217.

Gates, Frederick Taylor, and Robert Swain Morison. *Chapters in My Life*. New York: Free Press, 1977.

Gergen, Mark P. "The Case for a Charitable Contributions Deduction." *Virginia Law Review* 74 (1988): 1393–1450.

Gil, Moshe. "The Earliest Waqf Foundations." *Journal of Near Eastern Studies* 57 (1998): 125–140.

Gilens, Martin. *Affluence and Influence: Economic Inequality and Political Power in America.* Princeton, NJ: Princeton University Press, 2012.

Giving USA Foundation. "Giving USA 2017: The Annual Report on Philanthropy for the Year 2016." Chicago: Giving USA Foundation, 2017.

Glazer, Amihai, and Kai A. Konrad. "A Signaling Explanation for Charity." *American Economic Review* 86 (1996): 1019–1028.

González-Ricoy, Iñigo, and Axel Gosseries, eds. *Institutions for Future Generations.* Oxford: Oxford University Press, 2017.

Grant, Ruth W. *Strings Attached: Untangling the Ethics of Incentives.* Princeton, NJ: Princeton University Press, 2011.

Groenewegen, Peter. *Eighteenth-Century Economics: Turgot, Beccaria and Smith and Their Contemporaries.* London: Routledge, 2002.

Gygax, Marc Domingo. *Benefaction and Rewards in the Ancient Greek City: The Origins of Euergetism.* Cambridge: Cambridge University Press, 2016.

———. "Gift-Giving and Power Relationships in Greek Social Praxis and Public Discourse." In *The Gift in Antiquity,* edited by Michael Satlow, 45–60. Hoboken, NJ: John Wiley, 2013.

Hall, Peter Dobkin. "Philanthropy, the Nonprofit Sector & the Democratic Dilemma." *Daedalus* 142 (2013): 139–158.

Harbaugh, William T. "The Prestige Motive for Making Charitable Transfers." *American Economic Review* 88 (1998): 277–282.

———. "What Do Donations Buy? A Model of Philanthropy Based on Prestige and Warm Glow." *Journal of Public Economics* 67 (1998): 269–284.

Havens, John J., Mary A. O'Herlihy, and Paul G. Schervish. "Charitable Giving: How Much, by Whom, to What, and How?" In Powell and Steinberg, *Nonprofit Sector,* 542–567.

Hodgson, Marshall G. S. *The Venture of Islam.* 3 vols. Chicago: University of Chicago Press, 1974.

Horowitz, Steven J., and Robert H. Sitkoff. "Unconstitutional Perpetual Trusts." *Vanderbilt Law Review* 67 (2014): 1769–1822.

Howard, Christopher. *The Hidden Welfare State: Tax Expenditures and Social Policy in the United States.* Princeton, NJ: Princeton University Press, 1999.

Independent Sector. *The New Nonprofit Almanac and Desk Reference.* San Francisco: Jossey-Bass, 2002.

James, Russell N., and Deanna L. Sharpe. "The Nature and Causes of the U-Shaped Charitable Giving Profile." *Nonprofit and Voluntary Sector Quarterly* 36 (2007): 218–238.

Jefferson, Thomas. *The Papers of Thomas Jefferson, Federal Edition.* Vol. 15. Princeton, NJ: Princeton University Press, 1958.

Kaiser, Brooks A. "The Athenian Trierarchy: Mechanism Design for the Private Provision of Public Goods." *Journal of Economic History* 67 (2007): 445–480.

Kant, Immanuel. "The Metaphysics of Morals." In *Practical Philosophy: The Cambridge Edition of the Works of Immanuel Kant*, edited by Allen Wood, translated by Mary Gregor, 353–604. Cambridge: Cambridge University Press, 1996.

Karl, Barry D., and Stanley N. Katz. "Foundations and Ruling Class Elites." *Daedalus* 116 (1987): 1–40.

Keppel, Frederick P. *The Foundation: Its Place in American Life*. London: Macmillan, 1930.

Klausner, Michael. "When Time Isn't Money: Foundation Payouts and the Time Value of Money." *Stanford Social Innovation Review* 1 (2003): 51–59.

Kozol, Jonathan. *Savage Inequalities: Children in America's Schools*. New York: Broadway Books, 2012.

Kuran, Timur. "Institutional Roots of Authoritarian Rule in the Middle East: Civic Legacies of the Islamic Waqf." Economic Research Initiatives at Duke Working Paper 171, 2014.

———. "The Political Consequences of Islam's Economic Legacy." *Philosophy and Social Criticism* 39 (2013): 395–405.

———. "The Provision of Public Goods under Islamic Law: Origins, Impact, and Limitations of the Waqf System." *Law and Society Review* 35 (2001): 841–898.

Kymlicka, Will. "Altruism in Philosophical and Ethical Traditions: Two Views." In *Between State and Market: Essays on Charity Law and Policy in Canada*, edited by Jim Phillips, Bruce Chapman, and David Stevens, 87–126. Toronto: McGill-Queen's University Press, 2001.

Lamarche, Gara. "Democracy and the Donor Class." *Democracy* 34 (2014): 48–59.

Laski, Harold J. "Foundations, Universities and Research." In *The Dangers of Obedience and Other Essays*, 153–171. New York: Harper, 1930.

Lev, Yaacov. *Charity, Endowments, and Charitable Institutions in Medieval Islam*, Gainesville: University Press of Florida, 2005.

Levmore, Saul. "Taxes as Ballots." *University of Chicago Law Review* 65 (1998): 387–431.

Levy, Jacob T. "There's No Such Thing as Ideal Theory." *Social Philosophy and Policy* 33, nos. 1–2 (2016): 312–333.

Levy, Jonathan. "From Fiscal Triangle to Passing Through: Rise of the Nonprofit Corporation." In *Corporations and American Democracy*, edited by Naomi Lamoreaux and William Novak, 213–244. Cambridge: Cambridge University Press, 2017.

Ma, John. *Statues and Cities: Honorific Portraits and Civic Identity in the Hellenistic World*. Oxford: Oxford University Press, 2013.

MacAskill, William. *Doing Good Better*. New York: Gotham Books, 2015.

Macedo, Stephen. "The Constitution, Civic Virtue, and Civil Society: Social Capital as Substantive Morality." *Fordham Law Review* 69 (2001): 1573–1593.

MacFarquhar, Larissa. "What Money Can Buy." *New Yorker*, January 6, 2016.

Machiavelli, Niccolo. *Discourses on Livy*. Translated by Harvey C. Mansfield and Nathan Tarcov. Chicago: University of Chicago Press, 1996.

Madoff, Ray D. *Immortality and the Law: The Rising Power of the American Dead*. New Haven, CT: Yale University Press, 2010.

———. "When Is Philanthropy? How the Tax Code's Answer to This Question Has Given Rise to the Growth of Donor-Advised Funds and Why It's a Problem." In Reich, Cordelli, and Bernholz, *Philanthropy in Democratic Societies*, 158–177.

Manuel, Frank Edward. *The Prophets of Paris*. Cambridge, MA: Harvard University Press, 1962.

Mauss, Marcel. *The Gift: Forms and Functions of Exchange in Archaic Societies*. Translated by Wilfred Douglas Halls. London: Routledge, 1990.

Max, D. T. "Jim Simons, the Numbers King." *New Yorker*, December 18 and 25, 2017.

Mayer, Jane. *Dark Money: The Hidden History of the Billionaires behind the Rise of the Radical Right*. New York: Anchor Books, 2017.

Mettler, Suzanne. *The Submerged State: How Invisible Government Policies Undermine American Democracy*. Chicago: University of Chicago Press, 2011.

Mill, John Stuart. *Autobiography*. London: Longmans, Green, Reader, and Dyer, 1873.

———. *Collected Works of John Stuart Mill*. Vol. 4. Edited by J. M. Robson. Toronto: University of Toronto Press, 1963–1991. http://oll.libertyfund.org/titles/165.

———. "Educational Endowments." In "Report of Commissioners on Education in Schools in England, Not Comprised within Her Majesty's Two Recent Commissions on Popular Education and Public Schools." *Parliamentary Papers* 28, pt. 2 (1867–1868): 67–72

———. "Endowments." *Fortnightly Review*, April 1869, 377–390.

Miller, David. *Justice for Earthlings*. Cambridge: Cambridge University Press, 2013.

Montesquieu, Baron de. *The Complete Works of M. de Montesquieu*. Vol. 2. London: T. Evans, 1777. http://oll.libertyfund.org/titles/838#Montesquieu_0171-02_632.

Morris, Ian. "Gift and Commodity in Archaic Greece." *Man* 21 (1986): 1–17.

———. *Why the West Rules—for Now: The Patterns of History and What They Reveal about the Future*. London: Profile Books, 2010.

Muniz-Fraticelli, Victor M. *The Structure of Pluralism: On the Authority of Associations*. Oxford: Oxford University Press, 2014.

Murphy, Liam, and Thomas Nagel. *The Myth of Ownership: Taxes and Justice*. Oxford: Oxford University Press, 2002.

Musgrave, Richard A., and Peggy B. Musgrave. *Public Finance in Theory and Practice*. 4th ed. New York: McGraw-Hill, 1984.

New State Ice Co. v. Liebmann, 285 U.S. 262 (1932).

Nielsen, Waldemar A. *The Big Foundations*. New York: Columbia University Press, 1972.

Nozick, Robert. *Anarchy, State, and Utopia*. New York: Basic Books, 1974.

Ober, Josiah. *Democracy and Knowledge: Innovation and Learning in Classical Athens*. Princeton, NJ: Princeton University Press, 2008.

———. *Mass and Elite in Democratic Athens: Rhetoric, Ideology, and the Power of the People*. Princeton, NJ: Princeton University Press, 1991.

Owen, David Edward. *English Philanthropy, 1660–1960*. Cambridge, MA: Harvard University Press, 1964.

Page, Benjamin I., Larry M. Bartels, and Jason Seawright. "Democracy and the Policy Preferences of Wealthy Americans." *Perspectives on Politics* 11 (2013): 51–73.

Perry, Suzanne. "The Stubborn 2% Giving Rate." *Chronicle of Philanthropy*, July 17, 2013.

Pettit, Philip. *Just Freedom*. New York: Norton, 2014.

Pevnick, Ryan. "Democratizing the Nonprofit Sector." *Journal of Political Philosophy* 21 (2013): 260–282.

Portes, Alejandro. "Social Capital: Its Origins and Applications in Modern Sociology." *Annual Review of Sociology* 24 (1998): 1–24.

Posner, Eric A., and E. Glen Weyl. *Radical Markets: Uprooting Capitalism and Democracy for a Just Society*. Princeton, NJ: Princeton University Press, 2018.

Posner, Richard. "Charitable Foundations." *Becker-Posner Blog*, January 1, 2007. http://www.becker-posner-blog.com/2006/12/charitable-foundations-posners-comment.html.

Powell, Walter W., and Richard Steinberg, eds. *The Nonprofit Sector: A Research Handbook*. 2nd ed. New Haven, CT: Yale University Press, 2006.

Powers, David. "Orientalism, Colonialism, and Legal History: The Attack on Muslim Family Endowments in Algeria and India." *Comparative Studies in Society and History* 31 (1989): 535–571.

Pozen, David. "Remapping the Charitable Deduction." *Connecticut Law Review* 39 (2006): 531–601.

Putnam, Robert D. *Bowling Alone: The Collapse and Revival of American Community*. New York: Simon & Schuster, 2000.

Putnam, Robert D., Robert Leonardi, and Raffaella Y. Nanetti. *Making Democracy Work: Civic Traditions in Modern Italy*. Princeton, NJ: Princeton University Press, 1994.

Ravitch, Diane. *The Death and Life of the Great American School System*. New York: Basic Books, 2010.

Rawls, John. *The Law of Peoples*. Cambridge, MA: Harvard University Press, 1999.

———. *Political Liberalism*. New York: Columbia University Press, 2005.

———. *A Theory of Justice*. Cambridge, MA: Harvard University Press, 1971.

Reckhow, Sarah. *Follow the Money: How Foundation Dollars Change Public School Politics*. Oxford: Oxford University Press, 2012.

Reich, Rob. "Gift Giving and Philanthropy in Market Democracy." *Critical Review* 26 (2014): 408–422.

———. "Not Very Giving." *New York Times*, September 4, 2013.

———. "Philanthropy and Caring for the Needs of Strangers." *Social Research* 80 (2013): 517–538.

———. "Philanthropy and Its Uneasy Relation to Equality." In *Taking Philanthropy Seriously: Beyond Noble Intentions to Responsible Giving*, edited by William Damon and Susan Verducci, 27–49. Bloomington: Indiana University Press, 2006.

———. "Repugnant to the Whole Idea of Democracy: On the Role of Foundations in Democratic Societies." *PS: Political Science and Politics* 49 (2016): 466–471.

———. "Strings Attached: Untangling the Ethics of Incentives. By Grant Ruth W. Princeton: Princeton University Press, 2011." *Perspectives on Politics* 12 (2014): 223–225.

———. "Toward a Political Theory of Philanthropy." In *Giving Well: The Ethics of Philanthropy*, edited by Patricia Illingworth, Thomas Pogge, and Leif Wenar, 177–195. Oxford: Oxford University Press, 2011.

———. "What Are Foundations For?" *Boston Review* 38 (2013): 10–15.

Reich, Rob, Chiara Cordelli, and Lucy Bernholz, eds. *Philanthropy in Democratic Societies: History, Institutions, Values.* Chicago: University of Chicago Press, 2016.

Reich, Rob, Lacey Dorn, and Stefanie Sutton. "Anything Goes: Approval of Nonprofit Status by the IRS." Stanford, CA: Stanford University Center on Philanthropy and Civil Society, 2009.

Reich, Rob, Christopher Wimer, Shazad Mohamed, and Sharada Jambulapati. "Has the Great Recession Made Americans Stingier?" in *The Great Recession,* edited by David B. Grusky, Bruce Western, and Christopher Wimer, 294–313. New York: Russell Sage Foundation, 2011.

Reiser, Dana Brakman. "Is the Chan Zuckerberg Initiative the Future of Philanthropy?" *Stanford Social Innovation Review,* Summer 2018.

Rhees, William, ed. *The Smithsonian Institution: Documents Relative to Its Origin and History.* Washington, DC: Smithsonian Institution, 1879.

Robbins, Kevin C. "The Nonprofit Sector in Historical Perspective: Traditions of Philanthropy in the West." In Powell and Steinberg, *Nonprofit Sector,* 13.

Rosenblum, Nancy L. *Membership and Morals: The Personal Uses of Pluralism in America.* Princeton, NJ: Princeton University Press, 1998.

Rosenblum, Nancy L., and Robert Post, eds. *Civil Society and Government.* Princeton, NJ: Princeton University Press, 2002.

Rudman, Harry. "Mill on Perpetual Endowments." *History of Ideas Newsletter* 3 (1957): 70–72.

Sabel, Charles. "Dewey, Democracy, and Democratic Experimentalism." *Contemporary Pragmatism* 9, no. 2 (2012): 35–55.

Salamon, Lester M., and Stefan Toepler. *The International Guide to Nonprofit Law.* New York: John Wiley, 1997.

Saunders-Hastings, Emma. "Plutocratic Philanthropy." *Journal of Politics* 80, no. 1 (2018): 149–161.

Scanlon, Thomas. *What We Owe to Each Other.* Cambridge, MA: Harvard University Press,1998.

Schneewind, Jerome B., ed. *Giving: Western Ideas of Philanthropy.* Bloomington: Indiana University Press, 1996.

Sears, Jesse Brundage. "Philanthropy in the History of American Higher Education." U.S. Department of the Interior, Bureau of Education, Bulletin 26, 1922.

Sen, Amartya. *The Idea of Justice.* Cambridge, MA: Harvard University Press, 2009.

Silber, Norman I. *A Corporate Form of Freedom: The Emergence of the Nonprofit Sector.* Boulder, CO: Westview, 2001.

Simmons, A. John. "Ideal and Nonideal Theory." *Philosophy & Public Affairs* 38, no. 1 (2010): 5–36.

Simon, John, Harvey Dale, and Laura Chisolm. "The Federal Tax Treatment of Charitable Organizations." In Powell and Steinberg, *Nonprofit Sector*, 267–306. New Haven, CT: Yale University Press, 2006.

Singer, Amy. *Charity in Islamic Societies.* Cambridge: Cambridge University Press, 2008.

———. "The Persistence of Philanthropy." *Comparative Studies of South Asia, Africa and the Middle East* 31 (2011): 557–568.

———. "Soup and Sadaqa: Charity in Islamic Societies." *Historical Research* 79 (2006): 306–324.

Singer, Peter. "Famine, Affluence, and Morality." *Philosophy and Public Affairs* 1 (1972): 229–243.

———. *The Life You Can Save: How to Do Your Part to End World Poverty.* New York: Random House, 2010.

———. *The Most Good You Can Do: How Effective Altruism Is Changing Ideas about Living Ethically.* New Haven, CT: Yale University Press, 2015.

Skocpol, Theda. *Diminished Democracy: From Membership to Management in American Civic Life.* Norman: University of Oklahoma Press, 2003.

Skocpol, Theda, and Morris Fiorina, eds. *Civic Engagement in American Democracy.* Washington, DC: Brookings Institution Press, 1999.

Steinhauer, Jennifer. "A Billionaire Philanthropist in Washington Who's Big on Patriotic Giving." *New York Times*, February 20, 2014.

Stemplowska, Zofia. "What's Ideal about Ideal Theory?" *Social Theory and Practice* 34, no. 3 (2008): 319–340.

Stemplowska, Zofia, and Adam Swift. "Rawls on Ideal and Nonideal Theory." In *A Companion to Rawls*, edited by Jon Mandle and David A. Reidy, 112–127. Chichester, West Sussex: John Wiley, 2014.

Steuerle, C. Eugene, and A. M. Sullivan. "Toward More Simple and Effective Giving: Reforming the Tax Rules for Charitable Contributions and Charitable Organizations." *American Journal of Tax Policy* 12 (1995): 1–46.

Stith, Kate. "Congress' Power of the Purse." *Yale Law Journal* 97 (1988): 1343–1396.

Surrey, Stanley S., and Paul R. McDaniel. *Tax Expenditures.* Cambridge, MA: Harvard University Press, 1985.

Taylor, Robert S. "Donation without Domination: Private Charity and Republican Liberty." *Journal of Political Philosophy* (forthcoming).

Terpstra, Nicholas. "Charity, Civil Society, and Social Capital in Islamic and Christian Societies, 1200–1700: Models and Hypotheses for Comparative Research." In *Philanthropy and Civic Engagement in Arab Societies*, edited by B. Ibrahim et al., 184–195. Cairo: American University of Cairo, 2012.

Thompson, Dennis F. "Representing Future Generations: Political Presentism and Democratic Trusteeship." *Critical Review of International Social and Political Philosophy* 13 (2010): 17–37.

Thoreau, Henry David. "Walden." In *Political Writings*, edited by Nancy Rosenblum, 23–102. Cambridge: Cambridge University Press, 1996.

Tocqueville, Alexis de. *Democracy in America*. Translated by Henry Reeve and Francis Bowen. New York: Vintage, 1945.

———. *Memoir on Pauperism*. Translated by Seymour Drescher. London: Ivan R. Dee, 1997.

Tomasi, John. *Free Market Fairness*. Princeton, NJ: Princeton University Press, 2012.

Tompkins-Stange, Megan E. *Policy Patrons: Philanthropy, Education Reform, and the Politics of Influence*. Cambridge, MA: Harvard Education Press, 2016.

Turgot, Anne-Robert. "Fondation." In *The Turgot Collection*, edited by David Gordon, 461–469. Auburn, AL: Mises Institute, 2011.

U.S. Congress, Commission on Industrial Relations. "Report of the Commission on Industrial Relations: Final Report and Testimony." 1912.

Veyne, Paul. *Bread and Circuses: Historical Sociology and Political Pluralism*. London: Penguin, 1992.

Walsh, Frank. "Perilous Philanthropy." *Independent* 83 (1915): 262–264.

Warren, Mark. *Democracy and Association*. Princeton, NJ: Princeton University Press, 2001.

Weisbrod, Burton A. "The Pitfalls of Profits." *Stanford Social Innovation Review*, Winter 2004. https://ssir.org/articles/entry/the_pitfalls_of_profits.

Wilson, Peter. *The Athenian Institution of the Khoregia: The Chorus, the City and the Stage*. Cambridge: Cambridge University Press, 2003.

Wolpert, Julian. "Redistributional Effects of America's Private Foundations." In *The Legitimacy of Philanthropic Foundations: United States and European Perspectives*, edited by Kenneth Prewitt, Mattei Dogan, Steven Heydemann, and Stefan Toepler, 123–149. New York: Russell Sage Foundation, 2006.

Wuthnow, Robert. *Saving America? Faith-Based Services and the Future of Civil Society*. Princeton, NJ: Princeton University Press, 2004.

Yetman, Michelle H., and Robert J. Yetman. "How Does the Incentive Effect of the Charitable Deduction Vary across Charities?" *Accounting Review* 88 (2012): 1069–1094.

Zurcher, Arnold J. "Foundations: How They Operate as Society's Risk Capital." *Challenge* 4 (1955): 16–19.

INDEX

accountability: democratic, 120, 144, 162, 191; foundations' lack of, 144–46, 156, 161–62, 191; marketplace, 144, 162, 191

alms: mandatory in Islam, zakat as, 36–37; theory of, 25

altruism, 116, 126, 182, 198

Andrews, William, 115–17

antidosis procedure, 32–35

Aristotle, 11–12

Athens, classical, 29–35, 64, 108

Azim Premji Foundation, 9

basic needs of the poor as recipients of charitable giving: foundations and, 150; income of donors and, 125–26; in the U.S., 87–89, 92, 124–26. *See also* distribution of charitable gifts

Becker, Gary, 50, 206n36

Beerbohm, Eric, 164

Berlin, Isaiah, 70

Bittker, Boris, 115

Bloomberg, Michael, 152

Bob Jones University v. United States, 155, 216n33

Brandeis, Louis, 138, 142, 160

Brody, Evelyn, 215n23

Brunner, Eric, 211n39

Buffett, Warren, 9

Calhoun, James, 213n6

California: local education foundations in, 96–100

California Consortium of Education Foundations, 97

Carlos Slim Foundation, 9

Carnegie, Andrew, 9, 63, 136, 142, 149, 164

Carnegie Corporation of New York, 141

Catholic Church, 52–55

Chan, Priscilla, 199

Chan Zuckerberg Initiative, 199

charity: benefits to donors of, 116; distribution of (*see* distribution of charitable gifts); giving in the United States, 10, 72–74; incomes of donors, 78; justice and, distinction between, 25; philanthropy and, interchangeable usage of the words, 19–20; public charities, IRS approval of, 211n26, 215n25; subsidizing (*see* taxation); as voluntary assistance of those in need, 67. *See also* philanthropy

climate change, 221n30

Clotfelter, Charles T., 92

Condorcet, Marquis de (Marie Jean Antoine Nicolas de Caritat), 46–47

Constitution, U.S., Appropriations Clause, 109–10

corporations, 58–59

DAFs. *See* donor-advised funds

democracy: accountability in, 144; in ancient Athens, the liturgy and, 30–31; experimentation, need for and limited ability to achieve, 160–61; liberal (*see* liberal democracy); the pluralism rationale for donation incentives and, 128–33; presentism in, problem of, 161–62, 174, 190; and private foundations (*see* democracy and private foundations, relationship of); public goods in, provision

democracy (*continued*)
of, 154; structuring philanthropy to support, Mill on, 60–61, 63; the waqf system and, 44

democracy and private foundations, relationship of: the accountability issue, 144–46, 156, 161; arguments for a positive, 152–53, 168; the compatibility issue, 44–45, 60–61, 63–64, 136–38, 140, 143; discovery argument for a favorable, 152–53, 159–66, 174; donor-directed purpose in perpetuity, issue of, 147–48; foundations as institutional oddities and, 144; intergenerational justice and (*see* intergenerational justice); liberal democracies, role of foundations in, 136; pluralism argument for a favorable, 152–59; questions and arguments regarding, 150–52; tax subsidization of foundations, issue of, 148–50; the transparency issue, 147

dependence, philanthropy and development of, 197–98

Diderot, Denis, 47

dirty/blood money, problem of, 112

discovery/innovation: foundations and, 159–66, 174, 191–93

distribution of charitable gifts: basic needs (*see* basic needs of the poor as recipients of charitable giving); equality and, 82–89; by foundations, 90–92, 150; local private fund-raising to supplement funding of local public schools, 94–103; redistributive outcomes and, 85–92, 122–27

donor-advised funds (DAFs), 146, 198–99, 210n25, 219n24

donor direction, 7, 10, 42, 60, 136, 143, 147–48, 155, 189; as donor discretion, 197; as donor intent, 8, 22, 28, 38, 40, 42, 44, 47–52, 62, 107–8, 135–36, 147, 150, 155, 208n13; future generations and, 16, 147–48

Dowie, Mark, 148–49

education: inequality exacerbated in, 101–2; Laski on the deleterious effect of foundation grants to universities, 146; local private fund-raising to supplement funding of local public schools, 94–103; as recipient of charitable giving, 85, 87, 91

effective altruism, 12, 198, 201–2n12

"eleemosynary" aims, 68, 127, 209n6

Eliot, Charles, 5

Elizabethan Statute of Charitable Uses (1601), 27, 63, 68

Embree, Edwin, 167

Emerson Collective, 199

endowments: intergenerational requirements for, 183; perpetual (*see* perpetual endowments); time-delimited, Mill's case for, 55, 60–61, 63, 137

equality: distribution of charitable gifts and, 82–89; distribution of gifts from foundations and, 90–93; focus on, reasons for, 67; liberty and, 70, 100–101, 103–4; philanthropy and, 68–71; taxation and (*see* taxation). *See also* inequality

exempt organizations. *See* nonprofit organizations

Fack, Gabrielle, 215n24, 216n31

family foundations, 43

Fidelity Charitable Gift Fund, 199

Fleishman, Joel, 167

Ford, Henry, II, 206–7n36

Ford Foundation, 206–7n36

Foundation Center, 90

foundations: aggregate assets of, 9, 171; democracy and (*see* democracy and private foundations, relationship of); distributions from, equality and, 90–92, 150–51; as exercise of power and plutocratic voice, 143; family, 43; growth in number of, 9, 141–42; intergenerational justice and (*see* intergenerational justice); legitimacy of, 104, 150–52, 168; local education foundations (LEFs),

94–99; origin of general-purpose grant-making (private), 1–7, 136–40; payout rule, 84, 145–46, 171, 210n25; percentage of private giving from, 90; plutocratic bias of, 123–24, 132, 158; purposes of private, 140–43; small, disadvantages of, 157–58, 165; small, growth in number of, 156–57; suggestions for, 166; taxation of net investment income of private, 76; time horizons of, 164–66, 191–93; underperformance of, 167–68; the waqf as precursor to contemporary, 42–44, 140. *See also* endowments; nonprofit organizations

foundations, arguments against: eighteenth and nineteenth century concerns, 45–46, 52–54; Mill's, 54–62, 108, 135–36, 165; negative effects of foundations, 48; perpetual endowments, objections to, 49–52, 54–60, 62, 135; self-aggrandizement of donors, foundations as, 48–49; Turgot's, 46–55, 62, 108, 135

foundations, arguments for: discovery and innovation, as a source of, 159–66, 174; intergenerational justice, working towards (*see* intergenerational justice); Mill's time-delimited proposal, 55, 60–61, 63, 137; pluralism, as a source of, 152–59; the political theory of philanthropy and, 197

Future of Humanity Institute, 189

Gabrielsen, Vincent, 30, 33–34, 203–4n11, 203n5, 204n15
Gaspart, Frédéric, 170
Gates, Bill, 9, 143, 145, 152, 201n3
Gates, Frederick, 1–4
Gates, Melinda, 9
Gates Foundation, Bill and Melinda, 9, 92, 94, 120, 145
Gates Trust, 9
generosity: expectations about, 25
gift aid, 121
gift exchange, 24–25

gift giving, liturgies in ancient Athens as, 30
Giving: Western Ideas of Philanthropy (Schneewind), 35
Gompers, Samuel, 4
Good Ventures, 200
Gosseries, Axel, 170
Granger, Robert, 218n11
Grant, Ruth W., 212n2
Groenewegen, Peter, 206n30

health care: as recipient of charitable giving, 85, 87, 91, 211n29
history of philanthropy: absence of Islam from the standard, 35–36; foundations, lengthy history of, 140; foundations, public scorn for, 141; the liturgical system of ancient Athens, 29–35; origins, 27; tax incentives as contemporary anomaly, 107–10
Hodgson, Marshall, 38
Holmes, Rev. John Haynes, 4–5, 8, 138, 142
Howard, Christopher, 214n22

ideal theory, 65–66
inequality: exacerbated by charitable giving, 101–2; the input/supply side of philanthropy and, 69, 78–81; local private fund-raising for public schools as a contributor to, 94–103; the output/demand side of philanthropy and, 69, 82–89; philanthropy and, 9, 69; taxation and, 80–81 (*see also* taxation); worsened by public policies, 93–103. *See also* equality
institutional forms of/design of philanthropy: the Athenian liturgical system and antidosis procedure, 33–34 (*see also* liturgical system); foundations (*see* democracy and private foundations, relationship of; foundations); liberal democratic justice and, 104–5; the state and, 25–27, 63 (*see also* state, the); time

institutional forms of/design of philanthropy (*continued*)

horizons and, 164–66, 191–93 (*see also* intergenerational justice); the waqf, 36, 39–40 (*see also* waqf, the)

intergenerational assistance, principle of, 177

intergenerational justice: charitable transfers of wealth and, issues of, 170–75, 193–94; the difference principle and, 183–84; the discovery argument, 190–93; global perspective on, 189–90; limits of democracies regarding, 190–91; the precaution against remote risks argument, 184–90; probabilities and magnitudes in assessing, 185–88; Rawls' theory of, 175–78; the reproduction of social capital argument, 178–84; state encouragement of intergenerational transfers to foundations, reasons for, 173–74

intragenerational justice, 170

Islam: absence of from standard history of philanthropy, 35–36; Judaism and, 205n20; sadaqa, 37–38; the waqf (*see* waqf, the); zakat, 36–37

Jefferson, Thomas, 165–66, 219n30

justice: distinction between charity and, 18, 25; distributive, 111–12, 118, 124, 186 (*see also* distribution of charitable gifts); reparative, 151

justification of incentives for philanthropy, 104–5, 108, 114, 133–34, 149–50; efficiency rationale, 119–27; framework for, 110–13; indefensibility of current U.S. policy, 134; pluralism rationale, 128–33; tax base rationale, 115–19

just savings principle, 23, 173–79, 183–86, 188–90, 193

Kant, Immanuel, 52, 111–12

Kennedy, Caroline, 95

Keppel, Frederick, 218–19n23

Kozol, Jonathan, 96

Kuran, Timur, 44, 205n23, 205n26–27

Kymlicka, Will, 18, 202n14

LaMarche, Gara, 167

Landais, Camille, 215n24, 216n31

Laski, Harold, 146

law: nonprofit organizations/foundations and, 26–27

LEFs. *See* local education foundations

legitimacy of foundations, 104, 150–52, 168

Levmore, Saul, 216n34

liberal democracy: foundations in, role of, 136; the institutional setting of philanthropy and, 25–26; intergenerational justice and (*see* intergenerational justice); intragenerational justice and, 170; justification of incentives for philanthropy in (*see* justification of incentives for philanthropy). *See also* democracy; equality

liberty: equality and, 70, 100–101, 103–4; giving, questions of, 107–10; philanthropy as an expression of, 67–70

Li Ka Shing Foundation, 9

limited liability companies (LLCs), 199–200

liturgical system, 29–35, 64

LLCs. *See* limited liability companies

local education foundations (LEFs), 94–99

Macchiavelli, Niccolo, 108–9

Mauss, Marcel, 24–25, 30

Mayer, Jane, 200

Mettler, Suzanne, 77, 209n14

Mill, John Stuart: criticism of foundations by, 21, 28, 45, 106, 108, 192; democratic constraint of foundations supported by, 142; perpetual and time-delimited endowments, case against and for, 54–64, 135–37, 165; regress, state intervention to prevent, 189

Montesquieu, Charles-Louis de Secondat, Baron de, 53

Moskovitz, Dustin, 200
Murphy, Liam, 92–93, 118–21, 216–17n35
Murphy, Starr, 5–6

Nagel, Thomas, 92–93, 118–21, 216–17n35
national security, philanthropy as a threat to, 46
New York City Fund for Public Schools, 95
Nielson, Waldemar, 167–68
nonideal theory, 66
nonprofit organizations: distributive/ redistributive benefits of, 92–93, 125–26; growth of the sector, 93, 215n25; tax exemption, rationale for, 130–31; tax subsidies for, 75–76 (see also taxation). See also foundations
Nonprofit Sector, The: A Research Handbook, 35
Nozick, Robert, 70

Ober, Josiah, 30–31, 33–34
Omidyar, Pam, 200
Omidyar, Pierre, 200
Omidyar Network, 200
Open Philanthropy Project, 189
Open Society Institute, 148–49
Owen, David, 219n31

Packard, David, 206n36
Packard Foundation, 206n36
parent-teacher associations (PTAs), 94–95
paternalism in philanthropy, question regarding, 197
patriotic philanthropy, 35
payout rule, 84, 145–46, 171, 210n25
percentage philanthropy, 133
perpetual endowments: the Catholic Church in France and opposition to, 52–54; the church in Britain and opposition to, 56–59; intergenerational justice and, 171, 189, 192–93; Kant's objections to, 52; Mill's objections to, 54–60, 62, 108, 135–36, 165; Posner on, 135, 148; Turgot's objections to, 49–52, 62, 108, 135; United States law regarding, 207n43
philanthropy: as an artifact of the state, 8–9, 25–27, 63, 71, 107, 172; charity and, interchangeable usage of the words, 19–20; compulsory, the liturgical system of ancient Athens as, 29–35; equality and, 68–71 (see also equality); examining contemporary, reasons for, 7–11; for-profit, 199–200; institutional frameworks for (see institutions for philanthropy); Islamic (see Islam); justification of incentives for (see justification of incentives for philanthropy); liberty and, 67–70; origin of the word, 27; patriotic, 35; percentage, 133; political theory of (see political theory of philanthropy); remaining questions and developments to explore, 197–200; theoretical perspective on, 11–19, 195–97; value of/esteem given to, 14–15. See also charity
Plato's Academy, 140
pluralism: associational life as a site of, 181; foundations in a democracy, as a positive role for, 152–59; as rationale for donation incentives, 128–33
plutocratic bias, 123–24, 132, 158
Police Department, hypothetical case of, 102–3
political philosophy: questions about philanthropy from the perspective of, 12–13; reasoning in ideal vs. nonideal modes, methodological debate over, 65–66
political theory of philanthropy: conclusions drawn from, 196–98; development of, 13–19. See also justification of incentives for philanthropy
poor, basic needs of the. See basic needs of the poor as recipients of charitable giving
Posner, Eric A., 204n16

Posner, Richard, 135, 192
Powell, Lewis, 130, 155–56, 216n33
Powell Jobs, Laurene, 200
power, philanthropy as an exercise of, 7–8, 15–16, 18, 25, 64, 137–39, 143, 148
Pozen, David, 213n10
private foundations. *See* foundations
property rights, 111–13, 118
public finance: the liturgical system of ancient Athens as a source of, 29, 31–32, 34; taxation (*see* taxation); the waqf as a vehicle for, 38–39
public goods, 153–56
public policy: distribution of charitable gifts and, 82–89; goals of, equality and, 103–4; inequality worsened by, 93–103; taxation (*see* taxation)
Putnam, Robert, 129, 178, 180, 182

Ravitch, Diane, 145
Rawls, John, 23, 173, 175–80, 183
religion: charity and, 27, 214n18; as recipient of charitable giving, 85–87, 90, 117
risk capital, philanthropic foundations as, 159–61, 165, 192, 219n26
Robert Bosch Foundation, 9
Rockefeller, John D., 1–7, 9, 63, 136–40, 149, 201n3
Rockefeller Foundation, 1–8, 137–41, 201n9
Roosevelt, Theodore, 4, 138
Rubenstein, David, 204n17

sadaqa, 37–38
Sage, Russell, 63, 149
Saunders-Hastings, Emma, 208n4
Scanlon, Thomas, 186–87
Schneewind, J. B., 35
Schumpeter, Joseph, 206n30
Sen, Amartya, 66
Simons, James, 218n12
Simons Foundation International, 218n12
Singer, Peter, 12, 201n12

Skocpol, Theda, 180
Smith, Adam, 47
Smithson, James, 213n6
Smithsonian Institution, 213n6
social capital, 173, 178–84
social norms: the activity of philanthropy and, 25–26; liberal democracy (*see* liberal democracy)
Sonstelie, Jon, 211n39
Soros, George, 148
state, the: funding associational life through, shortcomings of, 181–82; philanthropic endowments and rights of, 54–60; philanthropy as an artifact of, 8–9, 25–28, 63, 71, 107, 172; policies of (*see* public policy); private foundations and, 42–43; submerged, 77; tax expenditures subsidizing charitable giving (*see* taxation)
status signaling, 116, 202n1
Stith, Kate, 109, 212–13n5
Surrey, Stanley, 209n14

Taft, William, 4, 6, 138–39
Talleyrand, Charles Maurice de, 53
taxation: charitable deduction, alternatives to, 81, 127, 132–33; charitable deduction, impact of 2017 legislation on, 210n17; charitable donors, treatment of, 78–81, 107, 114; distributive benefits of the charitable deduction, 92–93, 96, 122–27; of family inheritance compared to transfers to foundations, 171–72; 501(c)(3) organizations, 75–76, 83–84, 95, 117, 127, 130, 145, 215n25; incentives for philanthropy, 26, 74–77, 107, 148–50, 214–15n23; incentives for philanthropy, historical anomaly of, 107–10; incentives for philanthropy, justification of (*see* justification of incentives for philanthropy); itemized deductions, 78–79, 120; Nozick on, 70; philanthropy as a tax cheating strategy, 215n24, 216n31; tax rate and cost

of charitable giving, relationship of, 210n20, 213n11; upside-down effect of deduction, 79–80, 120–21, 123, 133; wasteful tax expenditures, impact of, 81–82

tax expenditures, 77, 119, 209n14

Thompson, Dennis, 161–62, 190

Thoreau, Henry David, 48

Tocqueville, Alexis de: on civic society in America, 63, 68, 180, 208n5; dependency as the result of charity, 48, 206n34; social capital, significance of, 178, 221n19

Tomasi, John, 113, 213n9

transparency: foundations' lack of, 144–46

triremes/trierarch/trierarchy, 30–32, 204n13

Tuna, Cari, 200

Turgot, Anne-Robert, 20, 28, 46–55, 57, 62, 64, 108

United States: charitable giving in, 72–74; federal charter for Rockefeller foundation, seeking of, 1–7, 137–40

upside-down subsidy, 79–80, 120–21, 123, 133

U-shaped curve of giving, 210n18

Voltaire (François-Marie Arouet), 53

Walsh, Frank, 5, 138

waqf, the: democracy and, 44; foundations, as precursor to, 42–44, 140; in Islamic civilization, 36, 38–39; kinds of, 40–41; mechanism and purposes of, 37–38; modern evolution of, 41–42; private provision of public goods, as a mechanism for, 39, 44; as religious and political entity, 39–40

warm glow, 116

Wellcome Trust, 9

Weyl, E. Glen, 204n16

Wickersham, George, 139

Wisconsin, University of, 141, 217n7

Wolpert, Julian, 91–92

Wuthnow, Robert, 86, 214n18

zakat, 36–38

Zuckerberg, Mark, 152, 199

A NOTE ON THE TYPE

This book has been composed in Adobe Text and Gotham.
Adobe Text, designed by Robert Slimbach for Adobe,
bridges the gap between fifteenth- and sixteenth-century
calligraphic and eighteenth-century Modern styles.
Gotham, inspired by New York street signs, was designed
by Tobias Frere-Jones for Hoefler & Co.